IF ONLY

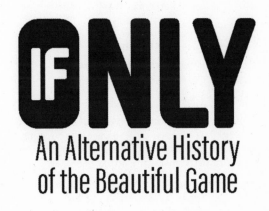

IF ONLY

An Alternative History of the Beautiful Game

SIMON TURNER

First published by Pitch Publishing, 2017

Pitch Publishing
A2 Yeoman Gate
Yeoman Way
Worthing
Sussex
BN13 3QZ

www.pitchpublishing.co.uk
info@pitchpublishing.co.uk

© 2017, Simon Turner

A CIP catalogue record is available for this book
from the British Library.

ISBN 978-1-78531-280-9

Typesetting and origination by Pitch Publishing

Printed in the UK by Bell & Bain, Glasgow, Scotland

Contents

This book is dedicated
to the memory of Jeremy Harber
1970–1994

'*History is not merely what happened: it is what happened in the context of what might have happened.*'

Hugh Trevor-Roper

Extract from *History and Imagination* by Hugh Trevor-Roper reprinted by permission of Peters Fraser & Dunlop (www.petersfraserdunlop.com) on behalf of the Estate of Hugh Trevor-Roper

Acknowledgements

I WOULD like to express my gratitude to Paul and Jane of Pitch Publishing, both for taking an interest in this book and for all the support that they have provided along the way. I also need to thank my father, Roger Turner, for his helpful remarks on an earlier, much lengthier, draft of this book and for persuading me to change the ending to the 'Clough vs. Cruyff' chapter. The book is undoubtedly better as a result. Whether I should thank him for his pivotal role in my becoming a Walsall FC supporter, however, is much more debatable. I am also grateful to Richard Mead for his useful comments on the book, to Duncan Olner for his innovative cover design and to Gareth Davis for his diligent editing. Finally, I must thank my wife, Val, for the incredible patience she has shown throughout the many long nights it has taken me to write this book.

Introduction

THE facts of football history are known. The winners have their names etched on to trophies for perpetuity, sometimes with nauseating regularity. But, behind all those triumphs, lie the countless disappointments of teams that were denied glory by the width of a crossbar, or by a dubious refereeing decision.

It is important that we do not fall into the trap of believing that successful sides were predestined to achieve greatness, and that those that failed to win were fated to end up as losers. The truth is that history can turn on what appear, at first glance, to be infinitesimally small events. Some great military battles have been determined by chance occurrences and freakish turns of fortune, and football matches are no different. There are countless paths that football history could have taken and, as I will attempt to show, some of them are quite remarkable.

The past wasn't always the past; it was once the future and was as unknowable as our own future is now. Football spectators of the past no more knew what the outcome of the games they were watching would be than we do with any match that we start to watch now.

Counterfactuals may appear, at first glance, to be a little frivolous, but they are becoming an increasingly important method for studying history. By considering what would have happened had key pivotal events turned out differently, such as the British not entering the First World War, or the D-Day landings ending in retreat, both of which were perfectly plausible outcomes, we can better understand the contingent nature of our nation's history. One of the purposes of the counterfactual is that it forces us to challenge our perception that what actually happened was inevitable; that the outcome of great clashes could never have been any different to what they actually were. The aim of this book is to use counterfactual techniques to reflect on what our football history could have been, what it might have been and, in some cases, what it probably should have been.

In the course of developing this book I have considered many alternative pretend fixtures but, often with a heavy heart, have whittled them down to the six matches selected. There are innumerable matches that I could have written about, but the ones chosen are those that intrigue me the most. The matches in this book encompass a wide span of football history, stretching from the first World Cup in 1930 to the modern-day Champions League.

I have chosen six matches that were never played but, if they had been, would have left us with a quite different history of the game. Imagine, for instance, a Scotland team running out for international matches with a gold star on their shirts to commemorate their victory in the first World Cup, or a replica of the European Cup sitting proudly in the Derby County trophy room. These are not far-fetched scenarios but credible events that could have happened, had circumstances been only a little different.

In selecting matches to write about, I have resisted the temptation to indulge in wild flights of fantasy. Therefore, you won't read of non-league teams fighting their way through a succession of giant-killings before thrashing Arsenal or

Liverpool in the FA Cup Final, or England prevailing in World Cups that they never had a hope of winning. The improbable has deliberately been discarded in favour of the plausible.

There is also another category of matches that I have not written about. The team most famous for not fulfilling its destiny were the great 'Busby Babes', many of whom perished in the snow at Munich in 1958. The Manchester United squad were on the way back from a quarter-final triumph over Red Star Belgrade in the European Cup when the accident happened. A year earlier they had narrowly succumbed to Real Madrid in the semi-finals of the same competition and, had the terrifying crash not happened, would probably have met them in that season's final. The Spanish side may have emerged victorious from that previous contest, but Busby's young side was a year older and much wiser to the ways of the European Cup. A clash between the majestic, all-conquering Real Madrid side of Di Stéfano, Kopa and Gento and Busby's home-grown talents of Taylor, Charlton and Edwards would, therefore, surely have been one of the game's greatest ever matches.

So why haven't I written about it? To my mind, the real tragedy of Munich was not that a great team failed to win the European Cup, but that so many young men lost their lives. The legacy of that terrible accident was a trail of broken lives and shattered dreams; mothers lost sons, wives lost husbands, children lost fathers. I cannot pretend that a football match matters more than that. For that reason, I have also not written about how Everton could have won the European Cup in 1986, having won both the Football League championship and the European Cup Winners' Cup Final a year earlier. The death of 39 innocent spectators in the Heysel Stadium at the 1985 European Cup Final, following rioting by Liverpool fans, resulted in all English clubs being banned from European competition, meaning that one of Everton's finest ever teams lost the opportunity to secure what would have been the club's greatest ever triumph. But that matters less than what happened at Heysel.

The same consideration also applies to the wonderful Liverpool side of the late 1980s, in which Beardsley, Barnes and Rush were all in their pomp. They may have cantered to a succession of domestic triumphs, but the crowning glory of European trophies was denied to them by the same ban. The dominant team of that era was the great AC Milan side of Gullit, Rijkaard and Van Basten, with the Italian club winning consecutive European Cups in 1989 and 1990. A clash between those two great sides would undoubtedly have been mouth-watering, but the shameful events at Heysel rightfully meant that it never took place.

The structure of each chapter in this book follows the same format. I tell the true story of each of the teams taking part in the fantasy encounter and then, interspersed among this, I imagine what would have happened had they actually played each other.

When I was a boy I would regularly re-enact football matches in the back garden, with my mother's rotary washing line helpfully acting as the upright of the goal frame. Surely it had been designed for just that purpose? Liverpool may have been the dominant team of my youth, but they won precious few matches in my garden, with a 6-0 thrashing by Walsall as they marched towards yet another FA Cup victory being a much more likely outcome. In imagining great matches that never took place I have therefore tried to conjure up the spirit of my younger self, liberated from the constraints of how things are and free to envisage what could have been. It may seem a little indulgent, but these games do need to be brought to life if counterfactual scenarios are to be considered properly, even if only in the imagination.

I hope that the six matches I have written about interest you as much as they fascinate me. I cannot contend that my final list of selected fixtures is in any way definitive, especially given that it focuses largely on the fortunes of British teams. Indeed, there may well be glaring omissions that other, more diligent, observers of the game immediately spot.

No matter; this book does not pretend to be an authoritative text of the key turning points in the game's history. Rather, it is a journey down some of the paths that fate did not take us and if my choices are viewed as being a little subjective or eclectic, then so be it. Some may think that my contentions about the alternative routes that football history could have taken are a little far-fetched and unrealistic. Perhaps, but sport can always produce the unexpected, and if you don't believe that just ask a Leicester City fan…

1
Triumph in Montevideo

World Cup Final, Centenario, Montevideo, 30 July 1930

Uruguay v Scotland

Uruguay	Scotland
Uruguay	**Scotland**
Enrique Ballestrero	Jack Harkness
José Nasazzi (captain)	Tommy Law
Ernesto Mascheroni	Jimmy Nelson
Álvaro Gestido	Jimmy McMullan (captain)
Lorenzo Fernández	Tom Bradshaw
José Leandro Andrade	Jimmy Gibson
Santos Iriate	Alan Morton
Pedro Cea	Alex James
Héctor Castro	Hughie Gallacher
Héctor Scarone	Jimmy Dunn
Pablo Dorado	Alex Jackson

Referee: Gilberto de Almeida Rêgo (Brazil)

Jimmy McMullan was afraid. There was a palpable menace in the air and he knew instinctively that he should be far away from this place. But there was nowhere else for him to go, for he was the captain of Scotland and a very important game of football had to be played. Every now and then McMullan could hear the unmistakable sound of a gunshot ricocheting through the air. For goodness sake, he thought, this was supposed to be a football match, not the Somme. When he had first played in the Centenario stadium he had thought that the fences separating the stands from the pitch were hardly necessary.

After all, there were only football fans standing behind them, not wild animals. Now he was glad to see the barriers there. The ground was packed full of Uruguayan supporters and he'd heard in the dressing room that there were thousands locked outside, still trying desperately to get in. There was nothing wrong with men getting passionate about a football match, he reckoned, but these Uruguayans were clearly taking it too far.

As McMullan peered beyond the fences he could see the odd Scot bravely wearing a Tam O'Shanter, but they were massively outnumbered by the home fans. A return trip to Uruguay was well beyond the means of Scotland's working-class supporters and consequently the only fellow countrymen in the stadium were those that had emigrated there. He had always thought that Hampden Park and Wembley were beyond compare but he had to admit that the Centenario was even more stunning; a huge, tiered bowl of concrete that climbed endlessly into the Montevideo sky. When McMullan had found out that he was going to spend his summer in South America he envisaged blazing sunshine and steamy tropical weather. He hadn't realised that July was in the middle of the Uruguayan winter.

Consequently, most of Scotland's matches had been played in biting winds on cold, misty days and there had even been some occasional wisps of snow. As McMullan felt the chill air at his back he smiled quietly to himself; this was just like being back in Scotland.

McMullan knew that his team would need nerves of steel to overcome the fine Uruguayan team, not to mention their fervent fans. But he fancied they could do it. After all, they had beaten every other team they had played so far. Belgium hadn't posed them much of a challenge; the Scots were 3-0 up at half-time and were able to spend most of the second half entertaining the small crowd rather than trying to extend their lead.

The Americans had been a bit of a surprise, even taking the lead, but when the Scots realised they had a game on their hands they'd responded firmly to the challenge, running out 4-1 winners in the end. Their last opponents in the group stage were Paraguay and they'd been repeatedly told by the locals that they mustn't underestimate them.

Apparently, they had even beaten Uruguay a year earlier. Scotland therefore took to the pitch in determined mood and made sure that the South Americans didn't get a foothold in the game. A 2-0 victory duly followed, as did a semi-final against Argentina.

The Argentineans were by far the best team that Scotland had played in the tournament until that point, their players possessed of silky skills, acute positioning and strong running. Unfortunately, they were also adept at making unsavoury tackles and the Scots were grateful for the strong refereeing of John Langenus, a Belgian whose officiating was as accomplished as any they had seen back home. McMullen's side eventually emerged victorious, but it had been a close-run thing. The two teams were level for most of the game and it was only a late strike that had won it for Scotland.

Nevertheless, McMullan felt their triumph was deserved as at least they had tried to play the game in the right spirit, which he couldn't truthfully say of the Argentineans. McMullan only hoped that the Uruguayans wouldn't be quite so ruthless.

• •

Uruguay and Scotland may lie at opposite ends of the planet, but there are several striking similarities between the two countries. They are both small, temperate lands with relatively modest populations, overshadowed by one large, football-mad port city. The football teams of Glasgow and Montevideo dominate their national leagues, with the duopoly of Celtic and Rangers being mirrored thousands of miles away by Peñarol and Nacional. Scotland and Uruguay also harbour similar football rivalries, both having a more populous and prosperous neighbour to the south which they rejoice in defeating whenever they have the opportunity. A Uruguayan will revel in a victory over Argentina just as surely as a Scot will delight in seeing his team overcome England.

Scotland, along with England, was one of the birthplaces of modern football, with the two nations competing in the first ever international match in 1872. The British were busy exporting goods all over the world in Victorian times and one of the things they took with them was football. The game was most probably taken to port cities such as Montevideo by visiting British seamen and it was their compatriots that settled there that helped to establish the game.

There was money to be made in fledgling nations such as Uruguay, especially in the construction and development of much-needed infrastructure, and the British had the necessary expertise. Expatriate British communities thus established themselves in the country, forming sporting clubs around the businesses in which they worked. Peñarol, for example, has its roots in the Central Uruguay Railway Cricket Club which, evidently, played more than just cricket. Over time the local inhabitants took these sporting clubs over from their foreign creators and, in doing so, started to make the game their own.

Uruguay played their first international match in 1901, almost three decades after Scotland had first taken on England. It was the first international fixture to take place outside of the British Isles and Uruguay's opponents, unsurprisingly, were near-neighbours Argentina. The capitals of the two nations, Montevideo and Buenos Aires, face each other across the bay of the River Plate, separated by just under 130 miles. By way of comparison, London and Edinburgh are more than twice that distance apart. The physical proximity of Uruguay and Argentina facilitated regular fixtures between them and, by the second decade of the 20th century, it wasn't unusual for them to play each other half a dozen times or more a year. Unsurprisingly, Uruguay versus Argentina soon set the record for being the most frequently played international match in the world.

Argentina initially had the upper hand in their confrontations with Uruguay, but the balance soon started to shift, with the two nations regularly trading victories. One of Uruguay's earliest triumphs came at the first South American Championships (the forerunner to the modern Copa America), which was held in Argentina in 1916 as part of the nation's centenary celebrations. Uruguay won that tournament, no doubt to the great chagrin of the Argentineans, and then showed that was no fluke by repeating the same triumph a year later back in Montevideo. Further victories then followed in 1920 and 1923, prior to Uruguay announcing themselves on the global stage at the 1924 Paris Olympics.

Uruguay had never previously played any international matches outside of South America, but were so determined to take part in the Olympics that they travelled in steerage across the Atlantic, sleeping on benches and playing friendly matches to fund their trip. Given that they had never encountered European opposition before, they arrived as unknown quantities and consequently little was expected of them.

The Uruguayans, however, proved to be a revelation. They thrashed Yugoslavia 7-0 in the first round and then dismissed the USA to set up a quarter-final against their French hosts. Uruguay blew France away, beating them 5-1 at the same Colombes stadium that witnessed the great *Chariots of Fire* triumphs of Harold Abrahams and Eric Liddell. The Netherlands were Uruguay's next victims and then the Swiss were swept aside in the final, beaten 3-0. Uruguay's efforts were rewarded not only with gold medals, but also with the respect and admiration of all those that saw them play. They scored 20 goals in their five victories and conceded only two, with many observers duly concluding that the epicentre of football excellence had shifted from Europe to South America.

Gabriel Hanot, the prime mover behind the creation of the European Cup in the 1950s, was nearing the end of his playing career when he first saw the Uruguayans perform. At the time the British creators of the game were still largely considered to be its masters but Hanot concluded otherwise, referring to the British as 'farm horses' in comparison to the 'Arab thoroughbreds' from the new world. Whether this was a fair comparison will never be known as Great Britain did not send a team to the 1924 Olympics. The British had a strong record in football at the Olympics, winning the gold medal in 1900, 1908 and 1912 (they didn't enter a team in 1904) but became increasingly frustrated at the organisers' refusal to prevent professional players from competing in the tournament. It may seem like an arcane dispute to modern eyes, but the British believed strongly that the competition should only be for unpaid amateurs. Unable to get their way, the British simply stayed away.

Britain's long head-start in the development of the game resulted in their top players becoming professional well in advance of those from other nations. That meant that countries such as Uruguay, which were still making the transition from amateurism, were free to field their best players at the Olympics, whereas the British were not. There was, however, quite a hazy distinction between professionals and amateurs at the time. The Uruguayan captain, José Nasazzi, for example, was a marble-cutter by trade, yet it is likely that he and the other members of the Uruguayan team were still paid in some form to play football.

The Uruguayans returned to South America as heroes, duly proclaiming their status as the best side in the world. Argentina had not taken part in the Olympics and, displeased that their uppity neighbours were titling themselves as global champions, duly challenged them to a two-legged tie to determine who that honour should really belong to. Argentina were ultimately victorious, but Uruguay were undeterred, going on to win the South American Championship again later that year; a fifth triumph in comparison to Argentina's solitary title. Bragging rights clearly lay on the northern shore of the River Plate and would remain so for several years.

After trading victories in the South American Championship in 1926 and 1927, the two nations both sent teams to the 1928 Amsterdam Olympics, ensuring this time there would be no loose ends, buts, ifs or maybes. Argentina cantered through their half of the draw, thrashing the USA 11-2 in the first round, Belgium 6-3 in the quarter-finals and Egypt 6-0 in the last four. Uruguay, meanwhile, overcame a more challenging set of opponents, defeating their Dutch hosts 2-0 in the first round, Germany 4-1 in the quarter-finals and then Italy 3-2 to reach the final. The semi-final between Uruguay and Italy was one of those games played on the fault-lines of international football history; the former were in their pomp, defeating all-comers, while the latter were on their way to becoming the dominant international side of the next decade.

The rest of the world may have struggled to give the teams from the River Plate a stiff challenge, but they were more than a match for each other. The first final, in front of a packed stadium, ended in a 1-1 draw, necessitating a second game three days later. Uruguay eventually emerged triumphant in the replay, winning 2-1, their clinching goal coming 17 minutes before the end. Uruguay's second successive Olympic triumph was undoubtedly deserved, but the British had stayed away once again. The ongoing dispute over professionalism was so dogging the game that FIFA decided that they needed an international competition free from the confines of Olympian ideals and so, within two years, the World Cup was born.

. . . .

The referee selected for the World Cup Final was a Brazilian, Gilberto de Almeida Rêgo. The Scots had been impressed with how the Belgian, John Langenus, had officiated over their semi-final encounter with Argentina and had expected him to be appointed for the final as well. It therefore came as quite a surprise when Almeida Rêgo was allocated the task instead. He had made a real howler in Argentina's clash with France, ending the match six minutes earlier than he should have, and the Scottish delegation were staggered when he kept being handed more matches to referee. The Scots soon learnt that it was the Uruguayans who had objected to the proposed appointment of Langenus. Apparently, they feared that a European referee would favour a team from his own continent and so insisted that the Brazilian take charge instead. The Scots had considered raising a complaint of their own, if only to draw attention to the double standards of the Uruguayans, but eventually thought better of it. The growing tension within Montevideo was becoming increasingly worrying and the Scots also sensed, probably rightly, that this was an argument that they just weren't going to win.

To be fair to Almeida Rêgo, his performance in the opening minutes of the match didn't give the Scots any cause for concern. The two evenly matched teams took it in turns to attack, the play constantly ebbing backwards and forwards. The Brazilian allowed the game to flow, only stopping the match for the heftiest and most inexcusable of challenges and, thankfully, there weren't too many of those. The Uruguayan players seemed oblivious to the fierce demands of the rancorous crowd, concentrating instead on playing the quick passing football that had so delighted those who had watched them play at the Olympics. The Scots, to their credit, were just as entertaining, making their way up the pitch with a succession of small, accurate passes that fizzed across the dusty surface. The two sides were like similarly talented fencers, jabbing and thrusting with great skill, yet still managing to parry each blow that came their way. A goal was coming, but for which team was almost impossible to say.

· ·

A few months before Uruguay won the gold medal at the 1928 Olympics, Scotland also secured one of the most important triumphs in their long and proud history. Despite having played in international matches for almost 60 years, the Scottish FA still had very narrow horizons. The national side routinely played only three matches a year and they were always against the same three opponents. The British Home Championships was created just over a decade after Scotland's first international fixture against England in 1872 and, for the next 70 or so years, it was the only tournament that Scotland competed in. Indeed, not only were the three annual fixtures against England, Ireland and Wales the only internationals that Scotland played in but, from the 1890s onwards, they even held them in the same order nearly every year. The Welsh were normally their first opponents, followed by the Irish, and then came the end-of-season showdown with the English.

Prior to the start of the First World War it was the English that were the dominant force in British football, winning eight of the previous 11 Home Championships. That situation was reversed after the conflict ended, with the Scots dominating the 1920s. They won six of the eight championships held between the 1919/20 and 1926/27 seasons, enjoying a purple patch in the last three of these tournaments, with eight victories in the nine matches played. Probably the most pleasing aspect of their supremacy was their sequence of results against England, with four wins and two draws from their eight post-war encounters. It was, therefore, quite a surprise when they failed to make an effective challenge for the 1927/28 British Home Championship. A draw away to Wales wasn't too disastrous a start to the tournament, but a shock home defeat to the Irish (the first since 1903) put paid to their hopes of retaining the trophy.

England's performances in that season's championship were even more woeful than the Scots', with them losing away to the Irish and at home to the Welsh. That meant that the traditional end-of-season encounter between Scotland and England, so often the decider for the trophy, became no more than a contest for the wooden spoon. Those looking for the cause of Scotland's malaise soon settled on it being due to an over-reliance on home-based players. Ten of the side that lost to the Irish played for Scottish clubs and, three weeks before the forthcoming match against England, a representative team from the Scottish League lost the annual challenge match with the English League 6-2.

The reaction of the Scottish selectors, therefore, was to pick a team to play England which contained eight players that plied their trade there. A famous cartoon of the time pictured the three home-based Scots in a train carriage on their way south for the match bemoaning the fact there weren't even enough of them for a game of bridge. If nothing else, the selectors had certainly been brave. They had discarded popular players from Rangers and Celtic in favour of those who had moved to play their football in England, including two who had never even been capped for Scotland before. Back then these 'Anglo-Scots' were nowhere near as well-liked north of the border as those that stayed at home and, consequently, their compatriots would be unforgiving if they failed to win at Wembley.

The captain selected for the game was Manchester City's pint-sized left-half, Jimmy McMullan. He first played for his country in 1920 and was 33 by the time that Scotland played England in 1928, which was positively geriatric by the standards of the time. The principal reason why he was still playing when many of his peers had long since retired was his great understanding of the game. With his knowledge making up for the deficiencies of his limbs, McMullan was the team's conductor. He used his fine passing ability to give action to his carefully crafted plans, determining the speed and nature of attacks on the opposition's goal. Domestic honours passed McMullan by, as he missed Partick Thistle's 1921 Scottish Cup triumph through injury and then finished on the losing side for Manchester City in the 1926 and 1933 FA Cup finals. His record for Scotland, however, was almost immaculate as he won 12 of the 16 games he played in and lost only once.

The other long-standing Scottish stalwart selected to play against England was the outside-left, Alan Morton. He was the proverbial 'first name on the team sheet' during the 1920s, amassing a total of 31 appearances for Scotland between 1920 and 1932. That may appear quite paltry by modern-day standards, but it was a phenomenal achievement in the inter-war period when so few international matches were played. Any current-day player with an international career of the length of Morton's would easily amass over 100 appearances, and it is in that echelon that he truly belongs.

Morton's wing-play was legendary as he was capable of dribbling past opponents at ease, yet he never allowed the beating of a full-back to become an end in itself. After leaving bewildered defenders in his wake, Morton would send crosses into the penalty area with unerring accuracy. His speciality was a floating lob which often seemed to hang in mid-air, causing chaos among those trying to defend the goal and offering a tantalising opportunity to those trying to attack it. Morton spent much of his career with Glasgow Rangers, with his haul of nine championship titles being particularly impressive given that he didn't join them until he was 27 years of age. His record for Scotland was just as distinguished, with only six of the 31 international matches that he played in ending in defeat.

The player selected to play on the opposite wing was Huddersfield Town luminary Alex Jackson. He had an erratic start in professional football, playing first for Dumbarton and then spending a season in the USA, before returning to Scotland to play for Aberdeen. He spent only a season at Pittodrie before Herbert Chapman tempted him to move south and sign for Huddersfield. Chapman had transformed the fortunes of the Yorkshire side after the war, leading them to consecutive league titles in the two seasons preceding Jackson's arrival in 1925. Chapman left Huddersfield to manage Arsenal not long after signing Jackson, but the side he left behind was strong enough to win the championship again in 1926 without him.

It hardly seemed possible at the time, but that was the only medal that Jackson was to win in his entire career. Huddersfield continued to be one of England's strongest teams for the remainder of the 1920s, but all they had to show for their efforts was a series of near-misses. They finished as runners-up in the First Division in 1926/27 and then did the same in 1927/28, magnifying their pains that season by suffering a defeat in the FA Cup Final as well. If that wasn't bad enough, Huddersfield lost another FA Cup Final in 1930, to Chapman's Arsenal of all teams. Jackson's exploits meant that he was regularly picked for Scotland, making his debut at 19 years of age and missing only two British Home Championship matches over the next six seasons. His record over that period was certainly impressive, with 15 of the 17 matches in which he appeared ending in a Scottish victory and only one in defeat.

Jackson may have been a fine player, but he was also the type of man who made sure everyone else knew as well. He told team-mates early in his career that he would go on to play for Scotland and his subsequent feats did nothing to shrink his opinion of himself. Thankfully for Jackson, he had the talent to back up his boasts. His lightning pace and excellent ball control not only made him an impressive right-winger, but also gave him the confidence to cut inside full-backs and shoot at goal. When Dixie Dean selected the best team from his playing days he chose Jackson at outside-right, reckoning him to be a better footballer than even the great Stanley Matthews.

Playing in the forward line alongside Jackson was Hibernian inside-right Jimmy Dunn. He was probably the least naturally talented of the forwards that were picked to face England, but it would be a mistake to discount him simply on those grounds. Dunn was an energetic runner who passed the ball crisply and scored his fair share of goals in all the teams that he played for. His performance against England at Wembley was so impressive that, less than a month later, Everton bought him to partner their greatest asset, Dixie Dean. The plan backfired initially, with Dunn struggling to settle in his new environment. The Merseyside club finished bottom of the First Division in 1930, though their stay in the second tier of English football was mercifully brief. They won promotion in the subsequent year and followed that by winning the championship and FA Cup in consecutive seasons, with Dunn being a key part of both triumphs.

The leader of Scotland's five-man forward line was the diminutive, volatile Hughie Gallacher. At 5ft 5in tall, he was hardly a traditional, battering-ram centre-forward, having to rely instead on his prodigious natural talent for the game. He could run with the ball, turn and twist defenders, shoot with power and, despite his height, was good in the air, even when competing against much taller defenders. Perhaps Gallacher's greatest quality, however, was his tenacity. He was regularly subjected to brutal punishment by vengeful defenders but would never allow himself to be intimidated, striving endlessly instead for the goal that would confirm his superiority over the beasts that tried to maim him.

Unfortunately, Gallacher's commendable character traits also had their negative side, with his passion for winning often boiling over and leading him into all manner of troubles. He didn't only argue and fight with the opposition, but also with referees, club officials and even with his own team-mates. Gallacher was just as capable of getting into trouble off the pitch as he was on it, once receiving a two-month ban for pushing a referee into a bath after a heated match. He also ended up in court after fighting on the streets of Newcastle. Modern-day footballers may be prone to bouts of bad behaviour, but the template was laid down for them many years earlier by men such as Gallacher.

Thankfully, Gallacher's suspect temperament did not do irreparable damage to his career. His performances for his first club, Queen of the South, were so impressive that he only played nine times for them before being snapped up by Airdrie. With Gallacher in their line-up Airdrie's fortunes were transformed, finishing as runners-up in the league to Glasgow Rangers for three consecutive seasons between 1922/23 and 1924/25 and winning the Scottish Cup, for the first and only time in their history, in 1924. Newcastle United persuaded Gallacher to move south of the border in 1925 and the move worked out well, with his goals propelling them to a league title in 1926/27. Gallacher's total of 463 goals in 624 matches in Scottish and English football easily places him among the greats of the domestic game, but it's his goal scoring feats at international level which most clearly differentiate his talents from the rest.

The inimitable Gallacher scored a total of 23 goals for Scotland, making him the nation's third highest ever scorer. Denis Law and Kenny Dalglish may have found the net more times, but the difference in scoring rates between them and Gallacher is stark. Gallacher scored over a goal a game, whereas Law scored just over once every two games while Dalglish scored once in every three games (and that's being kind with the maths). Hughie Gallacher, meanwhile, rarely disappointed his expectant countrymen, finishing on the winning side 17 times in the 20 matches he played for them.

Scotland's inside-left against England in 1928 was Alex James, an old school friend of Hughie Gallacher. They had grown up together in the small town of Bellshill in Lanarkshire, playing football whenever they could and watching their beloved Celtic whenever it was possible. That they should both end up playing in the same forward line for their country is certainly a romantic story, though neither of them were particularly poetic figures. Gallacher could be irascible and tempestuous, while James could be indolent and not a little selfish. Despite being the younger of the two men, Gallacher was the first to be offered a professional contract. A relieved James was later taken on by Raith Rovers and, after a few seasons with them, moved south to play for Preston North End. The fact that the club played in the second tier of English football didn't stymie James's international career, with the striker making his Scotland debut shortly after joining them.

James's next move was the one that came to define his career. Herbert Chapman offered him a contract at Arsenal in 1929 and he never looked back, going on to become probably the most important player in a side that dominated English football in the 1930s. James didn't have much pace and was knocked off the ball fairly easily, but his natural talent for the game didn't reside in his physique; it lay between his ears. His speed of thought and imagination made up for the frailties of his limbs, enabling him to fashion creative moves that often flummoxed opposing defences. James was well rewarded for his efforts at Arsenal, winning four league championships between 1930/31 and 1934/35, as well as two FA Cups in 1930 and 1936.

Alex James's appearances for his native Scotland were inexcusably rare, with Preston and Arsenal often taking advantage of the rules that allowed them to refuse him permission to play for his country. James only played eight times for Scotland, but he couldn't blame that entirely on the selfishness of his English employers. He cried off a few days before Scotland's game against England in 1933, citing injury, but then proceeded to play for Arsenal on the very same day that his countrymen were battling the English. Unsurprisingly, James was never asked to represent Scotland again.

• •

As the first half progressed, the five-man Scottish forward line started to impose themselves on the game. Fed by a succession of accurate passes from McMullan, the left-winger Morton began to give his opposing number a torrid time. He dribbled past him with increasing ease, before sending looping crosses into the penalty area for Gallacher and Jackson to chase. The Uruguayan defence dealt manfully with the challenge, but their increasingly nervous supporters sensed that they wouldn't be able to keep the Scots out forever. Gallacher, in particular, was an ever-present threat; his movement and energy clearly troubling the Uruguayan back-line.

There was much to admire about how Gallacher was playing the game, but sadly the little Scotsman was also indulging in some rather ignoble tactics. The more eagle-eyed of the Uruguayan supporters spotted him aiming the odd kick at an opponent's ankles when the referee's attentions were elsewhere and his fierce temper was often in evidence. Gallacher's behaviour was no doubt a reaction to the increasingly harsh challenges that came his way, but there was a constant danger that one of his skirmishes with opposing defenders would escalate into an all-out brawl. Before the match he had stuffed cotton wool beneath his shin-pads, as was his usual custom, and no doubt felt the benefit as the Uruguayan defenders aimed retaliatory hacks at his battered legs.

There was little in common between Gallacher and Morton; the former a tempestuous firebrand who drank as hard as he played, the latter a clean-living mining engineer who spent more time sporting a bowler hat and briefcase than he did football boots. On the pitch, however, Gallacher and Morton formed an admirable alliance. They had combined well on many occasions before and it was now Uruguay's turn to feel the power of their partnership. The move started with the captain McMullan, who sprayed a well-aimed pass to the feet of Morton. He quickly flicked the ball past the lunge of the opposing defender and looked up to see where Gallacher was. Most of Morton's previous crosses had been played high into the air, but the diminutive Gallacher had been unable to make the most of them. This time Morton dispatched the ball from the left wing at chest height. Gallacher read the flight of the ball perfectly, getting a step ahead of his marker before flinging himself headlong at the ball. His forehead connected with the ball as he intended and the Uruguayan goalkeeper could only glance in despair as the net rustled behind him. The Scots had metaphorically drawn first blood, but if Gallacher continued to play the way he was playing there was a risk of real blood being spilt.

• •

The man selected to keep goal for Scotland against England in 1928 was Jack Harkness. He was still an amateur when the game took place, though he turned professional just over a month later. He grew up in Glasgow, began his career with local side Queen's Park and was only 19 years old when selected for his first international match; a 2-0 victory over Northern Ireland in 1927. Success came quickly to Harkness, but it was clearly deserved. He was a brave, agile goalkeeper who was more than capable of holding his own against strikers who routinely challenged keepers much more robustly than would be allowed today.

One of Harkness's principal rivals for a place in the international team was the Celtic goalkeeper, John Thomson. Like Harkness, Thomson had risen to prominence early in his career and great things were expected of him. He made his debut for Scotland in May 1930 and could well have been the first-choice goalkeeper if a squad had been sent to Uruguay that summer. Sadly, Thomson was to die in tragic circumstances just over a year later, following a collision with a Rangers striker during a match at Ibrox. He was rushed to hospital with a head injury but, despite undergoing emergency surgery, died a few hours later, aged just 22.

Playing in front of Harkness against England was right-back Jimmy Nelson. Of all those selected, Nelson had the loosest associations with Scotland. He was eligible for the national side by virtue of having been born in Greenock, but he spent little time there before his family relocated to Belfast. The struggle for independence made the island a troubled, violent place and Nelson escaped it as soon as he was able to, gladly accepting the offer of a professional contract with Cardiff City in 1921.

The Welsh team had most successful spell in their history in the 1920s and Nelson was a key part of it. The disappointment of near-misses in 1924 and 1925 (runners-up in the league and then the FA Cup) was banished by a cathartic victory over Arsenal at Wembley in 1927; Cardiff thus becoming the only club from outside England to win the FA Cup.

Cardiff's fortunes faded after that triumph and they were relegated from the First Division two years later, though Nelson and his fellow defenders were not the chief culprits for their demise. The Welsh club conceded fewer goals than any other team in the division that season, with even the title winners, Sheffield Wednesday, letting in more. Nelson only played in the Second Division for a season before moving back into the top flight with Newcastle United. He repaid their faith in him by captaining the side to another FA Cup triumph; a 2-1 victory over Arsenal in 1932. Nelson was only capped four times by his country of birth, though that could hardly be attributed to the quality of his performances for the national side. Scotland won all four of those matches, conceding only two goals in the process. The principal reason for the paucity of his international appearances was simply that he didn't play his club football in Scotland. In truth, for a man who grew up in Ireland and spent his career playing in the English league (with most of that being at a Welsh club), being awarded four Scottish caps was actually quite an impressive achievement.

Nelson's defensive partner, Tommy Law, was the youngest of the players selected to face England, with the teenager making his international debut. Law was raised in Glasgow but his talent for the game was missed by the local clubs. A Chelsea scout spotted his potential, however, and Law made his debut for the west London side in 1926, with his first cap for Scotland being awarded only a year and a half later. It was a rapid rise to the top and his selection for the national side was particularly remarkable given that Chelsea were only playing in the second tier of English football at the time. Law had little pace, but made up for it by reading the game well and making sure that he was in the right place at the right time. He was particularly adept at the sliding tackle; a skill that he was to demonstrate successfully on the sodden Wembley pitch against the English forwards.

The centre-half who played in front of Nelson and Law was Tom 'Tiny' Bradshaw. The nickname was a deliberately ironic misnomer as Bradshaw was a 6ft 2in, 14st stopper. Despite his size, Bradshaw was an adept ball player, though his predilection for trying to dribble his way out of difficult positions, rather than kicking the ball up the pitch, was often seen as the weakness in his game. The fledgling Bradshaw was given a trial by Hamilton Academicals but they passed up the opportunity to take him on and it was Bury that gave him his chance in the game. The Greater Manchester club may be a football outpost in modern times but they had a strong team in the 1920s, winning promotion to the First Division two years after Bradshaw joined them and then securing three top-five finishes in the following four seasons. That gave Bradshaw a stage from which he was able to attract the attention of the Scottish selectors and he was given his first, and only, cap against England in 1928.

Bradshaw had a marvellous game at Wembley, with his omission from future national sides having to be put down to a combination of misfortune and the selectors' preference for home-based players. Early in the 1928/29 season Bradshaw picked up a bad injury and Bury were duly relegated. Despite resuming his First Division career with Liverpool, Bradshaw never became Scotland's first-choice centre-half again. The selectors' preferred option in that position was the Glasgow Rangers player, Davie Meiklejohn, and it's not too hard to understand why. Rangers dominated Scottish football in the 1920s and 1930s and Meiklejohn was an integral part of that success. In the 16 seasons between his debut in 1920 and his retirement in 1936 Meiklejohn played 635 times for the club, winning 12 Scottish championships and five Scottish Cups. Not only was Meiklejohn a strong defender and decent ball player but, perhaps most importantly of all, he was also a great leader. Meiklejohn captained Rangers to many of those triumphs and regularly led the national side as well.

The final member of the Scotland line-up against England was Aston Villa right-half Jimmy Gibson. He was talented enough to excel in several positions, playing in all the half-back positions for Villa, as well as at inside-right, centre-forward and once, when the keeper was injured during a match, even in goal. He began his career with Partick Thistle but was tempted south by the greater financial opportunities on offer, being transferred to Aston Villa in 1927 for what was then a British record fee of £7,500. Villa were a strong team for most of his time there, achieving two second-, one fourth- and one fifth-place finish in the First Division between 1929/30 and 1932/33. Gibson's record for his country was just as impressive, with Scotland winning six of the eight matches he played in and only losing once.

Scotland went into the game against England as heavy underdogs. Not only were they playing away from home, but they also had to contend with an in-form Dixie Dean. He was at the peak of his career that season, scoring an unequalled record of 60 goals in the league and was clearly in confident mood for the game against the Scots. The night before the match he sent a bottle of aspirins to Scotland goalkeeper Jack Harkness with a note wrapped around it, advising him to get a good night's sleep before he faced the prolific Everton striker. Dean was to be the focal point of England's attacks, with balls played up to him as quickly as possible. The Scots, meanwhile, aimed to keep the ball on the floor, passing it swiftly between themselves, out of reach of the bigger and heavier English players. The Scots and the English may only have been playing for pride but, given the long, and sometimes bitter, history between the two nations, that was more than enough for the match to be a competitive one.

The weather conditions on the day of the game suited the Scots perfectly. Heavy rain resulted in a slippery pitch which favoured the Scottish forwards, enabling them to run at the English defenders secure in the knowledge that their opponents would be reluctant to dive in and tackle for fear of losing their footing. The Scottish forward line was one of the smallest to ever to take to the field; two of them were only 5ft 5in in height and another two were just an inch taller. Yet, on a muddy pitch, their lower centre of gravity became a positive advantage, helping them to torment an English defence which longed for a more physical, aerial battle.

England started the match well, nearly taking the lead after a minute of play when a well-hit shot struck a post. The home fans no doubt thought that augured well, but that was pretty much as good as it got for them that afternoon. After surviving the initial English onslaught, the Scots began to come forward. A swift interchange of passes took the ball to Alan Morton, who beat the opposing full-back and then sent a cross into the penalty area, where it was met by inrushing right-winger, Alex Jackson. He buried his header into the net and, with just three minutes on the clock, the Scots were in front. The two Scottish wingers were probably the most influential players on the pitch that afternoon, causing such trouble to the English full-backs that the right- and left-halves playing in front of them had no choice but to leave their usual positions in midfield to help them out. That left large gaps in the middle of the pitch, resulting in the Scottish half-back line seeing plenty of the ball and having more than enough time and space to use it wisely.

The English were thus pinned down in their own half of the pitch, with Bradshaw subduing Dixie Dean so effectively that the great English hope was reduced to a peripheral figure. Scotland's second goal was perfectly timed, coming just before the half-time break, serving to further demoralise the hosts while reassuring the visitors. The goal was scored by Alex James with a half-volley from the edge of the penalty area; a strike so good that he later considered it to be the finest of his career.

England came out fighting at the start of the second half, but the Scots were in no mood to relinquish their hard-won lead. Their third and fourth goals came in quick succession, in the 65th and 66th minutes, thus effectively ending the match as a contest. Jackson scored the first of these two goals with a header after another fine cross from Morton. It was not just the left-winger that Jackson had to thank though, as Gallacher's contribution was just as important. He might not have scored any of the team's goals that afternoon, but his unselfish running frequently took his English centre-half marker out of position and so left space for Jackson to come in from the wing and take advantage.

Gallacher was also influential in Scotland's fourth goal, going on a weaving run soon after the kick-off which was halted only when he was upended on the edge of the penalty area. The loose ball then ran into the path of James who smashed it gleefully into the back of the net. After that the Scots really started to enjoy themselves, stringing long sequences of passes together to demonstrate their superiority over the English. Their fifth goal came five minutes from the end of the match and they could probably have scored more, had they concentrated on finding the net rather than on humiliating their opponents. The creator of the goal, once again, was Morton who crossed the ball for Jackson to volley into the goal from only a few yards out. It was a historical hat-trick for Jackson; the first player to score three goals at Wembley and the first to do so for Scotland against England since Robert McColl in 1900.

The English did manage to get a goal back one minute from time but, given the galling afternoon they had endured, it was hardly much of a consolation. Each man in the Scottish team played his part in the victory, but the glory inevitably shone on the five-man forward line. They had been dismissed before the match as midgets but left the pitch as giants, mobbed by the Scottish fans that ran on to the Wembley turf to congratulate their heroes. Gallacher, generous in victory, happily deflected the glory on to his captain, Jimmy McMullan, who he reckoned to have been the best player on the pitch.

The victorious Scottish players were christened for posterity as the 'Wembley Wizards', but the selection committee never picked the same XI again. In retrospect, it appears to be a bizarre decision. The selectors stumbled, almost by accident, upon a team that was good enough to humiliate the English on their own turf and yet they never gave them a second game.

Perhaps the best explanation is that priorities were just different back then. International caps were often given as a reward to players who had done well for their clubs and, as a result, were shared around much more equitably than they would be now. In addition, the pressure to select home-based players was simply too great for the selection committee to bear. Despite the result secured by the Anglo-Scots at Wembley, the sides picked for the 1929 British Home Championship were once again dominated by players from Scottish clubs.

. . . .

Uruguay tried to come back at the Scots, but their search for an equaliser floundered on the rocks of the well-drilled Scottish back-line. Law had looked uncomfortable from the start, clearly intimidated by the bloodcurdling cries from the terraces, but McMullan shielded him from most of the Uruguayan attacks. The home side tried to make progress down their left flank instead, but Nelson made full use of his experience to deny them that possibility. Scotland's most effective defender, however, was the centre-back, Bradshaw. It didn't matter whether the Uruguayans played the ball on the ground or in the air as he rose to the challenge of both, either dismissing aerial attacks with thumping headers or crashing into tackles with colossal force.

As the match edged towards half-time the Scots sensed that there was another goal there for the taking. Uruguay were playing higher and higher up the pitch, trying desperately to level the scores before the referee blew his whistle for the break. That resulted in the Uruguayan back-line becoming increasingly isolated and it was much more vulnerable as a consequence. Scotland's chance to take advantage of the situation came when Gibson won the ball and played it forward to Jackson, who was standing just inside the halfway line. The four other Scottish forwards immediately galloped towards the opposition goal, outnumbering the abandoned Uruguayan defenders.

Jackson quickly passed the ball to Dunn, who then flicked it into the path of Gallacher, the ball being moved sideways across the pitch as if they were playing rugby. When the ball found its way to James he was completely unmarked; the slanting passing movement having stretched the Uruguayan defence beyond its breaking point. With time on his side, he was able to stop, look up and spot Jackson's run to the right-hand edge of the penalty area. James took aim and fired a 20-yard pass straight into Jackson's path. The ball bounced a foot into the air after landing and Jackson caught it full on the volley, sending it crashing into the back of the net. The Uruguayan goalkeeper didn't even have a chance to move.

Scotland's goal was greeted with a crescendo of jeers from the home supporters, which only increased in volume when the referee brought the first half to a close a few moments later. Many of the Uruguayan fans had been in the ground for hours before kick-off, desperate not to miss what promised to be the national side's greatest ever triumph. Having made such an effort, they were angry to see the Uruguayan players not responding in kind, and so duly let them know how they felt. If the daunting atmosphere was alarming for the Uruguayan players, then it was several times worse for the Scots. As soon as they heard the first note from the referee's whistle they ran quickly to the sanctuary of the dressing room; not wanting to be out on the pitch a minute longer than they had to.

. . . .

The year 1929 witnessed not just the Wall Street crash, the St Valentine's Day Massacre and the first Academy Award ceremony, but also the decision over which nation would host the first World Cup. FIFA gathered in Barcelona to make its choice, with five European countries putting themselves forward as well as one from South America. As the tournament was the brainchild of a Frenchman, Jules Rimet, it may be reasonable to assume that his nation would want to host it. Yet, when applications for holding the tournament were invited, the French happily let the opportunity pass them by. They clearly wanted to have a party, but not in their house. The European nations that did offer to be hosts (Italy, the Netherlands, Hungary, Spain and Sweden) eventually all withdrew their bids in favour of one from Uruguay. It may seem to be a curious choice of location now, but there were strong moral and practical arguments at the time for holding the competition there.

Uruguay's consecutive victories at the 1924 and 1928 Olympics had put them firmly on the map as far as football was concerned and 1930 would also be special for their country as they would be commemorating 100 years of nationhood. What better way to celebrate that milestone than with an international football tournament? Lastly, and perhaps most importantly, the Uruguayans were prepared to back up their proposal with cold, hard cash. They promised to build a vast new stadium for the competition, capable of accommodating 100,000 spectators, and offered to meet the expenses of all competing nations. In light of such an attractive proposal the European nations agreed to withdraw their applications and Uruguay's bid was duly accepted.

The prize that the Uruguayans won, however, soon started to look more like a poisoned chalice. As the months to the beginning of the tournament ticked away it became doubtful whether any European nation would actually take part, with all of those that had volunteered to host it declining to attend. That may appear, at first glance, to be a case of sour grapes, but there were sound practical reasons for their reluctance to take part. There was no commercial air travel in 1930, meaning that teams would have no alternative other than to make the two-week journey to South America by boat. It would take a further month for the competition to be completed and then another fortnight would have to be spent at sea before they arrived back home again. Any European side that wanted to be part of the Uruguayan jamboree, therefore, had to commit to being away from home for over two months. It was little surprise, then, that most of them decided not to participate.

There were some brave pioneers, though. The French had little option but to take part, given that it was their idea in the first place, and they were joined, somewhat reluctantly, by Belgium, Romania and Yugoslavia. Over half of the teams in the tournament came from South America, with teams being sent from Argentina, Bolivia, Brazil, Chile, Paraguay and Peru. North America was represented by Mexico and the USA, while there were no entrants at all from Africa, Asia or Australasia. In total 13 teams took part, though it really should have been 14. The Egyptians were due to attend, but just missed the boat from Marseilles and so had to wait another four years before making their World Cup debut.

The Uruguayans had managed to get just about enough teams to take part to make the tournament worthwhile, though there were fewer than had taken part in the 1924 and

1928 Olympics. Most damaging for the fledgling competition, however, was the absence of so many of Europe's major football powers. Perhaps the strongest of the sides not to travel to Uruguay was the Austrian 'Wunderteam', which bewitched football watchers in the early 1930s with their fluid attacking play. Also missing were the Italians, who would win the next World Cup in 1934, and Spain, who, in 1929, became the first team from outside Britain to beat England. The Czechs, Hungarians and Germans were also absent.

Uruguay were so desperate for the World Cup to be a success that they invited British nations to take part, even though they were not members of FIFA at the time. The British had refused to participate in the football tournament at the previous two Olympics because of their concerns over the blurred definitions of amateur and professional players. The World Cup was to be free of Olympian ideals and so any player, be they amateur, professional, or something in between, could take part. The creation of a level playing field should have encouraged British nations to participate, but it didn't. The English received a polite invitation from the Uruguayans, but all they provided in response was a curt, two-sentence letter confirming that they wouldn't be coming. Given the insularity of the Football Association at that time, perhaps the South Americans should have been grateful that they got even that. The Scottish FA, sadly, also declined.

The FA may not have been a beacon of forward thinking at the time, but they were far in advance of the Scots in such matters. While both nations turned up their noses at the prospect of participating in a World Cup, the English were far less averse to taking on continental opposition in friendly matches than the Scots were. The first match played by the English outside Britain was in 1908, when they travelled to Vienna to challenge Austria. It took over 20 years for the Scots to follow their lead, not journeying abroad until 1929 when they crossed the North Sea to play against Norway. By that time England had played 25 international matches against eight different continental nations, only two of which had been played at home. The Scottish FA, by contrast, was an inward-looking body that clearly lacked the more progressive outlook of its southern neighbour, let alone the vision of the Uruguayans who were so determined to make a success of the first World Cup.

The Scots really should have ventured abroad much earlier than 1929, as they soon found that there was little to fear. They played three matches on that end-of-season tour and none of them ended in defeat. Norway were crushed by 7-3, the Netherlands beaten 2-0 and Germany held to a 1-1 draw in Berlin. This sequence of results was particularly impressive given that the Scottish squad couldn't be described as being anything better than a second- or third-string outfit. None of the 'Wembley Wizards' were included, with all of the great luminaries of the day such as Gallacher, Jackson and James being absent.

To be fair to the Scottish FA, sending a side to the 1930 World Cup would have been a mighty challenge. They would have required an enormous amount of co-operation from others if they were to have sent such a team, but it's doubtful they would have received it. The Scottish League, and the clubs who played in it, would have taken a vast amount of persuading that the tournament was worth bothering with, not least because it would have entailed reorganising the following season's fixture list.

The 1930/31 Scottish League season started on 9 August, just ten days after the World Cup ended, meaning that any home-based players in the Scottish squad would have been somewhere on the Atlantic Ocean when it kicked off. Their clubs would either have been forced to commence the new season without them, or else have appealed to the Scottish

League to delay its start until their top players returned. Either way, it's hardly likely that Scottish clubs would have looked favourably on their players travelling to and from Uruguay, missing pre-season training and a host of league matches, before arriving back out-of-shape after lounging about on a boat for a fortnight. After all, it was the clubs that employed and paid the players, and it was hardly in their interests to make a sacrifice for the greater good of the nation.

An indication of the most likely outcome of a tussle between the Scottish FA and their leading clubs can be found by looking at the international side that was put out against France in May 1930. At first glance it may appear curious that there were no players from Glasgow Rangers in the team, given that they had just completed a league and cup double. Yet there was a perfectly sound reason for their absence: they were thousands of miles away in the USA on an end-of-season tour, organised by their club as a reward for their achievements that season. If that tour took priority over the match in Paris, then there seems little likelihood that the World Cup would have been looked on any more favourably.

It's even more doubtful that English clubs would have allowed their Scottish players to be involved in an expedition to South America. The 1930/31 league season didn't begin in England until the end of August, which meant that Scottish players could have made it back from Uruguay in time for the start. However, given the antipathy of English clubs at the time towards releasing 'foreign' players for international duty, even for British Home Championship fixtures, it seems unlikely that they would have sanctioned their involvement in the World Cup.

Even if the Scottish FA had obtained the co-operation it required from Scottish and English clubs, the players would still have needed persuading that the trip was worth making. No doubt some of them would have relished the challenge, but others would have taken a lot of convincing. The Scottish full-back Tommy Law went on a tour of Argentina, Brazil and Uruguay with Chelsea in 1929, but did not return with happy memories of the experience. The west London side were greeted with unruly crowds that thought nothing of trying to intimidate players and officials by firing gunshots into the air during matches. One Chelsea player was punched by a spectator and a match in Buenos Aires had to be abandoned because of crowd disturbances. The English couldn't even rely on the native referees who, quite understandably in the circumstances, blatantly favoured the home teams and rarely interpreted the rules of the game in the same way that the British players did.

It's unlikely that Law would have relished a return trip in 1930, and his experiences would hardly have encouraged other Scottish players to participate in the tournament. Interestingly, one of the 'friendlies' played by Chelsea on that tour was against Peñarol, who supplied several players for Uruguay's World Cup challenge. The hosts may have won the game 2-1 but that is scant evidence of the superiority of Uruguayan football, given that Chelsea had just finished ninth in the second tier of the English league.

Another player that would not have been keen on the trip was Alex James. He was a reluctant traveller at the best of times, which was hardly surprising given what he had experienced earlier in his career. James was taken on Raith Rovers' end-of-season tour to the Canary Islands in 1923, but the journey nearly ended in disaster when his ship was wrecked just off the coast of northern Spain. The captain had to ground the ship in order to avoid hitting rocks but, in doing so, caused so much damage to his vessel that all the crew and passengers had to be evacuated.

Understandably, James was never keen on travelling by sea after that and avoided even relatively short sea trips whenever possible. He pulled out of Arsenal's summer tour to Denmark and Sweden in 1931 and then refused to play for the Gunners in a friendly match in Ireland in 1933. James also regularly missed the annual match played by Arsenal in aid of First World War veterans against Racing Club of Paris. The thought of a two-week sea voyage to Uruguay would no doubt have filled him with horror, and he would probably have sought any excuse not to go.

. . . .

The Scots' dressing room was a riot of noise at the interval, with almost every occupant trying to make himself heard above the din. Some of the players were talking excitedly about the first half and the goals the team had scored, while others spoke about what they needed to do after the break. Alex James happily stepped aside from the fray, deciding to let the younger men have their say for a few minutes. As he sat down on one of the benches his eyes settled on Jimmy McMullan, who was seated at the opposite end of the room. James was immediately concerned by what he saw, for the team's ageing captain was clearly exhausted.

Even though McMullan had been resting for a few minutes, he was still breathing heavily; his body struggling to restore its equilibrium. James started to lift out of his seat, so as to walk toward his captain, but then thought better of it. The last thing McMullan needed was someone fretting over him, especially given that there was little that James could realistically do to help.

James left his captain in peace and diverted his gaze to some of the Scottish FA officials that were moving among the players, congratulating them on their first half performance. James lifted his head back, closed his eyes and muttered something unrepeatable beneath his breath; this game was far from over and the last thing they needed was administrators patting them on the back as if the job was already done. When he opened his eyes again he noticed one of the officials talking eagerly to Alan Morton. From what he had heard, this was the young man who had moved heaven and earth to get Scotland to the World Cup.

The last thing James had wanted to do that summer was travel all the way to Uruguay; he hated boats at the best of times and he had better things to do with his break than sail halfway across the world. He didn't quite know how the young administrator had done it, but he had somehow convinced James's bosses at Arsenal that he had to be on that boat and they, in turn, had made sure he was. Wheels within wheels, no doubt, thought James to himself. God; how he hated the upper classes. They just organised the world around themselves and made sure that the little people did as they were told, regardless of what the little people may have wanted for themselves. Still, he had to admire what the young man had achieved. Apparently, the Scottish league season was even going to start a few weeks later than planned, just to give the players time to get back from Uruguay. How he had managed to do that he would never know.

• •

The World Cup of 1930 has become a much more important event than it ever was at the time. We see it as the first episode in the history of the biggest sporting competition in the world but, back then, most viewed it as no more than a curious experiment that was unlikely to succeed. To the British it was simply a fledgling tournament in a faraway land, contested by teams of which they knew little that had nothing to teach those who had pioneered the game. Now, once every four years, the World Cup Final is the most watched television programme on the planet; mankind's activities grinding to a halt simply to see two teams of young men chase a ball around a grassy field. The 1930 final didn't just take place in a different era; it took place in a different world.

The squad that the Uruguayans assembled for the World Cup, unsurprisingly, was based around the players that had won two Olympic titles. The side was captained by the reliable left-back, José Nasazzi, who had been a key part of both of those triumphs. He was joined by five other double gold medal winners, four of whom were forwards. There was Héctor Scarone, who practised his shooting by knocking down bottles at a distance of 30 metres; Santos Urdinarán, a diminutive right-winger; Pedro Cea, who sold ice when he wasn't playing football; and Pedro Petrone, who was Uruguay's top goalscorer at both Olympics, even though he declined to head the ball lest it spoil his carefully greased hair. The other veteran from Paris and Amsterdam was wing-half José Leandro Andrade, the only black player in the side. Andrade came from a humble background, scraped a living by shining shoes and subsequently died in poverty from tuberculosis. There was, however, no paucity in his ability to play football. He was an extravagantly gifted player who, it was said, once crossed half the pitch during a game with the ball balanced on his head.

Uruguay's first-choice goalkeeper for the World Cup was due to be Andrés Mazali, but he was dropped after being caught breaking a curfew. The double Olympic winner had made a quick visit back home to spend some 'quality time' with his wife. One only hopes she was worth it. He was replaced by Enrique Ballestrero who, while not as good a goalkeeper as Mazali, did at least possess the merit of being able to resist his urges when it was asked of him. Other additions to the squad for the World Cup included the lanky right-back Ernesto Mascheroni, who would go on to be the longest-living member of the World Cup winning side, the side's centre-half Lorenzo Fernández, and Álvaro Gestido, a wing-half whose brother later became president of Uruguay. The squad was also strengthened by the inclusion of three forwards; the one-handed Héctor Castro (he lost his right hand in a chainsaw accident), Pablo Dorado, the youngest member of the team at 22, and Santos Iriarte, nicknamed the canary, apparently.

The playing formation adopted by Uruguay was that employed all over the world at the time. Two defenders (a right-back and left-back) played behind three midfielders (a right-half, centre-half and left-half) who supported a five-man forward line (an outside-right, inside-right, centre-forward, inside-left and outside-left). The Uruguayans played their own variation of 2-3-5, but it was still recognisably the same system that had been used since the game was developed in Britain in the 1880s. Tactical revolutions would come in the future but, in 1930, the victors were generally those that played the system best, rather than those which had the best system.

The structure of the first World Cup was not radically different to that used for modern tournaments, with the 13 teams being split into four first-round groups. Ideally there would have been enough sides to make up four groups of four teams, but the weakened field meant that the Uruguayan hosts had to make do with one complete group of four teams and three groups of three teams. Only the winners of each group progressed to the semi-finals, with there being no second chances for those who finished as runners-up in their first-round group.

There were five seeded nations in the draw: the hosts, neighbouring Argentina, Paraguay and Brazil and, rather curiously, the USA. Uruguay's great rivals, Argentina, drew the short straw by being placed in the only group that contained four teams. The hosts, meanwhile, were drawn in a not particularly tough looking three-team group with Peru and Romania. The hosts of modern World Cups invariably distribute the tournament's games across a number of different cities. The first World Cup, however, was held solely in the Uruguayan capital of Montevideo, with only three different stadia being used.

Uruguay may have invited the world to come and play football in their country but their citizens initially showed little enthusiasm for the competition. The tournament's opening match between France and Mexico attracted a crowd of just over 4,000 spectators, while only 300 souls turned up to watch Romania play Peru, the lowest attendance in World Cup history. Teething troubles no doubt, but it was hardly an advertisement for the fledgling tournament.

What the Uruguayans did want to see, of course, was their own team play. An impressive crowd of over 57,000 people gathered to watch their opening match against Peru in the still unfinished Centenario stadium. The Uruguayans got off to a successful start, winning 1-0, but it was a stuttering, uncertain performance and their expectant supporters were less than impressed.

Decisive action was needed and it was duly taken. Four changes were made to Uruguay's team for their second match against Romania and, except for one player, remained unchanged for the rest of the tournament. Right-back Domingo Tejera was replaced by Mascheroni, even though Uruguay hadn't conceded any goals against Peru, and the forward line was also rebuilt. If Petrone had thought that being the side's top scorer at the last two Olympics had made his position in the side safe, then he was wrong. He was dropped, as was Castro, even though he had scored the winner against Peru, and Urdinarán also had to give way. Their replacements were Dorado, Scarone and Peregrino Anselmo, an asthmatic whose illness was to get the better of him before the tournament was over.

The Romanians, whose team was selected by King Carol, the nation's German-speaking monarch, were not expected to present the hosts with many problems, and so it proved. Uruguay's remodelled team fulfilled expectations by dispatching the Romanians 4-0, all scored within the first

35 minutes of the game. Half-time rescued the Romanians from further punishment and, without needing to stretch themselves in the second half, the Uruguayans breezed into the semi-finals.

Uruguay's opponents in the last four were Yugoslavia, who had topped their group ahead of Brazil and Bolivia. Not too much should be read into that, though. The Brazilian side was not remotely close to the standard of the great teams that would compete in future tournaments, while the Bolivians were probably the weakest team in the entire competition. They had only played seven international matches in the years preceding the World Cup and had lost them all, conceding an average of six goals a game in the process. The fact that their two World Cup matches against Brazil and Yugoslavia both ended in 4-0 defeats, therefore, actually represented an improvement in form.

Uruguay fielded the same side that had crushed Romania but, against all expectations, it was Yugoslavia that drew first blood, scoring after only four minutes of play. In front of a crowd of nearly 80,000 eager spectators the hosts soon drew level, courtesy of a goal by Pedro Cea. By half-time they were 3-1 up, with the irrepressible Anselmo scoring twice. The build-up to the third goal apparently included a touch by a policeman, who kicked the ball back into play after it had rolled off the pitch. It was a curious incident but, in the end, not one that mattered terribly. Uruguay scored another three goals in the second half, with Cea completing his hat-trick and Iriarte scoring his first goal of the tournament. The semi-final, ultimately, was a desperately one-sided affair, with Uruguay scoring more goals in it than they had in their previous two games combined.

Uruguay's opponents in the final were their nearest neighbours and oldest foes: Argentina. They had a tougher route to the final as they were in the only first-round group with a full complement of four teams and also had to overcome France, the strongest of the four European teams in the competition. The French eased to a 4-1 victory over Mexico in their first match of the tournament and then met Argentina in the group's second game. The peculiar schedule of matches hardly helped the French as they had to face a fresh Argentina only two days after beating Mexico. Their cause was also not helped by early injuries to two of their players, which meant that they had to play most of the match with only nine fit men (no substitutes were allowed back then).

The French managed to hold out until nine minutes from the end when they conceded a goal from a poorly defended free kick. They almost got back into the match when their left-winger bore down on the Argentinean goal but he was halted by the referee blowing his whistle for full time. That would be irritating enough at the best of times, but the official had inadvertently ended the match six minutes earlier than he should have. Lengthy complaints from the French ensued and, after the referee finally accepted his error, the game was restarted. However, whatever drive the French had was gone for good and no further goals were scored. The spectators thought so much of the Frenchmen's efforts, however, that they carried some of them off the pitch on their shoulders. The watching Uruguayan players also commented afterwards that France should have won the game, though they may have said that just to antagonise their rivals from across the River Plate.

After that initial flurry of excitement events proceeded more smoothly for the Argentineans. They won their next two group matches at a canter; a 6-3 win against Mexico followed by a 3-1 victory over Chile. Then, in the semi-finals they encountered the surprise team of the tournament: the USA. Little was initially expected of the Americans but their unorthodox tactics caught both their Belgian and Paraguayan opponents unawares. Their approach of defending in large numbers and then counter-attacking was novel for the time and neither of their challengers in the first-round group could fathom out how to respond to it. The USA defeated Belgium 3-0 in their opening match and then repeated the scoreline against Paraguay to book their place in the last four. The latter victory was particularly impressive as Paraguay had finished as runners-up at the previous year's South American Championship, beating Uruguay 3-0 in the process.

The Argentineans were a much classier outfit than the Americans, however, and it soon showed. They overwhelmed their opponents, taking the lead after 20 minutes and then scoring a further five goals in the second half. It was an impressive performance by the men from Buenos Aires, though a serious injury to one of the American players just before the break also had some bearing on the outcome. Even the American trainer had a bad day. He ran on to the pitch to remonstrate with the referee over a foul, dropped a bottle of chloroform from his medical kit and had to be helped back to the stands by his considerably more alert colleagues.

It was fortunate for FIFA that Uruguay and Argentina were in opposite sections of the draw as only a clash between these two teams could produce a World Cup Final worthy of the name. None of the other sides in the tournament, with the possible exception of France, had been able to trouble either of the two South American neighbours and the competition desperately needed a well-contested final. Argentinean fans sailed across the River Plate in their thousands for the game, eager to see their team avenge the defeat suffered at the 1928 Olympics.

The new Centenario stadium was full and many disappointed fans, some with valid tickets, were locked outside when the gates were closed half an hour before kick-off. Those that got in were searched by the police for handguns and revolvers and the tension rose even higher when it emerged that one of the key Argentinean players, Luis Monti, had received death threats in his hotel on the morning of the game.

If anyone was to receive such a word of warning, then it was bound to be Monti; the pantomime villain of 1930s international football. If you wanted to be charitable about his style of play, you would call it robust. Those on the receiving end of his challenges probably had some rather more choice words to describe it, however, and Monti courted trouble throughout the tournament.

The match against France was only two minutes old when he caught an opposing striker's ankle and left him limping for the rest of the game. Then, in the clash with Chile, he started a brawl on the pitch in which over 30 players and officials eventually became involved before it was broken up by the police. One suspects that the match between Argentina and Mexico only passed off without incident because Monti didn't play.

It would be unfair, however, to simply dismiss Monti as a bruiser. He was the pivot of the Argentinean team, acting as their playmaker when they had the ball and marker of the opposing centre-forward when they didn't. It's probably fair to say that Argentina's fate at the World Cup rested more heavily on his shoulders than on any other single player in their team. After 1930 he moved to Italy and, because of the more relaxed rules in place at the time, was able to play for their national team at the 1934 World Cup.

He ended up on the winning side that time, so becoming the only player in the history of the World Cup to have appeared in two finals for different nations. The nature of the man can perhaps best be summed up by an incident that took place in a match when Chelsea toured Argentina in 1929. In what was supposed to be a friendly game Monti offered to shake the hand of one of the Englishmen and, as the gesture was about to be reciprocated, promptly kicked him. Nice. Monti may not have been the captain of the Argentinean side but he was, without doubt, their most dominant, and brutal, character.

The 1930 World Cup Final was played in a febrile atmosphere. The referee selected to keep control of the incendiary fixture was a Belgian, John Langenus. He was familiar with the combatants, having been a linesman for their clash at the 1928 Olympics, and had already officiated over three World Cup matches involving either Uruguay or Argentina. However, he was so concerned by the fervour of the fans that he only agreed to take charge of the World Cup Final on condition that he was given a police escort to the port once the game was over, where a boat was waiting to take him and his family back to Europe. Clearly he didn't want to stay in a restless Montevideo a minute longer than he had to. Before the match started the two teams even had a row over which ball they were going to use, both wanting to use one made in their own country. The referee wisely resolved the dispute by suggesting that they play with the away team's favoured ball in the first half, and then the home team's in the second period.

Uruguay would have preferred to play the same XI that had thrashed Romania and Yugoslavia but, unfortunately, Anselmo had to miss the final after falling ill. His place was taken by the one-handed Castro, with the remainder of the team staying the same. The match started at a furious pace, with Uruguay making all the running. They scored the first goal through Dorado after 12 minutes of play, but were only able to hold on to their lead for eight minutes before the Argentineans breached their defence and scored an equaliser. Luis Monti may have been disconcerted by the threats he received but there was no evidence that it was affecting his football. He competed with his usual verve and vigour, playing a key role in the second goal which gave Argentina the advantage at half-time. The goal was scored by Guillermo Stábile, whose international career had all the brilliance and longevity of a firework. He made his debut at the 1930 World Cup, scored eight goals in four matches, finished as the tournament's leading scorer, left to play football in Italy and then never played for his country again. Curious days.

Uruguay played much better in the second half, following Nasazzi's half-time exhortations for them to raise their game. What was just as crucial, however, was Argentina's failure of nerve. Luis Monti was anonymous after the break, the death threats perhaps finally having the desired effect, while an injury to one of his team-mates only served to tilt the balance further in the hosts' direction. With their midfield warrior neutralised, Argentina were effectively doomed. Cea scored an equaliser after 57 minutes, Iriarte put Uruguay into the lead after 68 minutes and Castro made sure of the victory when he headed the ball into the net one minute from the end of the game.

It was, in retrospect, a truly grand final and Uruguay's victory meant they were able to claim, with some justification, that they still had the best football team in the world. Montevideo celebrated long into the night and the following day was declared a national holiday. Meanwhile, in the Argentinean capital, their bitter rivals hurled stones at the Uruguayan embassy. One can only wonder what would have happened if the final had been played on the other side of the River Plate. Perhaps with home advantage and an unthreatened Luis Monti, Argentina would have prevailed. Perhaps if they had volunteered to host the World Cup finals rather than let their neighbours take the strain, Argentina would have been the first holders of the Jules Rimet trophy. Perhaps.

• •

When the Scots arrived back on to the pitch for the second half the Uruguayan players were already standing there, patiently waiting for them. The pale-blue-shirted players made a point of fixing their glares on the Scots, making it abundantly clear that they were up for the challenge of clawing back the two-goal deficit. Some of the Scottish players returned the stares with fierce grimaces of their own, though others were clearly cowed; either averting their gaze or dropping their heads to the floor. Jimmy McMullan saw it all and was particularly concerned to notice that the left-back, Tommy Law, was one of those who had anxiously looked away. He had spent most of the first half protecting the youngster from the Uruguayan attackers but he knew he no longer had the energy to keep doing so. Law was about to embark on the longest 45 minutes of his life and there was little that McMullan would be able to do to help him through it.

If any of the Scottish players harboured any doubts about whether the Uruguayans really had the stomach for the fight, then they were soon disabused of them. The hosts came storming out at the start of the second half, not only taking the game to the Scots but also hurling themselves into some of the most committed tackles that the visitors had ever felt. Both sides had made a few full-bodied challenges in the first half, but they paled in comparison with the ferocious approach that the home team were now taking to the game. At the heart of the Uruguayan onslaught was the side's captain, José Nasazzi, who led by example; his tackling full of venom and attacking full of purpose. The Scots were rocked back on their heels by the sheer force of the Uruguayan attack and their five famed forwards could only watch helplessly as their defensive colleagues struggled to hold back the tide.

McMullan and Law, in particular, were having real trouble containing the hosts. The Scottish captain's ageing limbs had little left to give, leaving the unprotected Law at the mercy of Dorado's pace and Scarone's intelligent runs. The Uruguayan causing most damage, however, was their right-half, José Andrade. His first-half battle with McMullan had been an evenly balanced struggle, but the shattered Scotsman was no longer able to match the younger man's energy. Andrade duly made the right flank his own, running with the ball into the Scottish half of the pitch almost at will and spraying passes around with ease. Bradshaw did his best to protect the penalty area but was unable to prevent every attack from getting through and Harkness was soon called on to make a couple of fine saves.

It had been clear from early in the second half that a goal was coming for Uruguay and the only surprise was that the Scottish defence lasted out as long as it did; the second period of the game being almost 15 minutes old when the hosts finally got the goal that their determined fightback deserved. The move started, rather inevitably, with Andrade who effortlessly skipped past another tired challenge from McMullan. He had time to look up and see Castro peeling away from Bradshaw, whose attention was distracted by Scarone's darting run. Andrade lofted the ball up to Castro, who had made his way to the edge of the penalty area, and now stood unmarked. The centre-forward turned his back to the Scottish goal, so that he could better judge the flight of the pass, and then jumped to intercept it. Castro flicked his head to the right, sending the ball straight into the path of the onrushing Cea. Nelson threw himself down towards the Uruguayan's feet but was too late to prevent Cea from striking the ball with all his might; the ball shooting off the forward's foot and crashing past Harkness's outstretched arm. Scotland may still have held the lead but even the few neutrals in the ground couldn't see them holding on to it for long. Uruguay were on the rise again.

· ·

Two months before the start of the World Cup Scotland played their fourth-ever international match outside of Britain. Their opponents were France, who departed shortly afterwards for South America. The Scottish team was a fairly strong one, with John Thomson in goal, Jimmy Nelson in defence and Alex Jackson and Hughie Gallacher in the forward line, though the absence of any players from the double-winning Glasgow Rangers side effectively prevented it from being a genuine first XI. The Scots won the match 2-0, both goals scored by Gallacher who could undoubtedly have had more had the French goalkeeper not been in such fine form. History may have forgotten this fixture but it is an important game in the context of this book as it is the only real tangible clue we have of how Scotland may have fared at the World Cup, had they taken part.

The French side that Scotland beat without too much difficulty performed pretty well at the 1930 World Cup, winning their opening game against Mexico before losing to a late goal against Argentina. The French played most of that game with only nine fit men, had had just one day's rest after beating Mexico and were playing a side that were as fresh as daisies. The slender margin of Argentina's victory over a tired French side thus speaks volumes for the prospects of a Scotland entry in the tournament. After all, if a below-strength Scottish side could beat the French in Paris then surely their best XI could have severely tested the Argentineans on neutral ground.

As it was, Scotland's focus was still fixed on the annual clashes with their British neighbours. After the aberration of the 1927/28 British Home Championships, when they finished a lowly third, normal service was resumed in 1928/29. Scotland won all three of their fixtures, putting four goals past the Welsh in Glasgow and seven past the Irish in Belfast. All 11 of these goals were scored by 'Wembley Wizards', with Gallacher notching seven, Jackson two and Dunn and James getting a goal apiece. The concluding game with the English at Hampden Park was a much more sedate affair, with the hosts winning by virtue of a goal scored in the game's dying minutes. The goal was notable for the fact that it was scored direct from a corner, the stiff wind helping to blow it in the right direction for the Scots. What also hindered the English was that their goalkeeper was rooted to the floor as the ball was crossed, his feet pinned down by a mischievous Gallacher.

The 1929/30 Home Championships got off to a familiar start for the Scots, with the Welsh being beaten 4-2 in Cardiff. Once again the 'Wizards' scored all of the goals; Gallacher getting a brace and James and Gibson a goal each. Gallacher was on the scoresheet again when the Irish were put to the sword in Glasgow, scoring twice in a 3-1 victory. England also recorded victories over the Welsh and Irish (scoring an impressive nine goals in the process) to set up another end-of-season showdown with the Scots for the trophy. It was the Scots' first visit to Wembley since the 'Wizards' had run amok two years earlier and English hearts were burning for revenge.

What Scotland should have done, of course, was field the same XI that had humiliated England in 1928. However, the selectors, in their wisdom, picked a side that omitted too many of the nation's finest talents. Six of the side were Glasgow Rangers players, including four of the team's five defenders. It was an understandable decision, given that Rangers had just won the Scottish league title for the fourth year in a row, but it turned out to be the wrong one. English-based players were also largely ignored, with only three being selected. In total, only five of the 'Wizards' from 1928 were picked again; Harkness, Law, Jackson, James and Morton. The most damaging omission from the side was undoubtedly the prolific Gallacher, though that couldn't be blamed on the selectors. He was due to play but decided that he should appear instead for his club side, Newcastle United, who were fighting against relegation and had a crucial fixture against Arsenal on the same day.

England duly took advantage of the poorly constructed Scottish side, taking the lead after only 11 minutes of play and then embarking on a five-minute goal frenzy which gave them a four-goal advantage at the half-hour mark. The Scots managed to get a goal back early in the second half, but England soon restored their four-goal lead and a further Scottish goal did nothing to change the game's inevitable outcome. Much of the damage was done by Derby County's flying winger, Sammy Crooks, who gave Tommy Law a torrid time and played a key role in four of England's five goals. The poor Law was never selected for Scotland again, though that may not have been entirely due to his woeful display at Wembley. In the 1930s the English Football League made it extremely difficult for the Scots, Welsh and Irish to select their best sides for international matches, decreeing that clubs were not obliged to release their non-English players when international fixtures clashed with league games, which, of course, they invariably did.

• •

In an attempt to halt the Uruguayan offensive, Scotland started to venture out of their half of the pitch and attack the opposition goal. That ploy was met with vicious resistance by the home side who hacked down the Scots at every opportunity. Fernández was one of the worst culprits, but it was Mascheroni that committed the game's most infamous foul. His failure to contain Morton in the first half had resulted in him receiving some harsh and unrelenting feedback at the interval and, determined not to be outdone by Morton again, the right-back decided he would do whatever was needed to neutralise the Scotman's impact on the game. His opportunity came when Morton received the ball wide on the left flank and, as the Scotsman pushed the ball forward slightly, Mascheroni hurled himself, two-footed, at both man and ball. The force of the challenge knocked Morton clean off the pitch, to the evident delight of the cheering home fans and the Uruguayan players.

The Scotsman tried to get back on his feet straight away, but as soon as he put pressure on his right leg intense pain wracked his limb. Morton managed to stifle his instinctive reaction, only allowing himself to reveal a desperate grimace; stiff upper lip and all that. While bearing his wounds with stoicism may have been achievable, walking was another matter altogether. The brutal tackle reduced Morton to a forlorn figure, limping along the touchline and unable to have any real impact on the game. In the future, more humane rules would be introduced to allow an injured footballer to leave the pitch and be replaced by a substitute. Back in 1930, however, that change was many years away; Scotland having no alternative other than to soldier on with only ten fit men.

Uruguay duly took full advantage of the situation and, with Scotland's left flank in ruins, they inevitably pushed all their attacking moves down that side of the pitch. McMullan did his best to keep Andrade in check, but the Uruguayan was not to be contained. He drove his side forward, even mocking the Scottish captain by slipping the ball between his legs and performing his party trick of balancing the ball on his head while skipping past another weary tackle. If facing a resurgent Uruguay with only ten players wasn't hard enough, the Scots also had to contend with a referee who didn't appear to have their interests at heart. Not only had the Brazilian official failed to restrain the Uruguayan's harsh tackling, he also opted not to punish Mascheroni for his ferocious tackle on Morton. The Scots were used to tough games back home, but at least the officials there knew when to intervene to prevent things from getting out of hand. If all of that wasn't bad enough, the referee then handed Uruguay the perfect opportunity to equalise.

The incident began when Dorado received a fine pass from Andrade and bore down on Law, who backtracked into the penalty area in an attempt to defend Harkness's goal. As the Uruguayan outside-left lifted his foot to strike the ball Law slid in with a tackle that took it cleanly away from him. The force of the challenge brought Dorado to the floor and, as he picked himself up, he was surprised to see the referee pointing to the penalty spot. It was a fair tackle but the bellowing crowd had clearly convinced the Brazilian official otherwise. The Scots protested vigorously but their complaints were to no avail, with the referee making it clear that he was not going to change his decision. Harkness made a decent effort of trying to save Castro's spot-kick, diving the right way and getting a hand to the ball, but the power of the shot took it over the line. There were still 20 minutes left to play and, to all those watching, that appeared to be ample time for Uruguay to find the winner.

. . . .

In the aftermath of the 1930 World Cup Final the football associations of Uruguay and Argentina severed relations. The match had evoked emotions so strong that even the administrators no longer felt able to talk to each other. It was a sad outcome, especially considering that it was the Argentineans who had helped to put forward Uruguay's case for hosting the tournament at the FIFA congress in Barcelona a year earlier. Even sadder was the fact that this began a period of 20 years during which Uruguay voluntarily cast themselves into the football wilderness; the spirit of adventure that drove them across the Atlantic to compete in the 1924 and 1928 Olympics disappearing into a haze of recriminations. Uruguay didn't take part in either the 1934 World Cup in Italy or the 1938 World Cup in France, their absence commonly being attributed to them still being angry about being rebuffed by the Europeans in 1930. When Uruguay finally took part in another World Cup (in Brazil in 1950) they won it again, breaking the hosts' hearts with a surprise victory over them in the final game of the tournament.

The crest on the modern Uruguayan shirt displays four stars: two to celebrate their Olympic triumphs of 1924 and 1928 and two to commemorate their World Cup victories in 1930 and 1950. One can only imagine how differently Scotland would view its own football history if its team wore a shirt sporting a star. For better or worse, the history of the English national team revolves around the World Cup-winning team of 1966; the tests and trials that came before it, and the disappointments and frustrations that followed, often being referenced to that pivotal moment. Consequently, the England shirt has a star on it, reminding their long-suffering fans that at least their side reigned supreme once. The Scots were a similarly dominant force back in the inter-war period but, unfortunately, have little to show for it now.

The principal blame for Scotland's failure to make its mark on the global stage in the 1920s and 1930s must lie with the administrators that ran their game back then. They rarely sent the national side abroad to test themselves against unfamiliar opposition, with the height of their ambition being limited to beating England at Wembley. The Uruguayans, by contrast, had the vision to see what the game could be, rather than being obsessed with respecting its traditions. That foresight gave them the opportunity to become the best in the world while the Scots, sadly, didn't realise that it was already getting quite late in the day for them to have their hour in the sun.

Scotland still had a decent team when the next World Cup was held in Italy but, again, chose not to compete. However, even if they had, it's unlikely that they would have returned home with the trophy. Not only did the Italians have an impressive side that year, but they were also ably supported by Mussolini's fascist regime which was desperate for a morale-boosting victory on home soil. No British teams took part in the 1938 World Cup in France either, though by that time the English had supplanted the Scots as the strongest of the home nations.

The World Cup was suspended during the Second World War, but when it was revived again in 1950 the British nations finally deigned to take part. The Scots secured a place at the finals in Brazil but, bizarrely, turned it down. FIFA had agreed to the British Home Championship being used as a qualifying group, with the two top-placed teams going through. In what was probably the greatest act of hubris in the history of the competition, Scotland declared that they would only go to South America if they won the championship. They proceeded to thrash the Irish 8-2 and then beat the Welsh, but a narrow defeat at home to England resulted in a second-place finish. So they stayed at home.

Scotland belatedly made their World Cup finals debut in 1954 but they were heavily, and perhaps deservedly, punished for the arrogant stance that they had taken to the competition over the previous 24 years. They only played two games, losing them both: the first to Austria and the second, ironically, to Uruguay, 7-0. Scotland's history in the World Cup after that is well known; failure to progress beyond the first round of the finals being followed by the disappointment of not even qualifying for the finals at all. If Scotland were to have won a World Cup, then 1930 was not just their best chance; it was their only chance. Not only did they have one of the most talented groups of players that the country is ever likely to produce, but they could also have competed in a tournament which many of the best teams in the world had declined to attend.

The Scots had the players to win a World Cup in 1930 but lacked a visionary leader to show them the way. The French had Jules Rimet, who not only helped to make the dream of a World Cup a reality, but also ensured that the national team sailed halfway around the world in order to take part. What the Scots most desperately needed in 1930 was such a figure; a man who could bully and cajole clubs into releasing their best players; a man who could persuade recalcitrant players that the long journey was worth making; a man who could see where football was headed and what it would eventually become. If the Scottish FA had such a man in their ranks in

1930 then perhaps the national side would be playing today in shirts sporting a star proudly above the thistles and lion rampant. There was a brief moment in time when Scotland had the world at its feet, but it came and went before they even realised what they had missed. It's hard to see that they'll get another chance.

. . . .

With a man down and Uruguay in the ascendency the Scots should have been dead and buried. To their credit, however, they refused to lie down and die. Their left flank may have been of little use but their right-sided players were full of vigour and attacking intent. Gibson was clearly getting the better of Gestido, while Jackson's pace and movement were testing even the great Nasazzi. Dunn may have had a poor season with Everton but he was like a man reborn in Uruguay, playing the precise and delicate passes that had so attracted the attentions of the great Merseyside club in the first place. The last third of the half should have belonged to the home side but the Scots' refusal to give up the match as lost resulted in a frenetic final few minutes, with the game being as evenly balanced at its end as it was at its start.

Morton was still limping out on the left wing and the pitiful figure he struck greatly irked Gallacher. He dearly longed for a chance to mete out some retribution on Mascheroni but the opportunity just wouldn't present itself so, with time running out, he opted instead to settle the score with the first Uruguayan to cross his path. Gallacher's short fuse had already been exposed in the semi-final against Argentina, when he had clashed with their chief bruiser: Luis Monti. The Argentinean seemed to take exception to the diminutive Gallacher's refusal to be cowed by him, and, after a series of unsavoury tackles, the two of them began trading blows. It hardly looked to be a fair contest, with Monti towering over the undersized Scot, but Gallacher refused to be intimidated, aiming a volley of punches at his opponent's midriff. The Scottish striker had boxed as a youngster, with his fierce temper amplifying his natural pugilistic talents, and he was more than a match for the much larger Monti. As the saying goes, sometimes it's about the size of the fight in the dog rather than the size of the dog in the fight. The two combatants were soon separated, but the incident was not lost on the watching Uruguayans who noted just how fearsome the little Scot could be.

Gallacher had managed to contain his temper throughout most of the match against Uruguay, but when Fernández jabbed a sharp elbow in his ribs he finally exploded. Before the offending Uruguayan had the chance to move away, Gallacher launched his fist at his chin. The punch connected and Fernández collapsed to the floor, clutching his jaw in agony. The Brazilian referee may not have spotted Gallacher's strike, but many of the crowd did and they erupted in a din of indignation. It certainly wasn't a wise move to have provoked the volatile home fans and Gallacher's team-mates openly cursed him, fearing that his actions would affect the safety of them all. There were nearly 70,000 men screaming in rage at Gallacher and all that separated them from him were a few flimsy fences. The confrontation between Fernández and Gallacher threatened to boil over into an all-out brawl but the referee soon restored order, calming the bruised Uruguayan and taming the fiery Scotsman.

When the game finally restarted, there were less than five minutes left to play. Uruguay's forwards thundered towards the Scottish goal, desperate to get the goal that would give them the victory that their fans expected of them. Nelson was resolute in defence and, after taking the ball from Iriarte's feet, lofted it 20 yards upfield to Dunn's feet. The little Scotsman turned so quickly that his movement caught out the dazed Fernández, the Uruguayan accidentally clipping his heels as he tried to get to the ball. The referee immediately blew for a foul and Alex James sauntered over to take the free kick, midway between the halfway line and the edge of the Uruguayan penalty area.

Dunn noticed that James was starting to look a little weary, so he reminded him that extra time would be needed if the game was still level after 90 minutes. James puffed out his cheeks, shook his head, muttered something unrepeatable and then lofted the ball into the penalty area. The pass, played just in front of Jackson, was inch-perfect; the outside-right smashing his header past the helpless Ballestrero. The Brazilian referee came under great pressure to rule the goal out for some minor infringement that Gallacher was alleged to have incurred, but he stood firm and instructed the game to be restarted in the centre circle. The raucous Uruguayan crowd screamed at their players as they frantically retook their positions, urging them to find an equaliser in the last few breathless moments that remained of the match.

The closing minutes of the game passed in a blur for the Scottish players. They chased and harried the home side for all they were worth, dashing all over the pitch in one last fraught attempt to keep them away from their goal. Then, after what seemed like an eternity, the Scots finally heard a shrill whistle above the ceaseless clamour of the crowd. Against all odds, they had beaten the best team in the world in their own back yard and there were few neutrals there that day that begrudged them their brave victory. Would they hear about it in England? Well, maybe not that day, or even the day after but, for the next 36 years, barely an hour would pass without some Englishman being reminded of what happened on that great day in Montevideo when Scotland became the champions of the world.

2
The Italian Job

European Championship Final (Replay), Olympic Stadium, Rome, 10 June 1968

Italy v England

Italy	**England**
Dino Zoff	Gordon Banks
Giacinto Facchetti (captain)	Ray Wilson
Roberto Rosato	Bobby Moore (captain)
Sandro Salvadore	Brian Labone
Aristide Guarneri	Keith Newton
Tarcisio Burgnich	Alan Mullery
Giancarlo De Sisti	Martin Peters
Sandro Mazzola	Bobby Charlton
Luigi Riva	Alan Ball
Pietro Anastasi	Roger Hunt
Angelo Domenghini	Geoff Hurst

Referee: José María Ortiz de Mendíbil (Spain)

Monday night was not really a night to play football, mused Sir Alf Ramsey to himself as he watched his players limber up, nor was a quarter past nine any time to be starting a game. But then, what choice did they have? Even at this time of night the Rome air was sticky and uncomfortable, so playing any earlier was not a realistic option. He could see that some of the England players' white shirts were already starting to glisten with sweat and he felt for them. They'd all had a long, hard season and the last thing they needed was a replay. He could see in their eyes that they'd had enough, that they just wanted to get back home to their families and enjoy a few weeks of respite before the season began again. Inspiring them to make one last effort hadn't been easy, but he'd done his best. It was up to them now.

Glancing up at the stands, Ramsey was initially surprised to see how empty they were, but then he ruefully reflected that it was a Monday night. People would still be at work or had other plans or, perhaps, had been so bored by the first game that they hadn't returned for the replay. He'd seen some of the reports in the papers from back home and they hadn't been kind, either to his players or to the Italians. Ramsey didn't have much time for the press at the best of times but those reports had made him seethe.

Did they not understand how difficult it was to play in such conditions? Did they not appreciate that every game can't be a six-goal thriller? Did they really think that neither side were trying? Only fools could have written that stuff. He and his players were trying to win this damn trophy for queen and country and the press should support them, not denigrate them at every turn. What really made his blood boil, though, was how short their memories were. Had they really forgotten what it was like when England weren't the favourites to win? What it felt like when they repeatedly returned home empty-handed? Ramsey had made England into the best side in the world and a little gratitude, every now and then, really wouldn't go amiss.

· ·

The way in which football was played changed considerably during the 1960s, and not necessarily for the better. The previous decade had, arguably, been football's golden age, with a host of magnificent teams setting the game alight. Puskás's Hungary astounded and delighted all those that watched them play, Di Stéfano's Real Madrid dominated the newly founded European Cup and Pelé's scintillating Brazil deservedly triumphed at the 1958 World Cup. It was a glorious time to watch football, with teams placing much more emphasis on scoring goals rather than on not conceding them and coaches genuinely wanting their sides to entertain the spectators that paid to watch them play.

Sadly, however, the era of four- or five-man forward lines was nearly at an end and it was the Italians who were at the forefront of that development. Changes in tactics occurred gradually over the decade but if there was a watershed moment then, arguably, it came when Benfica met AC Milan in the 1963 European Cup Final. The Portuguese side had won the two previous editions of the tournament, with their 5-3 victory over Real Madrid in 1962 being one of the most thrilling European Cup finals of all time. In 1963, however, they came up against an Italian side that based its success on the miserliness of its defence. AC Milan triumphed 2-1 in a dull match at Wembley and, adopting similar tactics, their fierce local rivals Internazionale succeeded them as European champions the following year. Inter then went on to win the European Cup again in 1965 as well as the World Club Championship, thus confirming their status as the best club side on the planet, if not the most entertaining.

The two sides from Milan based their success on the use of a defensive tactic known as *catenaccio*, meaning bolt or lock, in which a sweeper, the *libero*, played behind the full-backs and centre-half. What was particularly novel about the system was that the *libero* protected space, rather than marking a particular player. The dominant tactical system at the time was the W-M formation, in which the centre-half marked the opposing centre-forward while the full-backs countered the threat from the wingers. The strength of the *catenaccio* system was that if the opposition breached the full-back and centre-back defensive line the *libero* was still on hand to help clear the danger. A team could only play with a *libero*, however, if they denuded their midfield or attack, thus weakening their offensive capacity.

Catenaccio wasn't a purely negative system but it became unpopular with spectators as it was often used in a particularly cautious way. Inter, for example, took a one-goal lead in the 1965 European Cup Final against Benfica and were content to defend it for the rest of the game, even though they were playing on their home ground against a side that had been reduced to ten men. *Catenaccio* seemed to have apprehension in its soul and in that, perhaps, lay its greatest weakness.

The two full-backs in the famed Inter defence were Tarcisio Burgnich and Giacinto Facchetti. Because of their effectiveness at club level they were also often paired together in the national side. The right-back, Burgnich, was a ruthless, aggressive man-marker whose defensive qualities led to him being nicknamed 'The Rock'. Facchetti, however, was a much more elegant player. Tall, well-built and handsome, Facchetti looked good before he even kicked a ball. As well as being a talented footballer he was also an accomplished sprinter, being capable of running 100 metres in less than 11 seconds. Facchetti played as a centre-forward prior to joining Inter as a teenager but, recognising his pace and energy, the team's coach, Helenio Herrera, decided to play him in an attacking left-back role instead. Consequently, he scored more than his fair share of goals, with one of his finest being a strike against Liverpool in the European Cup semi-final in 1965 when he ran 70 yards up the pitch to finish off a delightful passing move.

Despite being part of the robust Inter defence Facchetti was only sent off once during his career, and that was for sarcastically applauding a referee. He made his debut for Italy at the age of 21 and was a virtual ever-present in the national side for the next 14 years, playing his final international in 1977 at the age of 35. Facchetti played 94 times for his country in total and was the side's captain for an impressive 70 of those matches. He and Burgnich were virtually inseparable during their careers, both winning four Serie A titles, two World Club Championships and two European Cups. They even shared a room together on nights before games, leaving the former to lament that he spent more time with Facchetti than he did with his own wife!

While Inter's success was based on the strength of its defence, the team still needed creative players, such as their gifted inside-forward, Sandro Mazzola. He was the eldest son of Valentino Mazzola, who captained the great Torino side that won five consecutive Serie A titles in the 1940s. *Il Grande Torino*, as they became known, not only dominated domestic Italian football but also provided most of the players for the national side. They appeared to be an unstoppable force but, in May 1949, their plane's pilot lost his way in the fog as they flew home from a friendly game in Lisbon. The plane subsequently crashed into a wall at the back of the basilica at Superga, which overlooked Turin, killing everyone aboard. The club was left with just one first team player, who only survived because he had stayed behind to receive treatment for an injury. For Manchester United fans 'Munich' means only one thing, and for Torino supporters 'Superga' evokes the same emotions.

Sandro Mazzola was only six years old when his father perished and so had to endure a hard start in life. A friend of his father's later arranged for him to have a trial at Inter and he was duly taken on by the club. It was not a case of nepotism, however, as the young Mazzola was a very talented player in his own right. Herrera made best use of his pace and fine dribbling skills by playing him behind the centre-forward, thus giving him space to run at defenders with the ball at his feet. Mazzola had a powerful shot and scored some spectacular goals, with his two most important strikes coming in the 1964 European Cup Final. Inter beat Real Madrid 3-1 and after the match the great Puskás gave Mazzola his shirt, telling him that he had once played against his father and that his memory had been honoured by the youngster's performance. That shirt, unsurprisingly, became Mazzola's most treasured prize from his career in football.

AC Milan also had their own creative genius; Gianni Rivera. With his film star looks and prodigious talent, Rivera became known as *Bambino d'Oro* – the 'Golden Boy' of Italian football. He was only 15 when he made his Serie A debut for his hometown side, Alessandria, and his ability was soon spotted by the Milanese giants. They brought him to the San Siro and he stayed at the club for the remainder of his career, becoming the team's playmaker. Rivera had great vision and imagination, sensing scoring opportunities before opposing teams had even spotted that there was any danger. While he scored plenty of goals himself, his most valuable contribution to the team was his ability to create goalscoring chances for others. Managers of sides that are struggling to score goals often lament that none of their players are able to deliver the 'final ball'. This was what Rivera specialised in and was what made him such a revered talent.

If Rivera had a weakness, it was his obvious distaste for the more physical side of the game. He was not one for lunging into tackles or racing back to help out his defence and his detractors would often dismiss him as a luxury. In order to get the best out of Rivera, therefore, managers would often pair him with a midfielder who could win the ball and give it to him. Rivera soon proved his worth to Milan, helping them to win the Serie A title in his second season at the club and then inspiring them to their first European Cup triumph the following year. He arguably reached his peak in 1969 when he captained Milan to their second European Cup triumph as well as being voted European Footballer of the Year, thus becoming the first Italian to win the honour. Rivera's career was as lengthy as it was successful, with it starting in the 1950s and almost lasting into the 1980s. In that time, he played 60 games for his country, scored 14 goals and was the first Italian to appear in four World Cups; a feat that no English player has yet achieved.

The upsurge in the fortunes of Italy's leading clubs during the 1960s was mirrored by the renaissance of the national side. After winning two successive World Cups in 1934 and 1938 Italian football lost its way after the war, not only suffering the loss of the great Torino side in the Superga disaster in 1949 but also failing to retain the trophy in 1950: the former event having a crucial impact on the latter.

Italy didn't progress beyond the group stages at the 1954 World Cup and then didn't even qualify for the 1958 tournament after being knocked out by Northern Ireland. Italy did make the 1962 World Cup but, once again, crashed out before the quarter-finals.

In the years that followed, however, Italian football started to rise again. A new national coach, Edmondo Fabbri, was appointed and he had a talented new generation of players at his disposal, including those from the two Milanese clubs that had won three consecutive European Cups. His new-look side were soon beating all-comers, winning 18 of the 27 matches played prior to the start of the 1966 World Cup and losing just three.

Italy qualified for the 1966 World Cup without too much difficulty, despite being drawn in a fairly tough group which included Poland and one of the strongest Scottish sides of all time. Not only were Scotland able to call on all the Celtic players that won the European Cup in 1967, but such luminaries as Jim Baxter, Billy Bremner and Denis Law were also available for selection. The Italians suffered a 1-0 defeat at Hampden Park but then negated its impact with a 3-0 victory back in Naples. Indeed, it was Italy's strong home form that ensured their qualification for the World Cup, with both Poland and Finland being beaten 6-1.

Italy were one of the four seeded teams for the 1966 World Cup, alongside Brazil, England and West Germany. They were expected to reach at least the semi-finals and hopes of even greater success were raised further by a series of victories in the weeks leading up to the tournament. Admittedly they were all friendly internationals played at home, but Italy won them all in some style. Bulgaria, who had also qualified for the finals, were thrashed 6-1, Austria were beaten 1-0 and Mexico, who were drawn in England's group, were given a 5-0 battering. The most impressive result, though, was a 3-0 victory over the much-fancied Argentineans.

Italy's first-round group included Chile, the USSR and rank outsiders North Korea. With the top two sides qualifying for the quarter-finals Italy confidently expected to make it through. Their first match was against Chile and it gave few hints of the disaster that was shortly to befall them. Mazzola scored the game's first goal after only nine minutes and the Italians were never in much danger after that, going on to win 2-0. Worryingly, however, Rivera was curiously anonymous and he was subsequently dropped for the next game against the USSR. Both sides started the match cautiously, assuming that a draw would probably be sufficient to ensure their qualification for the next round. Unsurprisingly the score was 0-0 at half-time, but in the second half the Soviets scored the game's only goal to book their place in the quarter-finals. Unusually it was the normally reliable Facchetti who was at fault, giving too much space to a Soviet striker on the edge of his own penalty area and allowing him to cut inside and score with an excellent shot into the top corner of the net.

It was a disappointing defeat for Italy but hardly a disaster; a draw in their final game against North Korea would still see them reach the last eight. The task seemed simple enough as the Koreans had lost their first match 3-0 to the USSR and had only secured a 1-1 draw with Chile by grabbing an equaliser in the last few minutes of the game.

The diminutive Communists were allegedly only in the tournament to make the numbers up, having qualified for the finals almost by accident. In determining the make-up of the competition FIFA decreed that only one of the 16 teams in the finals would come from the vast continents of Africa, Asia and Oceania. The nations affected were, quite understandably, rather displeased with these bafflingly unjust arrangements and, consequently, all but two of them withdrew from the qualifying competition. That left just North Korea and Australia who, inconveniently, were technically still at war with each other. It was therefore agreed that they would contest a two-legged play-off at a neutral venue.

In the rather unlikely setting of Phnom Penh, Cambodia, the Koreans squared up to the Australians and won convincingly by an aggregate score of 9-2. One witness was the FIFA president, Sir Stanley Rous, who subsequently warned that the North Koreans should not be underestimated. Few listened to him, but they really should have.

Fabbri brought Rivera back into the side for the game against North Korea and persisted with playing Giacomo Bulgarelli in midfield, even though he knew he was not fully fit. The folly of that decision soon became evident when the

Italian captain was carried off the pitch on a stretcher with an hour still to play after suffering further damage to his already injured knee. It was no less than he deserved, though, as he had hurt himself in the act of trying to scythe a North Korean player in two. Substitutes were not yet allowed in World Cup finals matches so Italy had no option other than to soldier on with ten men, their task being made even harder when Park Doo-Ik scored with a low shot from just inside the penalty area shortly before half-time.

Italy fought back in the second half but the Koreans held on for a famous victory, leaving the favourites to trudge off the pitch disconsolately at the end of the game. The result was disappointing enough for the players but worse was to come when they arrived back at Genoa airport. They were greeted by jeering fans who expressed their disgust by pelting the players with rotten tomatoes and other assorted fruit and vegetables. The defeat was to have hefty consequences for those who were deemed to have disgraced the nation, with several of the players never representing their country again and the team manager, Fabbri, being sacked. The World Cup duly went on without the Italians and, for once, it was to have a happy ending for the English.

. . . .

The replay started in much the same manner as the previous match had finished, with both sides carefully guarding their goal and not committing men forward in attack. The game was only a few minutes old but Ramsey could already sense that the crowd was growing impatient. Weaker men may have felt impelled to respond but the England manager was impervious to their criticism. He had his plan and he would stick to it come what may. If it was entertainment that they really wanted, he muttered under his breath, they should go to the circus. This wasn't some trivial distraction, this was serious. This was football.

Almost as if to give the crowd something to be interested in, Burgnich clattered into an unsuspecting Englishman who had made the mistake of dwelling a little too long on the ball. It was a clear foul and, incensed, Ramsey instinctively rose to his feet to protest. The Spanish referee blithely waved play on and, with a barely perceptible shake of his head, a disgusted Ramsey returned to his seat. Dienst had been the referee on Saturday and he'd had a damn good game, just as he had in the World Cup Final two years earlier. Now they were back with this bloody Spaniard who'd given them nothing in the semi-final. Well, if that was how it was going to be, he thought, then that's how it was going to be.

The two coaches may have been strong-willed enough to resist the crowd's desire for a more open game, but not so the players. As the first half reached its midway point the Italians started to break ranks first, with Mazzola leading the way. Almost single-handedly he dragged his team up the pitch, taking the game to the English and pushing them back even further towards their own goal, if that were possible. The space left behind the Italian defence was too inviting a prospect for the visitors to ignore and they made repeated attempts to move into it, despite Ramsey's pleas for them to keep their shape. Almost in spite of itself, the match was threatening to turn into something worth watching.

• •

Alf Ramsey was appointed as England manager in 1962, with a brief to win the World Cup in four years' time. Ramsey was rightly feted for leading England to glory and, while he was undoubtedly an excellent manager, he was also quite a fortunate one. Not only did he have some genuinely world-class players at his disposal, such as Bobby Charlton, Bobby Moore and Gordon Banks, but he also had the advantage of playing a World Cup on home soil. Ramsey truly deserves his plaudits, but it must never be forgotten that no England manager has ever had a better chance of winning a World Cup than he did in 1966.

Before becoming a manager, Ramsey had been a formidable right-back, winning a league winners' medal in 1951 as part of Arthur Rowe's famous 'push and run' Tottenham Hotspur side. Ramsey was also selected to play for his country 32 times, though it was not a period of great success for the national side. He played in England's two most infamous defeats of that period; the shock 1-0 loss to the USA in the 1950 World Cup and the 6-3 mauling by Hungary at Wembley in 1953. That defeat to the Hungarians was the last game that Ramsey played for his country, and his club career didn't last much longer after that either.

Within a couple of years Ramsey had given up playing and had taken over as manager of Ipswich Town. He was a natural leader, having captained both Spurs and England, and he soon demonstrated his managerial genius by revolutionising the fortunes of the unfashionable Suffolk side. His first match in charge of Ipswich was a Third Division South fixture against Torquay United yet, within seven years, his side would be playing against AC Milan in the European Cup. Ramsey's team finished top of the Third Division at the end of his second season in charge and, four years later, were Second Division champions. That was a fairly impressive set of achievements, but it was as nothing compared to what was to come.

Most commentators confidently predicted that Ipswich Town would last no longer than one season in the First Division but they were proved badly wrong. Ramsey's side swept all opposition aside, including Bill Nicholson's magnificent Spurs team that had won the league and FA Cup double the previous season, and duly finished as champions. Ipswich couldn't afford to buy star players and so Ramsey sought competitive advantage by using tactics that baffled opposing teams. One of the key features of Ipswich's play was the use of a deep-lying left-winger to start attacks. That may not seem like much of a development, but at a time when English football was still in thrall to the standard W-M formation any well-planned deviation from it was sufficient to cause great confusion in opposition defences.

Ramsey's success with Ipswich was perfectly timed. He won the league title in 1962, shortly before Walter Winterbottom's last World Cup as England manager, and when that job became vacant Ramsey's name was inevitably near the top of the list. The post was initially offered to Burnley right-half Jimmy Adamson, who had been Winterbottom's assistant at the World Cup. He turned the job down so the FA instead offered it to Ramsey, who only accepted on condition that he would have full control over team selection. Winterbottom had had no such luxury, having had to suffer the unwelcome interference of a selection committee. It was an important step forward for the national side and one of many important changes that Ramsey was to insist upon.

Ramsey confidently predicted that England would win the World Cup in 1966, but it took much experimentation before he finally constructed a team that was capable of doing that. He knew that any fool could pick England's best 11 footballers, but was acutely aware that his job was to create a team that was greater than the sum of its parts. That meant selecting some players who fitted better into his overall plans ahead of others who were widely regarded as being the best in their position in the country. That often made for unpopular and initially questionable decisions, but Ramsey's judgement would eventually be vindicated.

Probably the most important player available to Ramsey was the incomparable Bobby Charlton. His talents were undeniable, but the challenge for Ramsey was how to make best use of them. Charlton started his career as an inside-forward before moving out to play on the wing, and this was where Ramsey used him at first. Ramsey had witnessed at close hand the damage done by Nándor Hidegkuti when he played as a deep-lying centre-forward in Hungary's trouncing of England in 1953. He therefore decided to use Charlton in a similar way, converting him into an attacking central midfield player. It was a role which gave him licence to do whatever he wanted to do and, within reason, to go wherever he wanted to go. Having settled on Charlton's best position Ramsey then proceeded to construct a side around him, making him the piece in the jigsaw puzzle that all the other pieces had to fit around.

Ramsey decided not only to remove Charlton from the wing, but to dispense with wingers altogether. England sides had played with wingers since their first international game in 1872 and Ramsey continued to persist with them for several years before it became obvious that his side would be more effective without them. The use of two wingers, either in a W-M or 4-2-4 formation, was still in vogue in English football at the time and it was almost heresy for Ramsey to select a team that didn't include them. Ramsey knew what he was doing, though. Times were changing and he realised that he could no longer afford to have wingers loitering on the touchline, simply waiting for the ball to be passed to them so that they could run at the opposing defence.

Thus, Ramsey's famous 'wingless wonders' were born. The profligate wide players were replaced with energetic, multi-tasking midfield players, of whom Alan Ball and Martin Peters were his favourites. Not only were they prepared to track back and tackle, a task many wingers thought beneath them, but they were also inventive enough to pose an attacking threat as well. Ramsey had a penchant for industrious footballers and his system made the most of players who were prepared to run up and down the flanks of the pitch for the entirety of a game. Ramsey's side were often described as playing in a 4-3-3 formation but, in reality, it was 4-1-3-2, with the combative Nobby Stiles playing as the '1' in front of the defence while Charlton spearheaded the midfield with Ball and Peters abreast of him.

Ramsey's new model army went on to capture the 1966 World Cup as planned, satisfying the hopes of a nation, many of whom viewed victory almost as their birthright. To characterise Ramsey simply as a tactical maestro, however, would be misleading. If that had been his only talent, then he would never have been able to lead England to glory.

Ramsey was also a consummate leader of men who created a tremendous spirit within the England squad. While he often came across as stand-offish and aloof in his dealings with the media, Ramsey was a popular figure with his players, many of whom would do anything for him. He expected loyalty from them, but was equally prepared to be faithful in return. After England defeated France to qualify for the quarter-finals of the 1966 World Cup Ramsey came under great pressure from the FA to drop Stiles from the team. The Manchester United player had committed a horrendous foul on the French midfielder Jacky Simon, though it was probably more due to over-zealousness than to any malicious intent. Ramsey's response was curt but clear: Stiles could be dropped but another manager would have to be found to do it. He effectively put his job on the line for one of his players and it was such acts of leadership that made Ramsey so revered by his men.

Ramsey could be ruthless with his charges, though, when he needed to be. After one training session, shortly before a trip abroad, some of the England players decided to enjoy a little light refreshment in a local hostelry. Ramsey was unimpressed and when the players arrived back in their hotel rooms early in the morning they found their passports lying on their pillows. It was not as if a horse's head had been put in their beds, but the warning was clear: disappoint the boss and you'll no longer be part of his plans. The offending players were given another chance and they never let the England manager down again.

Ramsey's goalscoring heroes of 1966 will probably always be remembered best, whether it's Charlton slamming the ball past the Mexican goalkeeper or Hurst's immortal hat-trick in the final. The foundation of England's success, however, lay in its rearguard. Ramsey's carefully constructed defence didn't concede a single goal in the first four matches of the tournament and it was only in the dying minutes of their fifth game, the semi-final against Portugal, that Gordon Banks finally had to pick the ball out of the back of the net. Indeed, no other World Cup-winning side has ever got so far through the competition without conceding a goal. Uruguay, Mexico, France and Argentina all failed to find a way past the English back four, and a team that doesn't let in goals doesn't lose all that often. While Ramsey tinkered with his choice of midfield players and strikers throughout the tournament, he noticeably never made a single change to his defence.

The figure at the base of Ramsey's rearguard was the unflappable Gordon Banks. He made his debut in Ramsey's second game in charge of England and the two men were inseparable for the next nine years. Banks kept a remarkable 35 clean sheets in his 73 appearances for his country and played 23 consecutive games between 1964 and 1967 without suffering defeat. During that period Banks was probably the best goalkeeper in the world, with only the ageing Soviet keeper, Lev Yashin, also having a legitimate claim on the title. Banks had superb reflexes, which were most famously exhibited when he made an almost miraculous save from a header by Pelé in the 1970 World Cup. Such was his importance to the England team that their quarter-final defeat in that tournament to West Germany is commonly attributed to his absence through illness.

The most important component in Ramsey's back four was one of the nation's greatest ever footballers; the imperious

Bobby Moore. Rudyard Kipling famously wrote that young men should aspire to keep their head while all those around them are losing theirs. It was a line that could have been written with Bobby Moore in mind, so perfectly does it capture his imperturbable nature. Moore's serene approach to the game sometimes gave the impression that he wasn't trying hard enough, but that was a mistake that only an untutored eye could make.

If there was one moment that encapsulated Moore's unhurried approach to the game it came in the dying seconds of the World Cup Final against West Germany. Moore collected the ball deep in England's half of the pitch, with Jack Charlton bellowing at him to kick it into the stands to protect their one-goal lead. Such crude behaviour, however, was just not in Moore's make-up. Instead he looked up, spotted that his West Ham United team-mate, Geoff Hurst, had been left unmarked and knocked a perfectly weighted pass up to him. Hurst collected the ball, galloped up the pitch and smashed the ball past the German goalkeeper. It was all over now.

If you were to nominate England's finest ever defender, then you probably wouldn't consider one that had little pace and wasn't particularly strong in the air. That was true of Bobby Moore, but which English defender would you ever choose ahead of him? Moore was only able to mask the deficiencies in his game because he could think faster than any other player on the pitch, thus gaining the extra half a yard that he needed. Bobby Moore won his first England cap just after his 21st birthday and played well enough to win a place in the squad for the 1962 World Cup in Chile. He gained valuable experience in that tournament and put it to great use when he led England to glory four years later, being one of the best players of the tournament. Moore had a natural air of authority and was captain of the England side for all but 17 of the 108 matches that he played for his country.

The other world-class defender available to Ramsey was Everton's diminutive left-back Ray Wilson. There were other players in Ramsey's World Cup-winning side that won more plaudits in the press but, among the players themselves, Wilson was never underrated. He was a clinical tackler who rarely allowed a winger to get the better of him, but perhaps his most distinguishing characteristic was his ability to deal with pressure. West Germany's first goal in the World Cup Final resulted from a weak defensive header by Wilson and, given the magnitude of the game and the potential seriousness of the error, lesser players may have crumbled. Wilson, however, continued playing as if it had never happened.

Italian sides may have been at the forefront of developing a more defensive style of play, but some of the blame for this direction of travel must also be placed at Ramsey's door. The success of his England side inevitably led other domestic managers to ape his tactics and, consequently, the number of goals scored in the league fell dramatically. When Spurs won the league in 1960/61 over 1,700 goals were scored in First Division matches. Within ten years, however, the total number of goals scored in the top division had fallen by over a third, to just over 1,000. Between 1960/61, when the W-M formation was the norm, and 1970/71 when it was virtually extinct, the average number of goals per game in the First Division dropped from nearly four to just over two. Tactics may have evolved, but from the perspective of the paying spectator it was a rather depressing type of progress.

. . . .

One of the most intriguing battles on the pitch was between Sandro Mazzola and Bobby Moore. Almost all of Italy's attacking moves were directed through the pencil-moustachioed striker and he ran repeatedly at the English back-line, with Moore often being the rock on which his efforts floundered. The England captain may have appeared to be well in control but

Mazzola was pushing him to his limits. Indeed, there were several occasions on which Moore's tackles only narrowly relieved Mazzola of the ball. Sooner or later Mazzola would get the better of Moore and, as he had shown so many times before, one chance was all that he needed.

One of the reasons why Italy were so reliant on Mazzola to drive them forwards was that their attacking left-back, Facchetti, was being well marshalled by Alan Ball. When England played Argentina in the quarter-finals of the 1966 World Cup Ramsey had used Ball to counter the threat posed by Silvio Marzolini, one of the best attacking left-backs in the game. Ball had a superb game, keeping Marzolini in check and also causing the Argentinean defence problems with his own attacking runs. Ramsey opted to use Ball in much the same way against Italy and it was working out just as he had planned, with the fiery-haired tyro neutralising Facchetti's impact on the game.

Italy's first real chance of opening the scoring came just after half an hour of play. The move started when Burgnich relived Bobby Charlton of the ball with a crunching tackle, the referee opting once again not to take any action. The Italian right-back was first to his feet and he managed to get the ball out to Mazzola, who was positioned just outside the centre-circle in his own half of the pitch. The Inter striker accelerated towards the England goal, with the ball seemingly glued to the toe of his boot, and then motioned as if he was going to play it out to the right wing. The waiting Moore instinctively swayed to his left in anticipation of the ball's flight, but was immediately wrong-footed as Mazzola darted to his right. The England captain tried to recover but the Italian's momentum was too great for him to be caught. The remainder of the England defence scrambled to fill the gap but, before they did so, Mazzola fired the ball hard at goal from the edge of the penalty area. Against most keepers it would have been a goal but Banks was equal to the strike, tipping it around the post with his fingertips. The match may have still been goalless but the impetus was clearly with the Italians. Surely it was only a matter of time before they scored.

. . . .

The manager given the unenviable task of redeeming the reputation of the Italian national side after the disaster against North Korea was Ferruccio Valcareggi. Technically he was one of the guilty men, as he had been Fabbri's assistant at the World Cup, and the price he had to pay was not being allowed to manage the side on his own. The Italian federation decided to establish a 'technical commission' to manage the team, which was composed of Valcareggi and the double European Cup-winning Inter manager, Helenio Herrera. It was to be a short-lived experiment, lasting only for four games, but results were good and some much-needed confidence began to return to the side. Their first match, four months after the debacle against the North Koreans, was a cathartic 1-0 home victory against the USSR.

Unsurprisingly only three of the side that fell to North Korea were picked to play against the Soviets, though some of the shamed players, such as Rivera, were eventually allowed to return from exile.

Italy's next match was their first qualifying game for the European Championship finals. The finals were scheduled to be held in the early summer of 1968, but their location was not due to be decided until after the qualifying games had been played. The finals back then were significantly smaller than the bloated modern-day tournaments, with the 31 competing nations being organised into eight qualifying groups and the winners of each group progressing to the quarter-finals. These were then played over two legs, with the four successful sides advancing to the finals. The finals themselves consisted of just four games: two semi-finals, a third and fourth place match and the final itself.

The 1968 European Championships were the third in the series, with the USSR winning the first tournament in 1960 and Spain taking the trophy from them in 1964. The idea for a European-wide competition for national sides was first suggested in 1927 by Henri Delaunay, head of the French Football Federation, but the proposal gained little traction until the creation of UEFA in 1954 provided the necessary impetus. Delaunay died before his plans reached fruition but he would not be forgotten, with the trophy that the nations competed for being named in his honour.

Italy's qualifying group did not look to be particularly taxing, with only Romania, Switzerland and Cyprus having to be overcome if they were to reach the last eight. Their first qualifying match was against Romania in Naples and Herrera's influence on team selection was clearly in evidence, with no less than eight of his Inter side being chosen for the game. Herrera was undoubtedly loyal to his players, but it must be questioned whether he really had the objectivity needed to be joint-manager of the national side.

Nevertheless, Italy got off to a winning start in the competition, though they were given an early scare by the Romanians who scored after just seven minutes. The visitors should have held on to the lead for longer but their goalkeeper gave away a poor goal after half an hour of play. Mazzola crossed the ball from the right wing and the Romanian goalkeeper, positioned with one foot either side of the goal line, caught it easily. He proceeded to bounce the ball on the ground but, to his horror, the linesman then signalled that it had crossed the line and duly awarded the goal to Mazzola. Italy got another goal just before half-time and, midway through the second half, Mazzola scored again with a delightful chip over the stranded goalkeeper from just outside the penalty area.

Italy's next qualifying game was against Cyprus in Nicosia and the side was once again dominated by Inter players.

Mazzola was missing, but Rivera was back in the side for the first time since the debacle against the North Koreans. It was a game that the Italians should have won easily but the Cypriots managed to keep them at bay until the last 15 minutes of the game. The deadlock was finally broken by Angelo Domenghini, whose low shot from just outside the penalty area evaded the goalkeeper's dive. Facchetti then made sure of the victory two minutes from time, heading home the ball from a corner.

Domenghini, a right-winger, made his debut for Italy in 1963 but got few chances to play while Fabbri was in charge. He was not selected for the 1966 World Cup squad but that turned out to be a blessing in disguise, as he consequently evaded being tainted by the disaster that unfolded in England. Domenghini's re-introduction to the national side was certainly helped by the fact that he was one of Herrera's Inter players, but he soon demonstrated his worth and went on to become a regular fixture in the team.

The rehabilitation of the national side was further demonstrated a few days later when they secured a 1-1 draw against Portugal in a friendly in Rome. The visitors had finished in third place at the 1966 World Cup and, having also beaten the fourth-placed Soviets a few months earlier, Italy were showing that they could still compete against the best. The clear impression given was that the defeat against North Korea had been no more than a blip and that normal service was being resumed. Buoyed by the decent run of results, the Italian federation showed their confidence in Valcareggi by allowing him to run the national side on his own. Valcareggi had been a decent inside-forward in his playing days, though he was never quite good enough to represent his country. He later went into football management and, after successful spells with Atalanta and Fiorentina, was offered the job of assisting Fabbri in managing the national side. A firm advocate of *catenaccio*, Valcareggi led the national side for eight years, losing only six games during that period.

Valcareggi's first game in sole charge of the national side was the European Championship qualifier away to Romania in June 1967. He soon showed that he was his own man by making a significant reduction in the number of Inter players in the side, with only three of them being picked instead of the seven or eight that had usually been selected when Herrera was involved. A draw would have been a decent result for Italy, and it looked like that was what they were going to get until they scored the winner nine minutes from time from a well-worked move. The victory lifted Italy to the top of the qualification group, level on points with Romania, who had played all of their six qualification matches. Italy then beat Cyprus 5-0 in their next home game to move clear at the top of the table, thus ending Romania's chances of reaching the quarter-finals.

The victory over Cyprus was particularly sweet for the Italian striker, Gigi Riva, who scored a hat-trick of goals in the first 15 minutes of the second half. He can lay claim to being one of the greatest Italian strikers of all time, if not the best of them all. He was tall, quick, and had a powerful physique which he was not afraid to throw around. His most potent weapon, though, was his left foot shot, which was once timed at 75mph. Apparently one of these thunderbolts was responsible for breaking the arm of a young boy who had unwisely stood behind the net during a training session. Riva made full use of his talents, often scoring with stunning shots from distance or brave headers.

Riva was that rarest of beasts: the one-club man who stays with his team through thick and thin, passing up lucrative offers from bigger clubs and staying loyal to adoring local fans. He spent virtually his entire career with the Sardinian side Cagliari, with his and the club's fortunes both following the same trajectory. When he joined them they were struggling in the lower divisions but he helped them to win promotion to Serie A and, after establishing themselves at that level, they went on to win the championship in 1970. It was an incredible achievement for a relatively small club and Riva was at the heart of it. He was the top goalscorer in Serie A in the 1966/67, 1968/69 and 1969/70 seasons and his exploits made it almost impossible for Valcareggi to ignore him.

Riva went on to become Italy's record goalscorer, with his tally of 35 goals in 42 games still standing as the national best. He was undoubtedly a courageous player, but his committed approach often resulted in him incurring injuries which interrupted his career. He broke his leg in the 1-1 draw with Portugal and then fractured it for a second time in 1970, also while playing for the national side. Perhaps inevitably, it was also an injury that ended his career. He damaged his thigh in a game in 1976 and, this time, there was no coming back. It was also the end of Cagliari's time at the top as they were relegated from Serie A that season.

Italy's final two qualifying games were against Switzerland, with the outcome determining which side would progress to the quarter-finals. The Swiss had got off to a poor start in the competition, losing away to Romania, before gaining ample revenge by thrashing them 7-1 in Zurich. The Swiss had then knocked five goals past Cyprus to put them in with a chance of qualifying, if they could get a couple of good results against Italy. The first game in Berne was predictably tight, with the Swiss twice taking the lead but Riva responding with two equalisers, the second a penalty with just five minutes of the game remaining.

That draw meant that Italy only needed to avoid defeat in the return fixture in Cagliari if they were to qualify. Rather than playing for a draw, Valcareggi's side took the game to the Swiss and reached the quarter-finals in some style. Mazzola settled early nerves with a goal after three minutes, and ten minutes later Riva scored in front of his delighted home crowd. Domenghini added another just before half-time and then scored again in the second half to give the Italians a well-deserved victory. Joining Italy in the quarter-finals were Ramsey's England, though their qualification had been a much more close-run thing.

. . . .

As the game neared half-time Ramsey was itching to talk to his players and explain what they needed to do to turn the game in their favour. One of the issues he needed to address was the increasing difficulty that Ray Wilson was having with Angelo Domenghini. The swift Italian right-winger was causing the World Cup winner all manner of problems with his pace, making him look every one of his 33 years. Football is no respecter of age and it appeared to be a tournament too far for the fading Wilson. Domenghini was seven years his junior and had already nipped past him a few times in the first half before delivering dangerous crosses into the penalty area. Ramsey recognised the problem and knew that it would only get worse as the match wore on.

Valcareggi was as keen for the first half to continue as Ramsey was for it to end. His team had pushed the English further and further back throughout the game and fully deserved a goal for all of the possession that they'd had. With the minutes ticking away to the break it seemed that England were going to escape the first period unscathed, but then came the moment that the home fans had been waiting for. Facchetti had the ball in his own half of the pitch and, with Ball blocking his path once more, he had no option other than to launch a long cross-field ball to Domenghini. The pass was hit with as much accuracy as it was with frustration and it landed straight at the right-winger's feet.

Domenghini immediately ran towards Wilson, skipped past his challenge and then hit a delightful, looping cross into the penalty area. Riva had done little during the first half but, like all great strikers, he was capable of sparking into life as soon as a goalscoring opportunity presented itself. He timed his run into the penalty area perfectly, climbing above the England defence and sending a thundering header down to Banks's left. From the moment the ball left Riva's head it looked certain to be a goal but the English keeper somehow managed to get a hand to it, flicking it on to the post. Moore tried to get to the rebound first but the swifter Mazzola beat him to it. With Banks still guarding the left-hand side of the goal Mazzola opted not to shoot, lifting the ball instead into the centre of the six-yard area where Riva was waiting to tap the ball into the net. It might not have been the most impressive goal he'd ever scored but, in the context of Italy's recent past, it threatened to be his most important.

• •

England embarked on the 1968 European Championships having never previously reached the finals. They had neglected to enter the 1960 tournament and were knocked out in the preliminary qualifying round of the 1964 competition. Their conquerors were France, who secured a 1-1 draw at Wembley before mauling England by 5-2 back in Paris. The second of these two fixtures was Ramsey's first game in charge and it was hardly an auspicious start to his tenure. Both Ramsey and England had moved on since then and, as reigning world champions, they were fully expected to progress from their qualifying group, though the composition of that group was a little unorthodox by modern-day standards.

UEFA had agreed that the fixtures in the 1967 and 1968 British Home Championships could also serve as the qualifying matches for the quarter-finals of the European Championships. It was a neat way of reducing fixture congestion and also had the benefit of guaranteeing that one of the four British nations would reach the quarter-finals. The drawback, of course, was that only one of them could progress to the next round, and that added an edge to the already feisty annual encounter between England and Scotland.

Before England took on the Scots, however, there were two fixtures against Northern Ireland and Wales to be taken care of. Ramsey's side met the Irish in Belfast and won 2-0, courtesy of strikes by Roger Hunt and Martin Peters. They then rounded out 1966 with a resounding 5-1 thrashing of Wales at Wembley, with the goals being shared between Geoff Hurst, the two Charlton brothers and a luckless Welshman. The first game against Scotland was played at Wembley in April 1967 and it has since become a much-remembered game, especially north of the border. Ramsey made only one change to his World Cup-winning side, bringing in Jimmy Greaves in place of Hunt. The Scots, bristling at the idea that their long-standing rivals could be considered to be the best in the world, fielded a strong side that included four of the Celtic team that would become the first British side to win the European Cup a month later. The side also included the belligerent, hard-tackling Billy Bremner, errant genius Jim Baxter and prolific Manchester United striker Denis Law.

Scotland, as expected, competed with great aggression, but there was also a petulant aspect to their play. Early in the match England were waiting to take a throw-in while the ball was returned to the pitch. The ball landed near a Scot who, rather than just pass it to the English player that was going to take the throw-in, simply volleyed it hard at his shins instead.

The outcome of the game was greatly affected by injuries to two England players, both of which occurred during the first half. Jack Charlton broke a toe in a collision with Bobby Lennox and then Ray Wilson sustained an ankle injury. With no substitutes allowed Wilson had no choice but to soldier on, though he was a much-diminished force, as was defender Charlton who bravely played on as an auxiliary striker. The

Scots took full advantage of the injury to Charlton, taking the lead while England were effectively down to ten men and keeping hold of it until 12 minutes from the end of time when there was a sudden glut of four goals in a frantic finish to the game.

Lennox scored the first with a low shot past Banks before the wounded Charlton got a goal back for England following some fine wing play by Alan Ball. Charlton was only on the pitch for nuisance value, rather than for anything else, but he played with so much grit and resolve that he outshone Greaves and Hurst, neither of whom played well. Jim McCalliog then restored Scotland's two-goal advantage with a run from deep which caught out the England defence. Even though they were two goals ahead, and there were only a few minutes left to play, the Scots' fractious behaviour did not improve. As England were about to take the kick-off one of the Scottish players, returning to his half of the pitch, kicked the ball away from the centre circle to delay the restart of the game. By beating England they may have considered themselves to be 'unofficial world champions', but they clearly didn't have it in them to behave like champions.

Hurst managed to get a late goal back for England with a header from a cross by Bobby Charlton, but it came too late to achieve anything other than to make the final scoreline look a little more respectable. The Scots had secured a famous victory, but it should be noted that they only did so by aping Ramsey's innovative 4-3-3 formation. The victorious Scots would never have admitted it but imitation is, of course, the sincerest form of flattery. The root cause of England's defeat lay in the injuries to Charlton and Wilson, which left them with only nine fit men on the pitch for most of the match and gravely weakened the defence on which so much of their success had been built. Scotland's triumph, meanwhile, not only won them the 1967 British Home Championship but also lifted them to the top of the qualifying group for the 1968 European Championships.

England's next game was a friendly at home to Spain. Ramsey retained most of the players that won the World Cup, but never again would he pick the side that beat West Germany. Nobby Stiles was unavailable for selection as he had gone on a tour of Australia with Manchester United so Ramsey replaced him with Tottenham Hotspur midfielder, Alan Mullery. An energetic, combative player, Mullery was nicknamed 'The Tank' by the Spurs fans; such was the force of his tackling. He was predominantly a ball-winner but, unlike many of his ilk, could do more with the ball once he had won it than just pass it to a more talented team-mate. This gave him an edge over the equally aggressive Stiles and he duly took advantage of his rival's Antipodean adventure to become Ramsey's first-choice defensive midfielder for the next few years. One of his finest performances in an England shirt came at the 1970 World Cup in Mexico, when he shackled Pelé in the group game against Brazil.

Ramsey also made a couple of changes to the defence for the game against Spain, with Everton captain Brian Labone replacing Jack Charlton at centre-half. At a time when most centre-halves made their names by scything down opposition strikers the graceful, composed Labone was a veritable rarity. He was only booked twice in over 530 games for Everton and was memorably described by his club manager, Harry Catterick, as being 'the last of the great Corinthians'. He may not have had Charlton's naked aggression, but he was just as strong in the air and was also a better passer of the ball. Labone's critics argued that he was too nice to be an effective centre-half but his achievements in the game belied their criticism. He won two league titles with Everton and also captained the club to an FA Cup triumph in 1966. Labone was initially included in Ramsey's squad for the 1966 World Cup finals but withdrew because he had already planned his wedding for that summer. Football meant a lot to Labone but, clearly, not everything. When Labone was given a second chance to prove his worth in an England shirt he took it, going on to become a regular fixture in the side between 1967 and 1970.

Ramsey's other change to the defence was to replace George Cohen with Blackburn Rovers full-back Keith Newton. He was a skilled tackler and good in the air, but the strongest part of his game was the attacking threat that he offered. Cohen also liked to attack down the flanks but the accuracy of his crossing, or rather lack of it, greatly hampered his productiveness. In an England team devoid of wingers Newton's ability to attack on the overlap and deliver precise crosses made him particularly valuable to Ramsey. Newton's other great strength was his versatility as he was capable of playing at left- or right-back, or even as a centre-half.

The changes that Ramsey made to the England team following the defeat by Scotland soon bore fruit. His side beat Spain 2-0 at Wembley and then a fine goal by Alan Ball gave them a victory over Austria in Vienna a few days later. The latter match was a drab affair, notable only for the fact that it was the last game that Greaves played for his country. He had been a regular fixture in Ramsey's side for several years, but lost his place after being injured in England's group game against France in the World Cup. Greaves then struggled to reclaim his place in the national side as Ramsey decided to keep faith in the partnership of Hunt and Hurst that had been so successful during the tournament.

The defeat to Scotland at Wembley meant that England could not afford any further slip-ups if they were to qualify for the quarter-finals of the European Championships. Their next game, away to Wales, could have been troublesome but they negotiated it with ease. England won 3-0 in Cardiff, with the midfield trio of Charlton, Ball and Peters all scoring. That was followed a month later by a 2-0 home victory over Northern Ireland, which put Ramsey's men into a much stronger position in the group. England's final match of 1967 was a friendly against the USSR side that had finished fourth in the World Cup a year earlier. The game was played on a snow-covered pitch at Wembley and the Soviets, clearly in their element, almost came away with a victory. Alan Ball put England ahead but two goals in two minutes gave the visitors the lead at half-time. The USSR held on to their lead until 15 minutes before the end of the game when Peters, much to Ramsey's relief, headed an equaliser.

England's final qualifying game for the European Championships was against Scotland at Hampden Park. Despite having lost to the Scots at Wembley England were top of the qualifying group and needed only a draw to progress to the quarter-finals. Not for the first time, or for the last, Scotland had managed to hurdle the most difficult challenge but had then slipped up against lesser sides. A draw away to Wales and, most damagingly, a defeat in Belfast handed the initiative to England, who duly capitalised on Scotland's mishaps by winning all of their other qualifying games. Ramsey, who had little time for the Scots, was so determined to prevail over them that he called up 35 players for a training session at Lilleshall to help his side prepare for the game.

The crucial qualifying match was played on a mud-heap of a pitch, deep in the middle of a Scottish winter, in front of a raucous crowd of over 130,000 expectant Scots. The huge attendance duly set a record for a European Championship fixture which, in all likelihood, will never be broken. England did have the advantage, though, of facing a Scotland side that were missing some key players, with their talismanic striker Denis Law and the ebullient Jim Baxter both sidelined with injuries. England drew first blood in the game when Peters scored with a rasping shot after 19 minutes of play, but the

Scots drew level shortly before half-time with a goal from Celtic's John Hughes. England were much the better side in the second half, but they resisted the temptation to risk everything for the win. They cautiously played the game out for the draw that they needed, delivering a controlled, mature performance that was fitting of a team that were world champions. The Scots may not have been vanquished, but the English had certainly subdued them once more.

• •

Ramsey may not have been one for making blood and thunder speeches, invoking the spirit of Agincourt and Dunkirk, but he rarely failed to get his message across. Once he was certain that he had all of his players' attention he spoke clearly and concisely, beginning with the observation that England shouldn't really be losing to an Italy side that was without the injured Rivera. 'He's the only player they've got!' he told his disbelieving players. 'He ripped my Ipswich team apart in '62! You should be thankful he's not on the pitch!' One of his charges wanted to mention Mazzola but then thought better of it; Ramsey didn't appear to be in listening mode.

The introduction of substitutes in international tournaments was still a couple of years away, so Ramsey had no choice other than to make best use of the players that he'd already put on the pitch. Recognising the difficulties that Wilson was having with Domenghini, he politely asked the England captain, Bobby Moore, to assist his colleague. Anticipating Moore's retort about the impact that would have on containing Mazzola, Ramsey turned to Alan Mullery and made clear that his principal task in the second half was to reduce the Italian playmaker to a peripheral figure. The Spurs player nodded his head silently, eager to accommodate the manager that had given him another chance after what had happened in the semi-final.

Ramsey reserved his harshest words for his forward players, though he pointedly excluded Alan Ball who was commended for his efforts at thwarting Facchetti. Encouraging them, courteously, to get more involved in the game, he then indicated which areas of the pitch he wanted to see them move into and what attacking ploys were most likely to be profitable. He finished his talk by reminding the players that England had never lost to Italy, not once in nearly 40 years of competition. 'And this is not the time to start now!' were the words ringing in their ears as they trooped back out of the dressing room for the second half.

• •

The quarter-final draw for the European Championships kept England and Italy apart, with the former being paired with Spain and the latter with Bulgaria. It may have seemed that Italy had received the easier draw but the Bulgarians were not to be underestimated, having qualified ahead of the Portuguese side that finished third at the 1966 World Cup. The first of the two ties was played in Sofia and Bulgaria took full advantage of being at home, taking the lead with an 11th-minute penalty. The Italians managed to equalise in the second half, when a Bulgarian defender put the ball into his own net as he tried to prevent the visitors from scoring, but the hosts responded with two goals in a seven-minute spell. That put the Italians in real trouble but, crucially, they managed to get one goal back before the end of the match, albeit a little fortunately.

As Italy attacked the Bulgarian goal one of the visiting players ended up lying motionless on the pitch, just outside the six-yard area. The Bulgarian defenders stopped playing, apparently presuming that the referee would stop the game. He didn't and the Italians, who had the presence of mind to carry on playing, duly scored. The prostrate Italian at least had the decency to remain still after the goal was scored, resisting the temptation to jump up and celebrate with his team-mates.

Italy's defeat to Bulgaria was their first since the North Korea debacle and it rang alarm bells. Valcareggi duly felt the need to make a number of changes to his team for the return game in Naples, one of which was putting the previously uncapped Dino Zoff in goal. Zoff went on to become one of the greatest goalkeepers in the history of Italian football, winning 112 caps in an international career that lasted for 15 years. During that period, he set a goalkeeping record for the longest time played in international matches without conceding a goal (1,143 minutes). A natural leader, Zoff captained Italy to third place in the 1978 World Cup and then led them to a 3-1 victory over West Germany in the final four years later. He was 40 years old when he lifted the trophy, so becoming the oldest player ever to play on the winning side in a World Cup Final.

Another casualty of the defeat in Sofia was the *libero*, Armando Picchi. He fractured his pelvis in the game, and although he courageously played on, the injury effectively ended his career. He was replaced in the side by Ernesto Castano, the Juventus centre-back. Valcareggi also decided to bring back Giorgio Ferrini, a tough-tackling Torino midfielder. It was a clear indication of how desperate Italy were to win as Ferrini's most infamous contribution to the history of the national side was his involvement in the 'Battle of Santiago'.

Italy's 1962 World Cup tie with Chile was easily one of the most violent matches ever played, with the two teams exchanging blows after only four minutes of play. A couple of minutes later Ferrini kicked out at a Chilean after being fouled which, unsurprisingly, resulted in his dismissal. The match was then held up for nearly ten minutes as Ferrini refused to leave the pitch, eventually necessitating the arrival of a dozen police officers to escort him away. Valcareggi's re-working of his team paid off as Italy went on to beat Bulgaria 2-0, thus giving them a 4-3 aggregate victory. The Italians dominated the match, with Pierino Prati scoring from close range after 14 minutes and Domenghini getting the winner with a tremendous free kick early in the second half.

If England were to join Italy in the last four they would have to overcome Spain, the holders of the trophy. For the first leg at Wembley Ramsey once again placed his faith in the midfield trio of Charlton, Ball and Peters. Arguably, Bobby Charlton was the most talented attacking player that England had ever had. A superb athlete, Charlton had great acceleration and could run all day long. He often used these skills to great effect when running at the opposition from deep in midfield, wrong-footing defenders with deceptive swerves before striking the ball at goal. He was famed for the power of his shooting and fans flocked to see him thump the ball at goal, mid-stride, from well outside the penalty area. Not only did Charlton have a superb aptitude for the game, he also played it in the right spirit. His sportsmanship was well-renowned, and though he inevitably came in for a lot of rough treatment from defenders he never retaliated or pretended that a foul was worse than it actually was.

Charlton's talent for football was obvious from an early age and he was selected to play for England at both schoolboy and youth level. Unsurprisingly, there were plenty of offers for his services and he eventually chose to sign for Manchester United, where he became one of the infamous 'Busby Babes'. He made his first team debut at the age of 18, scoring twice in a game against Charlton Athletic, appropriately enough. Two years later he survived the air disaster at Munich and, just a couple of months after the crash, made his England debut, scoring in a 4-0 defeat of Scotland at Hampden Park. Charlton went on to become a regular fixture in the national side for the next 12 years, amassing 106 caps and scoring 49 goals; a record that was to stand for over 45 years.

Playing on the right-hand side of Charlton was the fiery redhead, Alan Ball. He was a courageous tackler, a decent passer of the ball and effective in front of goal, though his greatest asset was probably his pair of lungs. Ball had tremendous stamina and Ramsey made full use of it by asking him to fulfil the two roles of right-midfielder and right-winger. His indefatigability was crucial to England's victory over West Germany in 1966 and he was widely acknowledged to have been the best player on the pitch that day. His endless running at the German defence, especially in extra time, slowly ground them down and he was instrumental in creating England's controversial third goal.

It was a remarkable turnaround in fortune for Ball who, only a few years earlier, had been turned down by Wolverhampton Wanderers and Bolton Wanderers for being too small. Indeed, the latter club even suggested that he might want to try becoming a horse jockey instead. Ball didn't give up and was eventually taken on by Blackpool. The knocks that he had taken early in his life did nothing to lessen his self-belief, with Ball even telling the legendary Stanley Matthews that he was after his place in the first team. Ball soon broke into the side and developed so quickly that Ramsey gave him his England debut at the age of just 19. He made a strong enough impression to force his way into the squad for the 1966 World Cup finals and, at the age of 21, was the youngest member of England's winning side. Ball continued to be a regular fixture in the national team for the next ten years, playing a total of 72 games for his country and scoring eight goals.

Playing on the opposite side of midfield was West Ham United's Martin Peters. He forced his way into the England squad for 1966 at the last possible moment, only making his debut a couple of months before the tournament began. His contribution to England's success was invaluable, with two highlights being his cross to Hurst for the winning goal in the quarter-final against Argentina and his strike to give England a 2-1 lead in the final.

Peters was easily England's most versatile player though, perversely, his ability to play in a multitude of positions hampered his early career at West Ham. As a youngster, he was often brought into the team to replace players who were injured, suspended or out of form. He was good enough to play in any of the vacated roles but, as a consequence, was never seen as first choice for any of them and that threatened to derail a promising career. Peters, however, eventually forced his way into West Ham's first team and was a key part of the side that won the European Cup Winners' Cup in 1965.

Peters famously played in all 11 positions for West Ham, including a spell in goal when their goalkeeper was injured during a game. He could play with either foot, had excellent ball control and was strong in the air. The only real weakness he had was a lack of pace, though his excellent positional sense meant that this minor chink in his armour was rarely exposed. One of the most effective aspects of his game was his ability to time late runs into the penalty area, thus catching defences unaware. That helped him to score 20 goals in his 67 appearances for England; an excellent goals-to-games ratio for a midfielder and a higher total than many strikers of his era, including Roger Hunt and Francis Lee. Peters could also deliver accurate and penetrating crosses from the flanks which, together with his ability to defend, made him the ideal player for Ramsey's 'wingless wonders' formation.

The first leg of the quarter-final against Spain was a tight game and it looked as if the visitors had done enough to get a valuable draw. Then, six minutes from time, Bobby Charlton scored with a majestic strike from just outside the penalty area. The Spanish came back in search of an equaliser and almost got it, forcing Gordon Banks into making an excellent save in the last minute. Ramsey's side may have won, but their lead was a slender one and defending it in front of a packed crowd in Madrid's Bernabéu Stadium would be no mean task. Ramsey therefore selected an even more defensive side than usual for the second leg in Spain, with Hunt as the team's sole spearhead and Norman Hunter playing in midfield to help protect the back four.

Hunter made his international debut against Spain in 1965 and, in doing so, became the first England player to appear as a substitute. Further appearances in the national side were limited, however, as his principal role in the squad was to be Bobby Moore's understudy. While the two men shared the same position on the pitch they were quite different types of player. Hunter had little of Moore's grace and composure and the rather indiscriminate nature of his tackling led to him being nicknamed Norman 'Bites Yer Legs' Hunter. While his hard man reputation was certainly deserved, it did detract from his other, less-well-observed qualities. He had a good passing range with his left foot and was sufficiently versatile to be used in a variety of different positions for England.

Hunter won 28 caps during his career, though it would undoubtedly have been many more if he had not had the misfortune to be born at the same time as the incomparable Moore.

As expected, Spain attacked England strongly but Ramsey's side managed to keep the hosts at bay until just after the start of the second half. A goal from Real Madrid's Amancio levelled the tie and jubilant Spanish fans raced on to the pitch to celebrate, clearly believing that the scalp of the world champions was within their grasp. Yet, just as they had faced down the Scots in Glasgow, Ramsey's men rose to the challenge once more, with Peters restoring their aggregate lead with a headed goal seven minutes later. The England defence continued to hold firm in the face of Spanish attacks and, eight minutes from time, an impressive victory was secured when perpetual understudy Norman Hunter scored the winner. England were in the European Championship finals for the first time and an expectant nation looked forward to the tournament in Italy, where surely Bobby Moore would lift the Henri Delaunay trophy.

. . . .

If the Italians had expected the second half to start as the first had finished, then they were to be disappointed. Ramsey's tinkering with his side's formation immediately had the desired effect, with Mullery's shackling of Mazzola stymieing many of Italy's attacking moves. The Englishman was back in the side after serving his one-game suspension, replacing the pugnacious Nobby Stiles who had been fortunate not to receive his marching orders in the first match against Italy. He had come up against the combustible Ferrini, veteran of the 'Battle of Santiago', and their feisty encounter had been one of the few memorable moments in a particularly dull game. The two men hadn't quite come to blows but the fierce tackles that they traded had made even the most hardened of football fans wince. Stiles and Ferrini were dropped for the replay, with both Ramsey and Valcareggi being wary of what would happen if the two combatants met again in a confined space.

With Mazzola struggling to have the impact on the game that he had in the first period, Italy tried to use Domenghini as an outlet. The right-winger had done well against Wilson in the first half but increasingly found Moore blocking his path instead. The England captain was equal to the task and soon Italy were reduced to knocking long balls up to Riva, hoping that his rumbustious style would unsettle the opposing defence. The Italian striker's style of play would have provoked many defenders into retaliating with hefty challenges of their own but Brian Labone was not the type of player to fall into that trap. He guarded Riva with grace and forbearance and, slowly, the Italian threat to the English goal started to recede.

Italy's retreat into defence was not a conscious tactical move, but England's new-found resistance to their attacks almost inevitably led to them opting to protect their one-goal lead rather than trying to increase it. Instead of attacking the central ranks of the massed Italian defence Ramsey's side advanced down the flanks, with Martin Peters revelling in the freedom provided to him now that Moore was shielding England's left wing from any Italian incursions. On the opposite side of the pitch, meanwhile, Ball and Newton were stretching Facchetti with their energetic, overlapping runs. Ramsey's side may still have been a goal behind, but Italy had been warned: the English were coming!

. . . .

It was decided after the quarter-finals that Italy would host the European Championship finals, with the USSR and Yugoslavia joining England in the four-team tournament. The draw pitched Italy against the Soviets and Valcareggi was well aware of the danger they posed. They had performed solidly in international tournaments throughout the decade, winning the inaugural European Championship in 1960, finishing as runners-up four years later and then securing fourth place at the 1966 World Cup. The USSR won their qualifying group for the 1968 European Championships comfortably, with victories in five of their six matches. Their quarter-final against Hungary, though, was a tougher affair, with the Soviets losing 2-0 in Budapest before winning 3-0 back in Moscow.

The semi-final was played in the same stadium in Naples in which Italy had beaten Bulgaria, with Valcareggi making only one change to the side that had started that game. The match was played in pouring rain and Italy got off to a bad start, with Rivera getting injured after only five minutes of play. With no substitutes allowed Valcareggi's side had to soldier on with ten men and, missing their playmaker, were even more defensive than usual.

Both sides had chances to score during the game but none of them were converted, with Zoff making a number of fine saves and Domenghini hitting the post near the end of extra time.

The rules of the competition made no provision for a replay or penalty shoot-out, with the winner having to be determined instead by the toss of a coin. The two captains went down to the dressing rooms with the referee and when he flicked the coin, Facchetti correctly called tails. He then went back out on to the pitch to communicate the good news to the patiently waiting spectators. Italy had reached the final by the narrowest of margins but, after so many disappointments, it was starting to appear that it might finally be their year.

England played two warm-up games shortly before the start of the 1968 European Championship finals, with the first being a morale-boosting 3-1 victory over Sweden at Wembley. Martin Peters got England's first goal with a header and then Bobby Charlton scored one of his trademark spectaculars. He picked the ball up near the halfway line, ran at the Swedish defence and then, from just outside the penalty area, struck a thunderous shot into the roof of the net. It was his 45th goal for his country and it secured him the national team's record (surpassing Jimmy Greaves's total of 44 goals which had been set the previous year). Roger Hunt then scored with a tap-in in the second half to finish off the Swedes, who could only manage a consolation goal in injury time in reply.

Roger Hunt's goal was the 18th and last that he scored for his country. Ramsey had selected the Liverpool striker for the odd international during his first few years in charge, but didn't give him a decent run in the side until Jimmy Greaves fell ill with jaundice in the autumn of 1965. Hunt impressed Ramsey with his performances, especially his two-goal display in a 4-3 victory over Scotland at Hampden Park in April 1966. Ramsey had a penchant for workaholic footballers and Hunt fitted the mould perfectly, running tirelessly when his side had the ball and chasing and harrying the opposition when they didn't. His constant running would also pull defenders out of position, creating space not just for himself but also for his team-mates to exploit.

One of the criticisms often made of Ramsey was that he was too loyal to some of his players for too long. Hunt continued to be a regular fixture in the England side after the World Cup, but it is questionable whether his form really justified his selection. In the 11 games he played between the World Cup Final and the start of the European Championships he scored just three goals. That was a poor return, especially when compared to his record of 15 goals in 19 international matches played up to and including the final against West Germany.

Before arriving in Italy for the European Championship finals England stopped off in Hanover to play an ill-advised friendly against West Germany. It was the first time that the two teams had met since the World Cup Final and, unsurprisingly, the hosts were looking for revenge. Hindsight is a wonderful thing, but it seems rather obvious now that Ramsey should have sought easier opponents for his side's last match before the finals.

Ramsey made a number of changes to the side that beat Sweden, including bringing back Geoff Hurst who hadn't played for England since the draw away to Scotland a few months earlier. What Hurst brought to the side was his ability to be a reliable outlet when the ball was played up to the forward line. His strong build and skill in the air helped him to latch on to the ball and keep hold of it until his team-mates could join him in attack. Hurst certainly had the courage needed to fulfil such a role as he was prepared to play with his back to defenders and take the hard knocks that inevitably came as a result.

The match wasn't much of a spectacle and it looked as if it was going to peter out into a 0-0 draw. Then, with just ten minutes remaining, Franz Beckenbauer scored a winner. It was the first time that the Germans had beaten England since their initial encounter in 1930 and, though it wasn't apparent at the time, the result marked a gradual shift in the balance of power between the two nations. It was a frustrating result for the England players, who blamed their defeat on the new boots that a sportswear manufacturer had convinced them to wear, and served only to put more pressure on them prior to the European Championship finals.

One of Ramsey's great bugbears as England manager was the amount of time, or rather lack of it, that he was able to have with his players in order to prepare for international matches. This was underlined by England's inadequate preparations for the finals in Italy which followed straight on from the end of the league season, with the warm-up matches against Sweden and West Germany having to be shoehorned into the schedule. Ramsey had been much better served by the arrangements for the 1966 World Cup as the tournament was held in July, thus giving his players time for a decent rest before they convened at Lilleshall at the start of June for intensive training.

Ramsey also had to cope with his most important player, Bobby Charlton, arriving in Italy in less than perfect condition. Shortly before the start of the tournament Charlton captained Manchester United to victory in the European Cup Final against Benfica. The match stretched into extra time and the occasion drained Charlton, both physically and mentally. The trophy had become something of a holy grail for the club after the disaster that occurred at Munich a few years earlier and Charlton was desperate to win it. Images of that famous night clearly show how exhausted Charlton was after the game and, understandably, he didn't play in the friendly against West Germany three days later. Charlton was back for England's European Championships semi-final against Yugoslavia, which took place a week after United's European Cup victory, but one suspects that he could have done with a longer rest.

On paper at least, England appeared to have received the most favourable draw possible for the semi-finals. Ramsey's side had avoided having to play the Italian hosts as well as the Soviets, who had finished fourth in the previous World Cup. England had a poor record against Yugoslavia, however, having won only two of their previous eight encounters. Both of those victories had come at Wembley and England had suffered three defeats in the four matches played in Belgrade. Yugoslavia's journey to the European Championship finals, meanwhile, had been as impressive as it had been unexpected. They were drawn in a qualifying group with West Germany and Albania and, unsurprisingly, the World Cup runners-up were clear favourites to progress to the quarter-finals.

The Germans started well, thrashing Albania 6-0 in Dortmund, but then lost narrowly to Yugoslavia in Belgrade. They then won the return fixture 3-1 in Hamburg, meaning that they only had to win their final match in Tirana by a single goal to qualify. That appeared to be a relatively straightforward task as Albania were one of the minnows of international football, having already lost all three of their qualifying games without scoring a single goal and conceding 12. Incredibly, however, the Germans failed to score and the match ended in a 0-0 draw, with the pleasantly surprised Yugoslavians progressing to the next round instead. Yugoslavia then cantered past France in the quarter-finals, drawing 1-1 in Marseilles before thrashing them 5-1 back in Belgrade.

Ramsey decided to field the same ten outfield players for the semi-final that had beaten Spain in Madrid, with Hunt playing alone in attack and Hurst being omitted. Norman Hunter was once again included in midfield, which may have helped to protect the back four but did little to improve England's creativity. The semi-final clash in Florence was the first time that the two teams had met on neutral ground but England's lamentable history against Yugoslavia continued.

Ramsey's side had plenty of possession of the ball but were unable to create many goalscoring chances against a side that were content to defend deeply and try and hit them on the counter-attack. What most frustrated the England players, however, wasn't Yugoslavia's negative tactics, but their overtly physical approach. It was an ill-tempered game, peppered with harsh tackles and cynical fouls, and Ramsey's side struggled to find any rhythm.

The dull game remained goalless until four minutes from time, when the Yugoslavians dashed England's hopes of being the first nation to become joint holders of the World Cup and European Championship. Unusually, it was the captain, Bobby Moore, who was at fault for the goal. The ball was played forward from the left side of midfield and Moore, the last man in defence, was caught in no man's land as the ball sailed over his head. The Yugoslavian winger, Dragan Džajić, sprinted in behind Moore, collected the ball on his chest and then thumped an unstoppable shot past Banks. If that wasn't bad enough events took a further turn for the worse when Alan Mullery became the first England player to be sent off while playing for his country.

Mullery, like many of his team-mates, had been on the receiving end of several bad challenges and his patience finally cracked when Dobrivoje Trivić raked his studs down the back of his leg. Mullery turned around and kicked the offending player in the groin, who then rolled around in apparent agony until the referee dismissed Mullery, upon which he made a miraculous recovery. Mullery expected Ramsey to tear a strip off him in the dressing room but, instead, found him surprisingly supportive. Ramsey had witnessed just how poorly his side had been treated by the Yugoslavians and was just as frustrated with their behaviour as his players were. So not only did Ramsey not lambast Mullery for his actions, he even paid the fine that the FA levied on him for being sent off.

The defeat was a big setback for England, though they had the chance to make some amends when they played the USSR in the third and fourth place play-off match. Such games are usually pointless but, for England, it was a much-needed opportunity to get back to winning ways after two consecutive defeats. Indeed, Ramsey hadn't suffered back-to-back defeats since losing his first two matches in charge after taking over as manager in 1962. He decided to field a more attacking side than he had against Yugoslavia, with Hurst being brought into the attack to accompany Hunt and Stiles replacing the suspended Mullery. Goals from Hurst and Charlton were enough to give England a cathartic victory, but it couldn't be pretended that the outcome of the tournament was anything but a great disappointment.

· ·

As the second half progressed England were clearly the prevailing force, dominating possession of the ball and pushing the Italian defenders closer and closer to an increasingly frustrated Zoff. The Italian goalkeeper tried to get his defenders to push further out, but their instinctive desire to protect the goal inevitably kept drawing them back closer to him. Clear-cut chances failed to present themselves, however, and the more pessimistic England fans openly wondered whether their side really had the imaginative spark needed to disturb Italy's well-drilled defence. England may have only needed one goal to level the tie, but Ramsey's side had always been more reliant on perspiration than inspiration. It wasn't clear whether that was going to be sufficient against arguably the best international defence in the world.

Ramsey was just as conscious of the minutes ticking away as the anxious England fans were, but he had faith that his players would manage to turn the game around. Few had given them much hope after Yugoslavia had scored late in the semi-final but his captain had rescued that situation, hitting a sublime pass up to Peters for him to head an equaliser in the dying seconds of normal time. Alan Ball's cool-headed extra-time penalty had then won the game and it seemed increasingly likely that the indefatigable youngster would be the one to salvage England's tournament again. His running was clearly troubling Facchetti, with even the normally implacable Italian starting to look a little flustered.

Despite the progress that Ramsey's side were making on the flanks, it was through the middle of the pitch that they finally made their breakthrough. Roger Hunt had tried manfully to trouble the Italian defence but there were simply too many men blocking his path for him to make much progress. He never stopped running, though, and it was one of his darting sprints that gave Bobby Charlton an opening. The balding genius hadn't made much of an impact on the tournament to date, clearly still worn out by his exertions with Manchester United in the European Cup. One opening was all he needed, however, and it was Hunt that created it, dragging one of the Italian defenders out of position for a split second. A small gap suddenly opened in the Italian rearguard and Charlton struck the ball with all his might, sending one of his inimitable screamers through the night air and past Zoff's flying dive.

. . . .

After winning the semi-final on the toss of a coin some Italians may have inferred that fate was on their side. Valcareggi, however, could be excused for not being one of them. Not only did he lose Rivera in the opening minutes of the semi-final, but injury also deprived him of the Juventus defender, Giancarlo Bercellino. Forced into shuffling his pack, Valcareggi decided to bring the experienced Aristide Guarneri back into the centre of his defence. Guarneri had played in the famous Inter back-line alongside Burgnich, Facchetti and Picchi but was transferred to Bologna after their 1967 European Cup Final defeat to Celtic. Valcareggi also decided to bring Giovanni

Lodetti, an energetic midfielder, into the side. Lodetti played as a ball-winner for AC Milan, thus earning him the epithet of Rivera's 'third lung'. The final change made by Valcareggi was to add Sicilian striker Pietro Anastasi to the forward line, even though he had never played for the national side before.

The Italians were favourites to win the final, but their visitors from across the Adriatic started the game better. The Yugoslav forward line caused a host of problems for the Italian defence, with Džajić scoring a rather scrappy goal shortly before the end of the first half. Italy nearly equalised when a well-hit free kick crashed against the crossbar but they were still behind at half-time and continued to struggle in the second half. Yugoslavia had a number of opportunities to make sure of the victory, including one where their player slid in towards the ball as it ran across the open goal but narrowly missed getting his foot to it. The chance was redolent of that missed by Paul Gascoigne in England's semi-final against Germany in Euro '96 and no doubt just as agonising.

Yugoslavia were only ten minutes away from winning the European Championships when Italy finally managed to find an equaliser. Tragically for the visitors, Italy's goal could have been avoided. They gave away a free kick on the edge of their penalty area and Domenghini smashed the ball straight through the defensive wall and past the goalkeeper. The players in the wall should have kept the ball out but Italy, fortunate at sneaking past the Soviets on the toss of a coin, were lucky once more. There were no further goals in extra time, though both sides had chances to score, and so a replay was required. It was bad enough to have to settle a semi-final by tossing a coin, but UEFA wisely drew the line at determining the winners of the trophy that way.

The replay was scheduled to take place just two days after the first game so Valcareggi opted to re-jig his side once more. He had a talented squad and was able to field five fresh players, bringing much-needed energy and vitality to a team that had played 120 minutes of football just 48 hours earlier. By contrast, the Yugoslavians made just one change to their side. The team that Valcareggi selected was much more adventurous than the one he had picked for the first match. He discarded two defensive midfield players, Lodetti and Juliano, and replaced them with Giancarlo De Sisti and a fit-again Mazzola. It was a particularly cruel blow for Juliano, who had played in every game in the competition until that point. Ferrini and Castano were also dropped in favour of Sandro Salvadore and Roberto Rosato, whose principal claim to fame was getting Pelé's shirt at the end of the 1970 World Cup Final, which he subsequently sold at auction in 2002 for the tidy sum of £157,750. Perhaps the most significant of the changes made by Valcareggi was to his forward line. Pierino Prati, who had failed to score in either the semi-final or final, was replaced by the totemic Gigi Riva, fit again after having broken a leg.

Riva had an immediate impact on the replay, using his strength and agility to unnerve the Yugoslavian defence. The game was only 12 minutes old when he received the ball near the penalty spot and rifled a low shot past the goalkeeper. He looked as if he may have been in an offside position but, despite anxious appeals from the Yugoslavian defence, the goal was given. The Italians then scored again on the half-hour mark; Anastasi receiving a pass from De Sisti on the edge of the penalty area before flicking the ball up and volleying it past the goalkeeper into the corner of the net. It was a delightful goal and it gave the much fresher Italians a lead that the exhausted Yugoslavians never really threatened.

Riva missed several chances to score in the second half but, in the end, it didn't really matter. The trophy was later handed to Facchetti and, as he lifted it up, the Rome night sky was illuminated by hosts of flares lit in the stands. The Italian team had certainly ridden their luck during the competition but who could begrudge them their celebrations? They had emerged from the shadow of the defeat to North Korea, restored national pride and were a force to be reckoned with on the international stage once more.

England missed out on the opportunity to be the first nation to simultaneously hold the World Cup and European Championship trophies and Italy almost succeeded where they had failed. They qualified for the 1970 World Cup finals with ease and arrived in Mexico as one of the favourites to win the tournament. All of their best players were fit and in their prime, with Facchetti, Mazzola, Riva and Rivera being between 25 and 27 years of age. They were drawn into a not particularly taxing first-round group with Israel, Sweden and Uruguay and, as expected, finished top, although their performances hardly set the tournament alight. A quarter-final victory over their Mexican hosts followed, with Riva scoring twice and Rivera once in a 4-1 triumph.

Valcareggi was still in charge of the national side and he continued his pattern of regularly changing players from match to match. His approach differed markedly to Ramsey who remained steadfastly loyal to the same small group of players. In the 1968 European Championships Valcareggi selected no less than 34 different players in Italy's 11 games compared to the 22 used by Ramsey in England's ten games. The Italian coach's lack of conviction over his best XI reached its apotheosis at the 1970 World Cup. Unable to decide whether Mazzola or Rivera should play in the creative role behind the strikers, he simply compromised by playing one of them in the first half and the other in the second.

Next up for Italy were the West Germans, with the two sides playing out one of the most thrilling World Cup matches of all time, though it didn't really get going until extra time. Valcareggi's side scored an early goal and then attempted to hold on to it for the remainder of the game. They would have done so, but for an injury-time equaliser that precipitated a frantic 30 minutes of football.

The Germans scored early in extra time only for Burgnich to score a rare goal four minutes later to level the game. Within six minutes Riva had restored Italy's lead with a fine goal, but they could only hold on to it for six minutes. Rivera was not a born defender but he somehow found himself guarding the near post when the Germans took a corner. The cross found a German head and, with the goalkeeper beaten, it fell to Rivera to clear the danger. He appeared to be allowing the ball to bounce out to safety but it somehow crept inside the post instead. His misjudgement immediately incurred the wrath of the Italian goalkeeper and the watching millions back home.

Rivera, however, refused to allow his career to be defined by one mistake and coolly re-established Italy's lead within a minute of the kick-off. There were still nine minutes of the game to play but the two exhausted teams had little left to offer, with Italy hanging on for a famous victory.

Italy's redemption from the embarrassing defeat to North Korea was almost complete, but a World Cup triumph proved to be beyond them. Valcareggi's side was a fine one but in the final they met possibly the finest of them all: Mario Zagallo's Brazil. The South Americans had dealt with every other challenge that had been laid before them in the tournament and the Italians were similarly dismissed, with the great side of Jairzinho, Pelé and Rivelino running out 4-1 winners.

That was the high watermark for Valcareggi's side as they failed to hold on to the European Championship trophy in 1972, crashing out to Belgium in the quarter-finals. They qualified easily enough for the World Cup finals in 1974, albeit from a relatively easy group, but then failed to get beyond the first group stage, with a 2-1 defeat to Poland eventually proving decisive. It was the end of the road for that great generation of Italian footballers, with Burgnich, Mazzola, Riva and Rivera never playing for their country again. As if to underline that the era had come to an end, Valcareggi also resigned as the national coach once the tournament was over.

England also entered the 1970 World Cup finals as one of the favourites, but the good fortune that Ramsey had four years earlier cruelly deserted him. Arguably he had an even stronger squad at his disposal than when he won the World Cup but his first piece of misfortune occurred when England were drawn in the same first-round group as Brazil. Victories over Romania and Czechoslovakia ensured qualification for the quarter-finals, but a 1-0 defeat to the South Americans meant that England only finished in second place in the group. To be fair, Ramsey's side performed magnificently against Brazil and the contest could have gone either way, but the defeat meant that Pelé's side got a relatively easy quarter-final tie against Peru while England had to face old foes West Germany.

For the first hour of the game against the Germans Ramsey's side were well in control, taking a 2-0 lead and looking well set for a place in the semi-finals. But then bad luck struck Ramsey once more. Gordon Banks fell ill on the day of the tie and his replacement, Peter Bonetti, did not have a game to remember. He conceded a poor goal to Beckenbauer midway through the second half and, with only eight minutes left, the Germans drew level. They were the stronger side in extra time and Bonetti was once again at fault for their third, winning, goal.

If Ramsey's side had managed to hold on to their lead they would have met Italy in the last four. The two nations had narrowly missed playing each other two years earlier and destiny kept them apart once more. It seems, sadly, that some matches are just fated not to happen. It is a curious fact that, despite being two of the world's top sides, Italy and England only played each other twice during Ramsey's 11 years in charge. Both of those games took place in 1973, well over a decade after he had taken on the job, and by that time both sides were a pale imitation of their former selves. Italy won the two matches, with future England manager Fabio Capello scoring in both games, but these were two worn-out boxers whose time had long since passed.

The Germans continued to be Ramsey's nemesis, with a quarter-final victory in the 1972 European Championships preventing England from reaching the finals of that competition. That was bad enough, but worse was to come when Ramsey's side failed to qualify for the World Cup finals in 1974 after being outdone by Poland. It was the first time that England had failed to reach a World Cup finals and, despite what he had achieved for his country, the knives were out for Ramsey. He lost his job shortly after and, just as with Valcareggi's Italy, a curtain was drawn on an especially memorable sliver of history.

. . . .

Sometimes even the most pedestrian of games can come alive in the last few minutes, and so it proved with the replayed 1968 European Championship Final. The prospect of yet more extra time clearly didn't appeal to either team and, eager for the tie to be over, they finally attacked with abandon. Facchetti happily dragged Ball out of position and ran at the heart of the English defence, requiring a fine tackle by Moore to bring the move to an end. Italy weren't done yet, though, and another bone-jarring challenge by Burgnich on Peters started their next move. De Sisti received the ball and ran at Mullery, allowing Mazzola to finally escape from his grip. The Spurs player attempted a sliding tackle in order to win the ball but De Sisti saw him coming and flicked it into Mazzola's path, willingly suffering the full force of Mullery's mis-timed tackle.

Mazzola ran towards the penalty area, drawing Labone towards him, and then caressed the ball out left to Riva, who immediately slammed the ball at goal. Banks was alive to the danger and his left hand was strong enough to divert the ball on to the post, after which it cannoned out to Anastasi who had made his way to the edge of the six-yard area. The ball was a little too high in the air for him but he managed to get his head to it, sending a looping header over towards the right-hand side of Banks's goal. It looked a certain goal but, somehow, the England goalkeeper managed to get back to his feet and hurl himself in the opposite direction that he had leapt for Riva's shot. Banks pushed the ball out for a corner and a relieved Bobby Moore duly sauntered over and calmly ruffled his hair. Breathless!

England dealt with the corner easily enough and Moore soon found himself with the ball at his feet, midway in his own half of the pitch. He instinctively looked up to see where Martin Peters was but, noticing that he was still limping after Burgnich's tackle, decided not to pass to him. Instead he knocked the ball over to Keith Newton, who had made his way up to the right-hand side of midfield. The Blackburn Rovers defender received the ball and ran up the flank, gesturing frantically for Ball to get ahead of him. The Everton midfielder complied, peeling away from Facchetti and, in doing so, forcing the Italian to decide whether he followed him or took on Newton. Taking the bait, the Italian captain tried to deprive Newton of the ball but, by the time his tackle arrived, the pass had already been released. The deep-lying Italian defence played Alan Ball onside and so he had plenty of space in which to control Newton's pass and run at the rapidly retreating rearguard. Rosato scampered across in an attempt to clear the danger but he was too late, Ball sending his cross flying into the penalty area. The Italian *libero*, Salvadore, had kept Geoff Hurst quiet for most of the game but the tall striker was to be England's hero once again. He timed his run into the penalty area to precision, getting in front of Salvadore and then rising to meet the cross, sending his header past the sprawling Zoff.

The last few minutes of the game saw the English players gleefully pushing the ball around between disheartened Italians, who simply didn't have either the heart or the energy to respond. Their only attempt on goal was Riva's ambitious 35-yard punt, which presented more of a danger to the glum Italian spectators than it did to Banks's goal. With only a few moments of the game remaining Keith Newton opted to waste a little time by kicking the ball back to Banks. It wasn't illegal in those days for goalkeepers to pick up a back-pass so Banks let the ball bounce in front of him, confident that it would rebound into his waiting arms.

To his horror the ball struck a divot in the turf and spun off wildly to his left, tracing a path towards the far corner of the goal. Banks turned quickly and chased the ball but its momentum outpaced his desperate dash, the England goalkeeper being no more able to influence its trajectory than anyone else in the stadium. Time then seemed to slow down for Banks as he watched the ball strike the foot of the post and curve round as it made its second attempt to cross the line. He threw himself headlong towards the goal-line, peeling the ball away for a corner that the Italians wouldn't have time to take. The stadium suddenly erupted as thousands of home fans beseeched the referee to award the goal, for surely the ball had crossed the line before Banks got his hand to it. Had it? Ramsey wasn't sure, nor were any of his players. The referee, personifying calm, marched over to his linesman and consulted him earnestly on what he had seen. They conferred for a short while before nodding their heads in agreement and announcing their rather controversial decision…

3
Clough vs. Cruyff

European Cup Final, Red Star Stadium, Belgrade, 30 May 1973

Ajax Amsterdam v Derby County

Ajax Amsterdam	Derby County
Heinz Stuy	Colin Boulton
Ruud Krol	David Nish
Horst Blankenburg	Colin Todd
Barry Hulshoff	Roy McFarland (captain)
Wim Suurbier	Ron Webster
Gerrie Mühren	Alan Hinton
Johan Neeskens	John McGovern
Arie Haan	Archie Gemmill
Piet Keizer	Alan Durban
Johan Cruyff (captain)	Kevin Hector
Johnny Rep	John O'Hare

Referee: Milivoje Gugulović (Yugoslavia)

Even though the sun had set, Belgrade was still stiflingly hot. It was one of those nights where the shirt sticks to your back, even if all you are doing is sitting in a shady street-side cafe sipping a cool beer. The city's Red Star Stadium had captured the day's heat like a cauldron, slowly boiling those who had unwisely chosen to step inside to watch the match. The last thing you would want to do on a night like this was run around with a ball at your feet, but that's what the Ajax and Derby players would have to do. And the more they wanted to be European champions, the harder they would have to run.

The Derby County players, clad in their already clammy change strip of yellow shirts and blue shorts, waited patiently for the referee to get the game started. Their left-winger, Alan Hinton, looked up towards the stands, to where the Derby County fans were. A few thousand had made the long trip to Yugoslavia but the gaps in the terraces were still painfully evident. It wasn't like being at the Baseball Ground, where all you could see from the pitch was a sea of expectant faces. The Derby fans, however, could hardly be blamed for their inability to travel to the final in large numbers. Times were tough back home, with the country racked by rampant inflation, never-ending industrial disputes and an oil crisis. Even Rolls-Royce, the backbone of the Derby economy, had been bailed out by the government.

Derby County had started their European Cup campaign against the Yugoslavian champions and now, against all the odds, they were back in the same country for the final. They might have been there on merit, but none of the watching neutrals gave them much hope of winning. Ajax were competing in their third successive European Cup Final, having won the previous two. Derby undoubtedly had a good team, with a host of English, Scottish and Welsh international players in their ranks, but they were facing the bulk of the

Dutch national side which was easily one of the strongest in the world. Outgunned on the pitch and outnumbered on the terraces, it was fair to say that Derby County were one of the least fancied European Cup finalists for years.

Back in Derby, however, there was hope. All across the city men huddled around television sets in crowded lounges and smoky pubs, cradling pints of frothy beer in their nervous hands. Steamy Belgrade seemed a world away from the muddy, often barely playable pitch at the Baseball Ground, but the European Cup Final was still just a game of football and it was there to be won. The referee's shrill whistle got the match underway and the watching Derby fans saw Alan Hinton sprint out to the left wing, where Clough always told him to play. Despite the roar of the crowd Clough's unmistakeable, nasally inflected tone could still be heard: 'Get the ball to Alan,' he was shouting. 'Get the ball to Alan.'

. . . .

Brian Clough arrived at Derby County in the summer of 1967; a year after England won the World Cup at Wembley. As a contemporary of Charlton, Hurst and Moore, Clough would have had an outside chance of being involved in that game had a horrific injury not ended his career.

Despite his playing days being well behind him, Clough was still a young man. He was only 32 years of age and yet already embarking on his second managerial post in the game. His first opportunity to run a club had come at Hartlepool United, who were in a desperate state when he arrived, having finished in the bottom two in the Fourth Division five times in the previous six seasons. Clough, who was in no position to wait for something better to come along, gladly accepted the offer.

Clough was recommended for the Hartlepool job by ex-Sunderland manager George Hardwick. When Clough's playing career ended, Hardwick threw the heartbroken striker a lifeline by putting him in charge of the Sunderland youth team. He enjoyed the experience tremendously and soon found that he had a talent for coaxing the best out of players.

Clough led the youngsters to the semi-final of the FA Youth Cup and Hardwick was so impressed that he planned to make Clough his assistant. That idea soon came to naught, however, as Hardwick lost his job at the end of the season. The club's directors were not interested in developing Clough's potential as a manager and decided instead to cash in on the insurance policy that they had taken out on him as a player. Clough was never the greatest fan of football club directors but, when they casually cast him aside, even though he had a young family to support and no trade or profession to fall back on, a lasting enmity was formed.

Clough was wary of taking on the job at Hartlepool on his own and persuaded his old friend, Peter Taylor, to join him as assistant manager. Taylor, who was nearly seven years older than Clough, had already embarked on a career in management and was having success with non-league Burton Albion at the time. Taylor never hesitated to join Clough, even though it meant a considerable drop in wages as well as a reduction in status. He was confident that his old team-mate would make an excellent manager and wisely judged that joining forces with him was his best chance of getting to the top in the game.

Clough and Taylor had first met when they played together for Middlesbrough, the former a budding striker-cum-local hero, the latter a journeyman goalkeeper. Taylor went on to make his name as one of the finest talent-spotters in the game and one of the first that he noticed was Clough. The young forward was only playing in Middlesbrough's reserves when Taylor arrived at the club, but the new recruit was impressed with what he saw. Taylor told anyone who would listen how good Clough was and pushed for his advancement into the first team. Unsurprisingly, a friendship soon blossomed between the two men. Clough duly got his chance and went on to become a prolific striker for his hometown club, scoring 204 goals in 222 appearances.

Clough and Taylor went on to build a long and successful partnership, though it was clearly a case of opposites attract. Their personalities differed considerably, with the younger man cutting a brash, opinionated, arrogant figure, while the older hand was much quieter and more studious. Curiously though, it was often Taylor who was the more adventurous of the two men, with his gambling instincts blending well with Clough's naturally more cautious stance to the game. The two unlikely lads quickly established their respective roles, with Taylor being responsible for finding talented players which Clough would then mould, motivate and manage.

At Hartlepool, Clough and Taylor inherited a playing staff with precious little to recommend it and they had virtually no money to spend on improving it. Yet, with Clough's drive and ambition and Taylor's eye for a bargain, they soon started to improve the club's fortunes. By the end of their second season in charge, Clough and Taylor had taken Hartlepool up to eighth place in the table and made enough of a name for themselves for Derby to take a chance on them. The legacy that they left behind at Hartlepool soon paid dividends, with the team they built winning promotion to the Third Division a year after they left.

The history of Derby County prior to Clough's appointment was long, but not particularly illustrious. Despite being one of the 12 founder members of the Football League in 1888 the club had never won the title. They finished second-bottom in the first league season and that was a strong hint of what was to come over the next 80 years or so. There was the odd second-place finish as Derby threatened to rise above their desultory past, but the great prize of being the best team in England consistently eluded them. For many years Derby found success in the FA Cup just as hard to come by, with the club reaching three finals in six seasons between 1898 and 1903 but still contriving to lose them all. Their moment of glory finally arrived in 1946 when they won the first post-war FA Cup Final, thus ending a barren run of over 60 years without winning a major trophy.

Derby County had a few decent seasons after their FA Cup triumph, but then went into a decline which ultimately ended with them being relegated to the Third Division North in 1955. They soon bounced back into the Second Division but were unable to climb back into the top tier of English football and, in the season before Clough's arrival, managed only a 17th-place finish. Given its lacklustre history, the club's decision to recruit Brian Clough and Peter Taylor as its new management team was probably made more in hope than in expectation. Both men were young, relatively inexperienced and only had a spell at lowly Hartlepool United on their CVs. Any thought that they would eventually lead Derby to the verge of European glory would, at that stage, have been almost laughable.

※ ※ ※

Ajax Amsterdam were founded 16 years later than Derby County and were immeasurably more successful in the years that followed. They were one of the Netherlands' dominant clubs and it was a rare year when they weren't challenging for either the league or cup or, more usually, both. Ajax were the reigning Dutch champions when Clough took over at Derby and were looking forward to another campaign in the European Cup. They had reached the quarter-finals the season before, having made short work of Bill Shankly's Liverpool in the second round. The first leg was played in a foggy Amsterdam and Ajax demolished Liverpool, scoring four goals before half-time and another in the second half to give them a 5-1 victory.

The English side tried to blame the result on the murky weather, claiming that the game had descended into farce as the players struggled to see each other through the gloom. The flimsiness of that excuse was exposed in the return leg when Liverpool failed to overturn the deficit in normal conditions, with Ajax securing a well-earned 2-2 draw.

Both of Ajax's goals in that game at Anfield were scored by a precocious 19-year-old called Johan Cruyff. He had a slender physique, appearing almost too delicate to be a footballer, but there was great strength in his thin frame. Cruyff could shoot strongly with both feet, had incredible stamina, decent heading ability and was quick, especially over those important first few yards. What most marked him out from other players, however, was his graceful style and perfect balance. There were times when Cruyff seemed more akin to a ballet dancer than to a footballer. Whereas other players ran, Cruyff glided. His poise and pace also helped him to avoid injury, enabling him to anticipate or avoid defenders that wanted to knock him out of his stride with clattering tackles.

Cruyff may have had many abilities, but he was not without flaws. He had little inclination or skill when it came to defending, and his supreme self-confidence could sometimes be interpreted as arrogance. Cruyff expected to be the leader on the pitch and, while most of his team-mates were happy to let him take this role, some did object.

The right-winger, Johnny Rep, was one of the few prepared to speak back to Cruyff, though such actions were not always without consequences. On one occasion Rep so infuriated Cruyff during a game that the latter responded by passing the ball slightly too far in front of his team-mate so that he couldn't get it, thus making it look like that it was Rep who was the weaker player.

Cruyff won an impressive list of honours while playing for clubs in his native Netherlands, including three European

Cups, nine league titles, six Dutch Cups, one European Super Cup and a World Club Championship. He later moved to Barcelona, winning the league in his first season at the club. Arguably, the peak of Cruyff's career came in the early 1970s, when he was voted European Footballer of the Year in 1971, 1973 and 1974 and captained Holland to a second-place finish at the 1974 World Cup.

Back in 1967, however, those triumphs were still in the future. The young Cruyff was unable to prevent Ajax from crashing out of the European Cup in the first round although, to be fair, the Dutch champions had a tough draw as they were paired with the Real Madrid side that had won the competition two seasons earlier. Ajax drew the first leg in Amsterdam and were still level on aggregate after 90 minutes of play at the Bernabéu Stadium, with the Spanish champions eventually prevailing in extra time. There was to be a measure of consolation for Ajax, however, as they went on to win another Dutch league title; their third consecutive triumph.

※ ※ ※

Meanwhile, in Derby, Clough's first season in charge started well enough, with seven wins from the first nine matches lifting the team to fourth place in the table. A promising season beckoned but the side proceeded to go on an awful run, winning only two of the next 15 matches which dropped them down to 12th place at the turn of the year. Their form levelled out after that and a mid-table finish would have been a fair reward for their efforts.

Derby had a poor run in their last six matches, however, with three draws and three defeats resulting in an 18th-place finish in the final league table. Clough had spoken confidently about how they were going to revitalise Derby's fortunes, so it was more than a little embarrassing for him that the club ended up finishing one place lower than they had the season before.

Indeed, if they hadn't had such a good start to the campaign they could easily have been relegated.

It was a disappointing start for Clough, especially given the efforts that he and Taylor had made to revitalise the playing squad. That initially involved deciding which players to weed out from the squad that they had inherited and which to persevere with. Interestingly, many of the players who survived that initial cull were still at the club when Derby competed in the European Cup six years later. One was the goalkeeper Colin Boulton, who joined Derby from non-league football in 1964. Boulton was a relatively short, unexceptional goalkeeper, but he had the merit of being consistent and reliable and was rarely out of the side as a result.

One of the few times that he didn't play was when he was suspended for two games in 1973 after shoving his muddy glove into the referee's face following a bad-tempered defeat at home to Leeds United. Also at the club when Clough and Taylor arrived were Peter Daniel, a versatile defender who could play at centre-half or as a full-back, and industrious right-back Ron Webster.

Brian Clough's predecessor was Tim Ward and he had good reason to be grateful to him for two acquisitions that he had made during his tenure. The first was the red-haired Welshman, Alan Durban, who was signed from Cardiff City in 1963. Ward used him as an inside-forward, but Clough and Taylor weren't sure that he was the type of player that they wanted. Durban clearly wasn't too enamoured with them either, requesting a transfer at the end of their first season in charge. Rather than letting Durban go, however, Clough and Taylor decided to play him as an attacking, right-sided midfielder instead. The change in role suited Durban well as he went on to become a regular goalscorer from midfield, often catching defences out by making late runs into the penalty area and latching on to loose balls.

Ward's other key legacy was a prodigious goalscorer, Kevin Hector. Clough and Taylor had noticed Hector's talent when he played against their Hartlepool side for Bradford Park Avenue. They marked him out as a player that they would come back and buy when they were at a bigger club, so to inherit him at Derby was undoubtedly a bonus. It would have appeared, therefore, that of all the players at the club when Clough and Taylor arrived, Hector's future was the most secure. However, they soon started to harbour doubts over him, fearing that he lacked the bravery and aggressiveness they expected of a centre-forward. They rashly attempted to swap him for Hull City striker Ken Wagstaff, who possessed such qualities in abundance, but fortunately for Hector the deal never came off.

In retrospect, Clough and Taylor's initial reservations about Hector appear harsh as he finished as Derby's leading goalscorer in their first season at the club, with 24 in all competitions. Hector continued to score regularly for Derby over the following years, ultimately notching 201 strikes in 589 appearances. Hector may not have been the most courageous of players but he had a strong shot, excellent balance and could run at speed with the ball. While Hector may have been revered in Derby, he found international recognition harder to come by. Like Clough, Hector played only twice for England, coming on both times as a substitute.

Clough returned to Sunderland to make his first acquisition for Derby. He had coached John O'Hare in their youth team and knew exactly what he was getting: a 19-year-old who had strength and courage in abundance. The Scottish striker would spend most of the game with his back to defenders, taking kicks and knocks, but always trying to get hold of the ball as it was played up the pitch.

O'Hare had excellent ball control and was adept at retaining possession until an opportunity came to lay the ball off to one of the team's more creative players. O'Hare went on to build an excellent striking partnership with Hector, their respective talents dovetailing perfectly. O'Hare became one of Brian Clough's favourite players, following him to Leeds United and then to Nottingham Forest, where he finished his career by winning the European Cup in 1980.

Clough and Taylor's next purchase was probably one of the most important of their careers. As with Kevin Hector, they had spotted Roy McFarland when he played against their Hartlepool side. Taylor was desperate to sign the 19-year-old Tranmere Rovers centre-half but, when he and Clough went to watch him play in a Friday-night match early in their first season in charge, it soon became obvious that they weren't the only ones that had their eye on him. The two men moved swiftly, agreeing a fee with Tranmere's manager after the game and then, rather than waiting until the following day to speak to the player, drove straight to his parents' house. The young McFarland had to be woken from his bed to speak to the late visitors and, though he was initially sceptical about joining Derby, he was eventually worn down by their passionate entreaties. Indeed, when a contract was thrust in front of him not only did Taylor give McFarland a pen, he still had his hand on his arm when he signed!

Taylor's faith in the young player was soon vindicated as McFarland developed into one of the finest English defenders of the 1970s, being capped 28 times for his country. A natural leader, McFarland was blessed with pace and composure, as well as a combative streak which his team-mates gladly relied on when matches got tough.

Clough and Taylor's third signing was a left-winger, Alan Hinton. He had started his career at Wolverhampton Wanderers and looked a fine prospect, making his England debut at the age of only 19. Hinton then moved to Nottingham Forest, but his career stalled there and Clough and Taylor gleefully found out that they were only too happy to sell him. Strangely their local rivals believed that Hinton had little left to offer in football, even though he was still only 24. His career was rejuvenated at Derby and he went on to become the club's most creative player, being quick and able to cross or shoot the ball accurately with either foot. Indeed, Clough so admired Hinton's ability at kicking a dead ball that he insisted he took all of the team's free kicks, corners and penalties. Clough also respected the way that Hinton always took on responsibility for building attacks when he had the ball, rather than pass it on to one of his other team-mates. Despite his success at Derby Hinton was never capped for England while he was at the club; a casualty of Sir Alf Ramsey's aversion to using wingers in his side.

Taylor's analysis of Derby's failure to make any progress in the Second Division was that the side lacked an experienced player that could lead the youngsters on the pitch. His suggested solution was to recruit the ageing Dave Mackay, who had been the heartbeat of the Spurs side that had won the league and cup double at the start of the decade. Mackay's playing career was coming to a close and he was planning to return to his native Edinburgh to be player-manager for Heart of Midlothian. Clough, therefore, had his work cut out in trying to persuade Mackay to join his struggling Derby side. That he succeeded was partly through his eagerness and self-belief, but was also down to the offer of a contract which made Mackay the best-paid player in the league.

Clough and Taylor's plan for prolonging Mackay's playing career was to play him as a defensive sweeper alongside Roy McFarland, rather than in his customary wing-half position. Mackay was sceptical initially, but it proved to be an inspired move. The change in role meant that he could stroll around the pitch, directing the younger players and initiating attacks and, crucially, it helped to spare his deteriorating limbs from the worst excesses of professional football.

Mackay's impact was hardly immediate as Derby failed to win any of their first five league games after his arrival for the start of the 1968/69 season, dropping almost to the foot of the table. Their form then picked up and 12 wins and only one defeat in the next 19 league matches lifted them to the top of the table at Christmas.

In the middle of this excellent run of form Clough and Taylor acquired a new midfielder, John McGovern. They had first come across him a few years earlier when they held a schoolboy trial at Hartlepool. He wasn't particularly quick but Taylor noticed that he could win the ball in a tackle, pass it well and also had a good understanding of the game.

Clough hadn't spotted anything in McGovern, but he had sufficient trust in Taylor's judgement to keep an eye on him until he was old enough to sign for the club on professional terms. That proved to be more difficult than he had anticipated as McGovern's mother wanted him to stay at school and take his 'A' levels. Clough eventually managed to win her round, however, and McGovern duly joined Hartlepool, making his debut for the club at the age of only 16. Clough and Taylor promised the youngster that they would come back for him when they were at a bigger club and they were true to their word, signing him for Derby for the grand sum of £7,000. McGovern was still only 18 and, when he first turned up for training on his bicycle, Dave Mackay mistook him for an overenthusiastic autograph hunter!

McGovern went on to become one of Clough's favourite players; signing for him again when he was manager of Leeds United and once more when he took charge at Nottingham Forest. Many fans couldn't see why Clough was so keen to have McGovern in the team as he had an awkward way of running (which was later diagnosed as being due to a missing muscle in his left shoulder) and he rarely did anything particularly exciting with the ball. His value to Clough, however, was as a reliable holding midfield player that broke up opposition attacks, dispatched the ball safely to a team-mate and then dutifully stayed in position as Derby made forward forays of their own. He would run tirelessly throughout the game, give fully committed performances and, crucially, follow Clough's instructions to the letter.

Derby's good run of form continued after Christmas, with five wins and two draws from their next nine matches. It was their final nine fixtures of the campaign, however, which demonstrated what an impressive side they had become. Clough's team won every single one of those nine games, including a 5-1 defeat of Bolton Wanderers to secure promotion, a 4-1 away victory over Norwich City and a grandstand 5-0 home victory over Bristol City in their last game of the season.

Clough's new-look Derby won the Second Division title by a margin of seven points, with the inspired signing of Mackay being crucial to their triumph. It wasn't only Derby fans that recognised what a huge contribution he had made, as the Football Writers' Association also voted him joint Footballer of the Year, along with Manchester City's Tony Book. It was an award that Mackay had never managed to win before, even in his glory days at Spurs. Mackay had retired from football by the time that Derby embarked on their quest to win the European Cup in 1972 but, without his vital contribution to their rise, the club probably wouldn't have been anywhere near such rarefied company.

※ ※ ※

Like Derby, Ajax also made great strides forward in the 1968/69 season, coming closer to winning the European Cup than they ever had before. They easily disposed of the West German champions, Nuremberg, in the first round and then won both at home and away against Fenerbahçe of Turkey in the second round. Confidence was high after those victories, and it rose even further when snow fell in Amsterdam prior to the first leg of their quarter-final against Benfica. The Dutch believed that the Portuguese players would struggle to cope with the inclement conditions, but they were to pay a heavy price for underrating their opponents. Benfica were a talented side, having won the competition twice earlier in the decade, as well as reaching the previous year's final. They duly prepared themselves sensibly for the match, arriving on the pitch suitably attired in tights and gloves.

Benfica surprised their hosts by taking a two-goal lead before half-time and, even though Ajax got a goal back early in the second period, the visitors scored again to restore their advantage. The home defeat was greeted so negatively in the Netherlands that the return match in Lisbon wasn't even broadcast on television, with the outcome being viewed as a foregone conclusion. Benfica certainly had an excellent home record, but this time it was their turn to underrate their opponents. Ajax tore into the Portuguese side in the first half, scoring three goals within the opening half an hour of play. The Dutch managed to hold on to their aggregate lead until 20 minutes from time when José Torres scored to level the tie. There were no further goals and the rules of the competition at the time required a third match to be played at a neutral venue to determine the winner.

The play-off was duly held in Paris. It was to become a seminal moment in the history of Dutch football, with over 40,000 Ajax fans travelling to France to watch the eagerly anticipated game. Never before had there been such a large exodus from Holland for a football match and it paved the way for the armies of Dutch fans that would travel abroad to support their teams in future years. The Ajax fans were rewarded for their efforts by a victory for their side, though extra time was needed before the two teams could finally be separated. There were no goals in the first 90 minutes of play, but a strike from Cruyff two minutes into extra time finally broke the deadlock and Ajax went on to win 3-0.

Ajax received the kindest possible draw in the semi-finals, being paired with Czech side Spartak Trnava, who had reached the last four without having to beat any teams of note. The Dutch team therefore avoided having to play either Manchester United, the holders of the trophy, or Italian champions AC Milan. The first leg was played in Amsterdam and a goal from Cruyff helped Ajax to win 3-0.

The return fixture, however, turned out to be a much tougher affair. The Czechs kicked Cruyff out of the match, got two goals back and it was only fine goalkeeping by the Ajax keeper that prevented them from drawing level and forcing the game to go into extra time.

Ajax's opponents in the final were AC Milan, who had narrowly prevailed over Matt Busby's Manchester United in the other semi-final. The game was played in front of a disappointingly small crowd in Real Madrid's Bernabéu Stadium and it proved to be a step too far for the Dutch side. The Italians took the lead after only eight minutes of play and were 2-0 in front by half-time. Ajax did manage to get a goal back 15 minutes into the second period, but were unable to halt the tide of Italian attacks. AC Milan scored a third goal seven minutes later and then soon got another to put the match well beyond Ajax's reach.

Alongside Cruyff, there were three other players in the Ajax side that lost to AC Milan who were still with the club in 1973. There was the combative right-back Wim Suurbier, who made use of his great pace to attack up the flanks, as well as the central defender Barry Hulshoff who, with his thick beard and long hair, looked every inch a product of the hippy age. On the left-hand side of the attack was Piet Keizer, the only member of the team with sufficient natural talent to rival that of Cruyff. He was adept at dribbling past defenders and also a fine passer of the ball, which he used to greatest effect when firing inviting crosses in from the wing or splitting defences in two with deft through balls. One of his most impressive party tricks was his ability to look one way while sending an accurate pass in the opposite direction.

A 4-1 defeat in such an important match was hard for the young Dutch players to take, but the experience would stand them in good stead for the future. It was a future, however, that didn't come quite as quickly as they would have liked. Their fierce rivals from Rotterdam, Feyenoord, won the league title that year and so became Holland's representatives in the following season's European Cup. Ajax had patiently built up experience in the competition over the previous three seasons but their failure to retain the league title, combined with their defeat to AC Milan, meant that their European Cup adventures were over for the time being.

The response of manager Rinus Michels to the defeat by AC Milan and the loss of the league title was to replace some of the older players with youngsters who he felt could take his team that little bit further. Heinz Stuy, who had the frustrating habit of making great saves as well as letting in easy goals, became the side's regular goalkeeper while a West German, Horst Blankenburg, was recruited to stiffen the defence. Blankenburg, who was the only non-Dutchman in the side, played as the defensive sweeper, with a brief to stop opposition attacks and then bring the ball out from defence. Ruud Krol was also brought in from the youth team to play on the left-hand side of defence. He was a tough left-back who, when not making crunching tackles on opposition strikers, would initiate attacks by surging forward quickly with the ball.

The Ajax side of the early 1970s may be remembered now for its majestic football and its wonderfully talented players but, like all successful teams, it also had its dark side. The player who operated most in the shadows was the team's principal ball-winner; the feisty Johan Neeskens. He was brought to the club by Michels in 1970 and soon gained a reputation for his merciless tackling. Neeskens came from a troubled background and seemed to tackle as if his life depended on it. It would be wrong, however, to categorise him simply as a destroyer. Neeskens was energetic, quick, a fine passer of the ball and became adept at taking penalties. Michels's other newcomers in the midfield were Arie Haan and Gerrie Mühren. Haan, another graduate from the Ajax youth scheme, was a clever, versatile player who usually operated on the right-hand side of midfield, while Mühren ran tirelessly on the opposite wing.

Michels's remodelled side wrenched the Dutch league title back from Feyenoord in the 1969/70 season, but it was their rivals from Rotterdam that had the last laugh. To Ajax's great chagrin Feyenoord not only replaced them in the European Cup, but also became the first Dutch club to win the trophy, beating Celtic 2-1 in the final. That meant that there would be two Dutch sides in the 1970/71 European Cup; a sure sign of where the power in European football now lay.

· ·

The opening 15 minutes of the match gave little clue as to whether Ajax or Derby would eventually emerge victorious. The ball barely moved outside of a 30-yard stretch of grass in the middle of the pitch, with the ball being taken from a player's feet almost as soon as he had received it. It was a battle that some of the combatants thrived on, with McGovern clearly relishing in his tussles with Neeskens. No punches were traded, but the scrap was no less intense than if they had have been. The short, spiky turf was hardly ideal for sliding tackles but that didn't deter those who had built their game on making such challenges. The referee's whistle was barely out of his mouth, with tackle after tackle being penalised for being late, over-aggressive, or even both. No cards were shown, however. This was still a man's game.

Every now and then a Derby player tried to get the ball out of the morass by knocking it forwards over the heads of the opposing Ajax defenders for one of their strikers to chase. Each time, however, the Ajax defenders simply stepped forward in unison, catching Hector, O'Hare, Hinton, or whichever player was brave enough to venture forward, offside. The Dutch defence had clearly perfected the art and there seemed little chance of them slipping up and letting a Derby player through. Meanwhile, Cruyff, of whom so much was expected or, in the case of Derby fans, feared, was strangely quiet. No doubt the close attentions of McFarland were partly responsible, but there was also the impression that he was carefully gauging this unfamiliar Derby side, patiently working out just where they were most vulnerable.

• •

The 1969/70 season was Derby County's first in the top division for 17 years and it started well, with seven wins and four draws in their first 11 matches lifting them to the top of the table. That excellent run of results culminated in a fabulous 5-0 thrashing of Tottenham Hotspur, with Dave Mackay relishing in a crushing victory over his former team-mates. If any Derby fans were starting to dream of back-to-back titles, however, they were quickly brought back down to earth. Clough and Taylor's side soon started to find top tier football more of a struggle as 11 defeats in the next 19 games dropped them down to ninth. Their home form was decent enough, but many of their performances on their travels were woeful, as evidenced by a 3-0 defeat to West Ham and a 4-0 hammering by Arsenal.

Clough and Taylor's customary response to such a predicament was to spend money on a new player, this time raiding local rivals Nottingham Forest for Welsh international Terry Hennessey. Hennessey wasn't a player whose appearance inspired confidence. He didn't look particularly athletic, was prematurely bald and, in a photograph taken alongside Clough and Taylor, looked to be the oldest of the three of them. Hennessey hadn't been bought for his looks, however, but for his ability to pass a ball accurately. He was capable of playing in midfield or central defence, with Clough and Taylor seeing him as a long-term replacement for Mackay who, though still playing well, couldn't be expected to go on forever.

Hennessey's impact at Derby was immediate. He played in their 12 remaining league games of the season, with eight of them won and four drawn. The resurgence in Derby's form propelled them up the table and they duly finished in a very creditable fourth place.

Derby qualified for the Inter-Cities Fairs Cup as a result, but their prize was soon withdrawn following an investigation by the football authorities into alleged financial irregularities at the club. No evidence of fraud or dishonesty was found, but sufficient problems were discovered with how its affairs were being administered for a fine of £10,000 to be levied, with the club also being banned from European competition for a year. It was a cruel blow for all involved with the club, especially given how far they had come in such a short space of time. When Derby qualified for the European Cup a couple of years later they embarked on the campaign without any history of playing competitive matches against continental sides. They still did well, but one can only wonder what they might have achieved had they competed in the Fairs Cup, gaining vital experience for the trials that they were to encounter later on.

Derby started the 1970/71 season positively, with three wins and a draw from their first five league matches lifting them to fourth place. If the fans thought that another successful season beckoned, however, they were soon to be disappointed. Derby proceeded to lose the next three matches so Clough and Taylor felt obliged to go into the transfer market once again. They deemed that the team needed a quick midfielder and settled on acquiring Archie Gemmill, a young Scotsman who was playing in the Third Division for Preston North End. Derby had some serious opposition for his signature, however, as Everton, the reigning league champions, were on the verge of agreeing a deal with him.

Clough and Taylor knew they had to move fast and travelled up to see Gemmill. The discussions started in a local hotel and carried on when Clough accompanied Gemmill back to his house. Gemmill made it clear that he wasn't going to make up his mind that evening and so Clough spent the night sleeping in his spare room, finally getting his man the following morning. Gemmill was so impressed with Clough's vision for Derby County that he accepted a contract much less lucrative than the one he had been offered by Everton, though he was also realistic enough to know that he was more likely to get a place in the first team at Derby. The Merseyside club had just won the league title with the great midfield trio of Alan Ball, Colin Harvey and Howard Kendall and they wouldn't have been easily displaced.

The team that Gemmill joined were finding their second season in the top division much harder than the first and he was on the losing side when he made his debut away at West Bromwich Albion, with Derby then going on to draw four and lose three of the next seven games. That left the club just outside of the relegation zone and Gemmill must have wondered whether he had made the right choice in joining Derby.

A couple of successive victories against Blackpool and Nottingham Forest in late November, however, helped them to turn the corner, and a further four wins and two draws from the next nine matches lifted them up to 15th place. Relegation was no longer a worry, but Clough and Taylor were not prepared to settle for mid-table obscurity, judging that another major acquisition was required if they were serious about challenging for honours.

Derby's inspirational captain, Dave Mackay, was 36 years old and nearing the end of his three-year contract with the club. His planned replacement, Terry Hennessey, was struggling with injuries and so an alternative was needed. Clough moved for Colin Todd, another player that he had coached in the youth team at Sunderland. The young Derby manager provisionally agreed the purchase of Todd with the club's chairman, Sam Longson, before the latter went on holiday to the Caribbean. What hadn't been settled, however, was the size of the transfer fee that was to be paid. In his chairman's absence Clough set a new British transfer record by signing Todd for £175,000, which infuriated Longson when he eventually found out about the size of the fee.

The breach of trust between the two men opened up a rift which, ultimately, was to prove fatal to their relationship. Thankfully for Derby, however, Todd proved to be a fine acquisition. He replaced Mackay as the side's defensive sweeper and formed an excellent partnership with McFarland; his pace and calm, measured approach complementing his team-mate's ferocious tackling and ability in the air.

Todd made his Derby debut in a home victory over Arsenal and played in all of the club's remaining league games that season. Clough's side won six of those 14 matches and drew three, resulting in a respectable ninth-place finish. To outside observers it may have seemed that Derby were slipping back, following their fourth-place finish the previous season. However, with Gemmill and Todd on board, Clough and Taylor had finally assembled a team that was capable of beating the best. Against all expectations, the following season was to become the most successful in Derby County's long, but often barren, history.

Shortly before the half-hour mark, while the ball was out of play, Cruyff trotted over to Neeskens and whispered in his ear. The midfielder nodded in agreement and Cruyff, seemingly happy with the outcome, made his way back to the centre of the pitch.

A few minutes later McGovern spotted Hinton running on Haan's blindside and quickly played the ball into his path. Hinton collected the pass with ease and, with Haan trailing in his wake, galloped towards the retreating Suurbier. If he could get past the full-back, then he would be free to bear down on the Ajax goal. Suddenly, the horizon shifted by 90 degrees and he felt his feet lose contact with the ground. The next thing he knew he was flat on the floor, and all he could see was Neeskens moving away with the ball at his feet.

As Hinton got to his feet he watched in horror as the Ajax players scythed their way through the Derby defence. Neeskens quickly released the ball to Cruyff, who had retreated to the centre circle to avoid the attentions of McFarland. The Ajax captain received the ball, turned sharply to evade the incoming tackle from Gemmill, looked up, and then played an inch-perfect pass to the feet of Keizer who was making his way down the left wing. Cruyff continued his run while Keizer skilfully hurdled over a sliding tackle by Durban.

Webster still blocked his path to goal but Keizer had no intention of taking him on. Instead, he simply kicked the ball past the Derby right-back and watched in delight as Krol sped past both him and the stranded defender. Krol reached the ball, took one touch, and then sent a looping cross towards the edge of the penalty area. Cruyff, who had not stopped running since he had passed the ball to Keizer, quickly gauged the flight of the ball and met it on the volley, crashing it between Todd and McFarland and past the despairing reach of Boulton: 1-0 to Ajax.

While Clough and Taylor spent the 1970/71 season laying the foundations for their future success, Rinus Michels's Ajax finally met with their destiny. They breezed through the first two rounds of the European Cup though, to be fair, only the Albanian and Swiss champions stood in their way. The challenge facing the Dutch side got a lot tougher in the quarter-finals when they were drawn against Glasgow Celtic. Jock Stein's Celtic were one of the strongest sides in the competition, having reached two of the four previous finals.

Michels's reworked Ajax side, however, were more than a match for them. The first leg was played in Amsterdam and the Scots managed to keep the hosts at bay until halfway through the second period. It was Cruyff who seized the initiative, scoring once before setting up goals for Hulshoff and Keizer. Ajax's three-goal advantage meant that their place in the semi-finals was never really in much doubt, though the Scots did manage to salvage some pride with a 1-0 win in the return fixture.

Ajax were drawn against Atlético Madrid in the semi-finals and they made things hard for themselves in the away leg by playing too defensively. They lost 1-0, but the defeat could have been much greater. Michels's side resorted to their usual free-flowing attacking football back in Amsterdam and were soon on level terms, with Keizer scoring from a fine free kick. It was now the Spanish team's turn to try and hold on, and they did so until 14 minutes from time when the relentless Dutch pressure finally told. Suurbier scored with a shot from outside the penalty area, and then Neeskens slotted home Ajax's third goal to put them into their second European Cup Final in three years.

The venue for the 1971 European Cup Final was Wembley and the game was played in front of a predominantly Dutch crowd. Ajax's opponents were the Greek side Panathinaikos, who were managed by the great Hungarian striker Ferenc Puskás. They had knocked out English champions Everton in a tempestuous quarter-final before being drawn against Red Star Belgrade in the last four. The Greeks lost the first leg 4-1 and seemed to be on the way out of the competition. They then fought back strongly in Athens, however, and gained a 3-0 victory, which was sufficient for them to reach the final on the away goals rule.

Panathinaikos had done well to get to the final but they weren't remotely good enough to challenge Ajax and, unsurprisingly, the match didn't turn out to be much of a spectacle. The Dutch side took the lead after only five minutes and they didn't have to work too hard to keep their advantage. The Greek keeper made a number of fine saves to keep the score down, but Ajax hardly helped matters by playing defensively in the second half. Michels's side finally made sure of their victory three minutes from the end of the game, when a shot from Arie Haan was cruelly deflected past the Greek keeper by one of his own defenders.

Ajax undoubtedly had great players, but what really gave them an edge over their rivals was their use of innovative tactics. Indeed, their way of playing of the game was so fresh and unique that it was even given its own name: 'Total Football'. Its principal architect was the side's manager, Rinus Michels. He had been a successful centre-forward for Ajax in the 1940s and 1950s and, after retiring from the game through injury, became a gymnastics teacher for a number of years. He returned to Ajax as manager in 1965, when the team was flirting with relegation from the top tier of the Dutch league.

A strict disciplinarian, Michels trained the players hard, building up both their stamina and skills. His dedicated, professional approach was also evidenced by his copying of the Italian practice of taking players away for intensive practice prior to important games. Michels had been quite a laid-back character as a player, fond of playing practical jokes, but he projected quite a different image once he became a manager. While he was affable with his players when they were away from the ground, he brooked no dissent on the training pitch or in the dressing room.

As Ajax became more successful and started to travel abroad to play matches the authoritarian Michels made sure that his players never considered such trips to be an opportunity to let their hair down, regularly patrolling the hotel corridors at night to ensure that they didn't go out drinking. After the away defeat to Atlético Madrid in the semi-finals of the 1970/71 European Cup he was so angry with the team's display that he refused to allow the players' wives to join them at the hotel after the game. That inevitably led to a huge quarrel between Michels and the players, which ended in them voicing their dissent by staying up all night in the bar, drinking heavily.

Michels initially deployed his Ajax team with four defenders, two midfielders and four forwards. This was a common formation for teams in the 1960s, having been popularised by the Brazil side that won consecutive World Cups in 1958 and 1962. Such an approach brought success in Holland, but proved to be ineffective against stronger foreign opposition, most notably in the heavy defeat to AC Milan in the 1969 European Cup Final.

The use of four forwards often led to Ajax being overrun in midfield and consequently made it difficult for them to regain the ball when they lost possession. Michels eventually remedied the problem by sacrificing one of the forwards for a midfielder and by encouraging the defensive sweeper to step up and join the midfield. This produced a 4-3-3 formation, which could morph quickly into a 3-4-3 when the team gained possession of the ball and started to attack.

The configuration of Michels's side, however, was not the key idea behind Total Football. Perhaps its most significant innovation was the freedom it gave to players to switch positions with one another during a game. While the swapping of positions between players wasn't particularly novel in itself, the way in which Ajax did it was. It wasn't uncommon at the time, for instance, to see a midfielder taking the place of another midfielder, or a forward taking the place of another forward.

The Ajax team of the early 1970s, however, sought to surprise their opponents by switching players along the flanks, or even in the middle of the pitch. That would mean a full-back becoming a winger, for example, or a central midfielder temporarily playing as a centre-forward. The swapping of positions between players gave the team a mentality that was focused on attack as the whole team was responsible for creating scoring opportunities, not just the midfielders and forwards. Another important feature of the Ajax style of play was their focus on using space as a way of controlling the game.

Put simply, when Ajax didn't have the ball they would restrict the amount of space that the opposition had to play in, making persistent use of the offside trap and pressing the other team until they lost possession. Then, once they had the ball, the players would use the full width of the pitch so that they had more space in which to operate as they attacked the opposition goal.

Michels may have created a novel concept in Total Football, but he still needed a lieutenant on the pitch to help implement his ideas. Having Johan Cruyff at his disposal, therefore, was a blessing in more ways than one. Cruyff's natural talents made him into a fine footballer, but what turned him into one of the greats was his tactical knowledge of the game. As talented as Cruyff was, he knew that he couldn't win matches on his own and so he learnt how to make best use of those around him.

Cruyff would talk constantly on the pitch, setting up attacks and encouraging movement while still ensuring that the shape of the team remained robust. Even as a teenager Cruyff would tell the older players how to play. They didn't object because it was obvious that, despite his tender years, he clearly knew what he was talking about. The positional flexibility of Total Football also suited the mercurial Cruyff perfectly, allowing him to drift out of his centre-forward position to play on the wings, or to drop deeper into midfield and orchestrate attacks from there.

Brian Clough, similarly, had a clear vision of how Derby County should play. He urged his players to keep possession of the ball, pass it crisply and, whenever possible, keep it on the ground. Derby would often build up attacks patiently from defence, with the players making short, simple passes to each other as they made their way up the pitch. The aim was for the ball to be passed around while they waited for gaps in the opposition defence to open up, which they could then seek to exploit. Clough also encouraged midfielders to run at defenders in a ploy to unsettle the opposition defence. The theory was that if the defender tried to tackle the midfielder then that created space for the forward he was supposed to be marking, but if the defender stayed close to the striker that just created more space for the midfielder to run into.

What Clough couldn't abide, however, was the long, hopeful ball launched out of defence. As a striker, he knew just how difficult it was to deal with, and so he discouraged his defenders from trying to attempt any such passes. Clough's Derby were also an effective team on the counter-attack as they had fast, energetic players, such as Gemmill and Hinton, who were well-suited to racing up the pitch and taking advantage of undermanned defences.

Clough's great rival, the Leeds United manager Don Revie, prepared detailed dossiers for his players which contained a wealth of information on the team that they were about to play. Clough was dismissive of this approach, preferring instead to see football as a simple game that didn't need to become unnecessarily complicated by over-preparation. Clough would give his players brief commands instead, such as telling Hinton to stay wide on the left-hand side of the pitch and encouraging O'Hare to hold up the ball, no matter how much he was kicked and jostled by opposition defenders.

Clough placed great value on the need for his team to maintain its balance and shape and so made sure that each player knew exactly what was expected of him in this regard. He stressed the need for his players to stay in their positions and look after their area of the pitch and, at half-time, would often only issue simple words of advice to ensure that the team kept their shape, such as telling the defenders to play higher up the pitch if he had seen them start to retreat too close to their own goal.

Clough was also a great believer in only asking players to do what they were capable of and so focused on developing their strengths, rather than trying to eradicate their weaknesses. Alan Hinton, for example, was the best kicker of a dead ball at the club but probably the side's weakest tackler (his distaste for the physical side of the game was so marked that he was nicknamed 'Gladys' as a result). Clough therefore insisted that he take all of the corner kicks and never asked him to track back and defend.

Clough's philosophy of how the game should be played was vindicated in the 1971/72 season, when his side finally delivered the success that Derby's long-suffering fans had been waiting for. Derby started the new campaign strongly and were unbeaten in their first 12 matches. Encouraging home wins over Arsenal, Manchester City and Everton followed, though away defeats to Liverpool and Leeds United helped to keep expectations in check.

It was in their first 12 matches of the new year that Derby laid the foundations for their league triumph, with nine victories and two draws lifting them up to second place in the table. While it was clear that the title was within Derby's grasp, they were not short of challengers for the trophy. It proved to be one of the closest-ever finishes to a league season, with the top four teams eventually all finishing within one point of each other. The run-in to the end of the season was particularly exciting for Derby fans as their side had to play all three of their title rivals (Leeds United, Liverpool and Manchester City) in their last seven matches.

The first of these fixtures was at home to Leeds, who had regularly thwarted Derby during Clough's tenure at the club. Clough never hid his disdain for Don Revie and their personal animosity added spice to what was already an enticing encounter. Clough, for once, emerged triumphant, with Derby winning 2-0. The victory lifted Derby to the top of the table for the first time that season, and two wins and a draw from their next four games kept them there. However, a defeat in their penultimate match of the season, away to Manchester City, dropped them back down to third place.

Derby's final league game of the season was a home fixture against title rivals, Liverpool. Clough's players knew that only a win would keep their dreams alive and they duly delivered it, by virtue of a majestic goal scored by John McGovern. The victory returned Derby to the top of the table, although Leeds United and Liverpool still had one game left to play.

The Derby players then went on an end-of-season trip to Majorca, fully expecting at least one of those two clubs to get the points they needed to become champions. To their utter delight and amazement both clubs then slipped up. Liverpool needed to win away at Arsenal but could only draw, while Leeds lost away at Wolverhampton Wanderers when a draw would have secured them the title. It was an incredible end to the season, with the Derby team becoming the first to win the league while sunbathing on a beach.

· ·

The pundits who had predicted an easy win for Ajax were sitting comfortably in their seats at half-time. The match had been tighter than they expected but, nevertheless, the Dutch champions were still in front and Derby hadn't created any meaningful chances to score. It might not have been the complete mismatch that many had anticipated, but there seemed to be little doubt which team would be lifting the trophy in an hour's time.

In truth, Derby's form away from the Baseball Ground had been woeful that season. They had mustered only four victories from their 21 away league fixtures and had suffered some real batterings on their travels, including a 5-0 thrashing by Leeds as well as 4-0 defeats to Manchester City and Stoke. They had also won only one of their four away ties in the European Cup, resulting in a clear suspicion that the Derby defence could be brittle away from home. The only real surprise, in fact, was that they weren't further behind to Ajax than they were.

The watching Derby fans, both in Belgrade and back home, weren't too downhearted at the interval, however. They had feared a bigger mauling than they were getting and were quietly proud that their team had gone toe-to-toe with the world's finest outfit and were still standing. True, they hadn't got a shot on target but then Ajax hadn't actually created that many clear-cut chances either. All they needed was a bit of magic from Hinton's white boots and they would be right back in the game.

Inside the Derby dressing room the players were a little more despondent. They had gone into the game with high hopes of upsetting the reigning champions, but now they knew just why Ajax had won so much in recent years; they were good, bloody good in fact. There was some chatter among themselves of what they could do to put more pressure on to Ajax, but there was no real conviction behind the words. In the backs of their minds they recalled some of the season's heavy away defeats and pondered quietly what they could do to avoid such an outcome from happening again. The brave fans that had travelled all the way to Belgrade deserved at least that. Brian Clough stood outside the dressing room, knowing that the next few minutes were probably the most important of his entire managerial career. He had watched his players troop off the pitch at half-time and had seen that they had lost confidence. Not only did he need to give them back their self-belief, but he also had to show them how they could get back into the game. Inspiring words wouldn't be enough on their own; he also had to put weapons into their hands. Could he do it? Well, he certainly didn't doubt so.

• •

After achieving his goal of making Ajax the best side in Europe, Rinus Michels left the club to become manager at Barcelona. Not all of the Ajax players were sad to see the disciplinarian go, with Piet Keizer jigging on a table in delight when he heard the news. The two men had rowed frequently about tactics as Keizer was never keen on running back and providing defensive cover when the full-back attacked, a key tenet of Michels's Total Football philosophy. Sadly, Keizer's habit of falling out with the manager didn't end with Michels's departure. After a row over tactics with one of his successors Keizer gave up football completely. Indeed, he was so soured with the game that he didn't play again for years, even moving away from the ball as it came towards him on the side of the pitch while he was watching his young son play.

Michels's successor, Ştefan Kovács, was a surprise choice. He was little known outside of his native Romania, where he had led Steaua Bucharest to a league title and a few cup wins. Kovács sensibly resisted the temptation to make his mark on the Ajax side that he had inherited, recognising that there could not be too much wrong with a team that had just won the European Cup. Ajax was an engine that needed fine-tuning rather than an overhaul, so the only changes he made were subtle and gentle. Kovács may not have changed many of the personnel at the club, but he did make some shrewd modifications to the way that they played. He encouraged the defenders Blankenburg, Suurbier and Krol to attack more than they had been allowed to under Michels, and he also gave senior players such as Cruyff and Keizer the licence to make tactical decisions on the pitch, rather than wait for directions to come from the dugout.

Kovács also gave the players greater freedom off the field, opting not to train them as hard as Michels had done. He was a much less authoritarian figure than his predecessor and so encouraged the players to sort out their problems for themselves. Once, after a fight broke out in training between Cruyff and the young Johnny Rep, it was the players rather than Kovács who decided that Rep was to be banished from the first team as a punishment.

Kovács may have delegated a lot of his authority to his senior players, but he still knew how to bring them back into line if they overstepped the mark. Before one game Cruyff complained of having an injured knee so Kovács, aware of the striker's fondness for money, duly rubbed it better with a banknote. Cruyff smiled and played on without any problems. Clearly, there were to be no malingering maestros on Kovács's watch. Rumours of ill discipline among the players dogged Kovács throughout his time in charge of Ajax, but the best riposte to this criticism was the success that he achieved with the club. In the two seasons that he was in charge Ajax won almost every competition they entered, including two European Cups and two league titles as well as triumphs in the Dutch Cup, UEFA Super Cup and the World Club Championship.

Ajax's defence of their European Cup in the 1971/72 season started easily enough. They knocked out Dynamo

Dresden without conceding a goal and then beat Olympique Marseilles home and away. Their quarter-final draw appeared much tougher, however, as they were pitted against English champions Arsenal. The London side, who had won the league and cup double the previous season, were confident as they had beaten Ajax in the semi-finals of the Fairs Cup two years earlier and fancied that they could repeat the triumph. Arsenal lost the first leg 2-1 in Amsterdam, but their away goal meant that they only needed a 1-0 victory at Highbury to reach the semi-finals.

Obtaining such a result seemed eminently possible, but things went badly wrong in the first quarter of an hour of the second tie, with young Peter Marinello missing a good chance before George Graham headed the ball past his own goalkeeper. Ajax then drew on their long experience of European football to protect their two-goal aggregate lead for the remainder of the game. Ajax were reunited with Benfica in the semi-finals, three years after their last epic clash in the competition. The Portuguese side had thrashed Feyenoord 5-1 in Lisbon in the previous round, but there was to be no further massacre of the Dutch. Kovács's side secured a 1-0 win at home in the first leg and followed that with a goalless draw in the away fixture.

Ajax's opponents in the final were Italian champions Inter Milan, who had beaten Celtic in a penalty shoot-out in the other semi-final. The final was held in Feyenoord's stadium in Rotterdam and initially the Ajax players were apprehensive about how they would be received at the home of their greatest rivals. Their fears proved to be unfounded, however, and they responded by giving what is often seen as their greatest ever performance. The defensive Italians had no answer to Ajax's intelligent, energetic, attacking football and kept ten men behind the ball for most of the first half. Inter managed to get to half-time unscathed, but Ajax's ambition was rewarded in the second half when Cruyff scored twice; the first an easy tap-in following a collision between the goalkeeper and a defender, and the second a powerful header from a Keizer free kick. Ajax were the champions of Europe again and there didn't appear to be a team anywhere on the continent that had the resources to match them. But was there?

· ·

Those who watched closely as the Derby County players ran out on to the pitch for the second half could see a slight spring in their step; a zest in their movement which simply wasn't there when they'd ambled off for the break. The demeanour of the Ajax players, meanwhile, was businesslike in most cases but there was a definite whiff of arrogance from some quarters. It was clear they believed that having already breached the English defence once, it was only a matter of time before they did so again.

The second period of the game started largely as the first had finished, with the Dutch side besieging the Derby defence. There was one subtle difference, however, as Clough's side were defending closer to their goal than they had in the first half, with McGovern playing only a yard or two in front of the centre-halves. At first glance all this appeared to achieve was to encourage Ajax to attack even harder. Within a few minutes of the restart, however, the purpose of the change of strategy became abundantly clear.

The move started with Todd, who dispossessed Cruyff with a tackle clean enough to bring back memories of Bobby Moore at the height of his powers. Todd looked up, saw Gemmill scampering off towards the right wing, and played the ball slightly in front of him. Gemmill, still in his own half, collected the pass, steered the ball around Mühren and then broke into a sprint. Keizer thought for a moment about chasing after him, but it was clear that Gemmill wasn't going to be caught. Krol saw Gemmill coming and, unable to rely on the offside trap, barrelled forward in an attempt to knock the little Scotsman off the ball. He clattered into Gemmill, but his challenge came too late as the ball was already making its way diagonally across the pitch towards Hinton.

The white-booted maestro was finally where he wanted to be; out free on the left wing, with the ball at his feet and Neeskens well out of kicking distance. The rapidly retreating Ajax defence had to make some quick decisions as there were only three of them left on their feet and there were three Derby players advancing quickly on their goal. Suurbier headed towards Hinton, while Blankenburg tracked Hector's run and Hulshoff kept a close eye on O'Hare.

Hinton saw Suurbier's challenge coming and lofted the ball forward towards O'Hare. The brave Scotsman leapt into the air, with Hulshoff at his back, and managed to get his head to the ball first. All he needed was the slightest of touches and he got it, with the ball skimming off his forehead and into the path of the onrushing Hector. The Derby striker had anticipated O'Hare's header a moment earlier than his German marker and his reward was half a yard of distance between them. There was only one chance of scoring from the opportunity and Hector took it cleanly, sliding the ball underneath Stuy's late dive. He wheeled away in celebration, soon being congratulated by Gemmill who had picked himself up from underneath Krol and carried on racing up the pitch. The three men looked towards the touchline, where Clough and Taylor had leapt up from the dugout. Taylor clapped his hands in applause while Clough gave them that so often desired, but incredibly rare, signal of affirmation; his single thumbs-up gesture. This really was going to be a game, after all.

· ·

Clough and Taylor embarked on the 1972/73 season knowing that if success had been hard to achieve, then maintaining it would be even harder still. One of the players they started to make greater use of was a striker that they had signed the previous season from non-league Worcester City. Taylor thrived on unearthing hidden gems and the acquisition of Roger Davies was another classic coup. There were other clubs that were showing an interest but they wanted to hedge their bets by only offering him a trial. Taylor trusted his judgement and signed Davies for £14,000, ignoring grumbles from Derby's chairman that it was a lot of money to spend on a non-league player. Taylor's faith in the hard-working Davies was vindicated as he went on to have a fine career with Derby, eventually being sold to the Belgian club FC Bruges for ten times the sum that Clough and Taylor had paid for him.

Davies may have been a purchase from the bargain basement but Clough and Taylor had no qualms about setting another British transfer record with their next acquisition. Taylor had recently watched the Brazilian team, Santos, in a friendly against Sheffield Wednesday and was excited by how their full-backs attacked from deep. In Leicester City's David Nish, he saw a player that could fulfil the same role for Derby. Nish had joined the neighbouring East Midlands club straight from school and was a prodigious talent. He represented England at youth and under-23 level and was appointed club captain at the age of only 21. Nish led Leicester to an FA Cup Final in 1969 and, in so doing, became the youngest ever captain of an FA Cup Final team. He was versatile enough to play in virtually any of the outfield positions and could pass the ball equally well with either foot.

As reigning league champions, Derby were England's sole representatives in the 1972/73 European Cup. It was the club's first foray into European competition and the challenge facing Clough and Taylor was not made any easier when the draw for the first round was made. Ideally, they would have been given a gentle introduction to the toughest club tournament in the world by being paired with the champions of Finland,

Luxembourg or Malta. Instead, Derby were handed a tough opening tie against the Yugoslavian champions, Željezničar Sarajevo.

Not only were Clough and Taylor completely inexperienced in taking on continental opposition, but they also had the unwelcome problem of their team not being in form. Derby's defence of their league title had started badly, with the side managing only two wins in the eight matches played prior to the first leg at the Baseball Ground. It was surely with some relief, therefore, that Clough and Taylor saw their side get off to a winning start in the European Cup. Goals from McFarland and Gemmill gave Derby the victory and, almost as importantly, the defence prevented the visitors from scoring a valuable away goal.

Derby expected a tough game back in Yugoslavia, though they probably didn't anticipate just how arduous a trip it would turn out to be. Their hosts soon made their intentions clear, refusing to provide Derby with any balls to practise with before the game. The crowd of over 60,000 hostile spectators also played their part in trying to cow the visitors, sounding sirens and letting off firecrackers. These were sights and sounds that the Derby players had never experienced before and they did well not to be intimidated by the menacing atmosphere.

The match, unsurprisingly, turned out to be a bad-tempered affair, with the Derby players being on the receiving end of some heavy and uncompromising tackling. Rather than losing their composure they responded in the most effective way possible; by ending the tie as a meaningful contest. Hinton scored after only nine minutes of play and O'Hare got a second six minutes later, both goals being scored on the counter-attack. The Yugoslavians did manage to get a goal back in the second half, but those two early strikes made it academic.

Derby County's prize for surviving the baptism of fire in Sarajevo was to be drawn against one of Europe's most revered sides: Benfica. The Portuguese club had played in five European Cup finals in an eight-year spell in the previous decade and were still a force to be reckoned with, having reached the semi-finals a year earlier. The side that faced Derby included six players that had played Manchester United in the most recent of those finals, including the legendary striker Eusébio. He was still only 30 years of age and continued to score goals at a prodigious rate. In Benfica's seven league matches prior to taking on Derby Eusébio had found the net 16 times. If that wasn't enough, there was also a vast gulf in experience between the two clubs. The tie at the Baseball Ground was Benfica's 66th game in European competitions, whereas it was only Derby's third.

Clough was sufficiently wary of the Portuguese side to undertake a rare scouting mission to watch them play. He wasn't particularly impressed, but decided not to tell his players for fear that it would make them complacent. Taylor took a different tack in the dressing room shortly before the game, making a few minor remarks about some of the Benfica side before tearing up the piece of paper that he was reading from and telling his players that there was no one to be concerned about. Not even Eusébio, apparently.

The low-key approach clearly worked as Derby dominated the opening half. The first goal came after only eight minutes of play when McFarland headed home a short corner from Hinton. Then, just before the half-hour mark, Derby scored a second.

McFarland got his head to a Hinton corner and knocked the ball back to Hector, who hit a wonderful, looping volley over the heads of the Benfica defenders, who could only watch as it sailed into the roof of the net. Just before half-time Derby scored a third goal, when Hector headed down a long, hopeful ball from Daniel into the path of McGovern who slid it past the goalkeeper from near the penalty spot.

Benfica, unsurprisingly, played much more cautiously in the second half, opting to limit the damage that had been done rather than trying to repair it. The resulting 3-0 victory over one of Europe's most prestigious clubs was arguably Derby's finest night of football. If there were still any lingering doubts over Clough and Taylor's ability to succeed at this level of the game, then this match banished them completely.

A three-goal lead was an excellent advantage to take into the second leg in Lisbon, but Clough and Taylor knew that their passage to the quarter-finals was far from secure. Derby's league form continued to be disappointing, with a 4-0 thrashing by Manchester City shortly before their trip to Portugal hardly lifting spirits. Clough was a great believer in the value of players being relaxed before a big game as he didn't think anybody could perform to their full potential if they were tense and anxious.

In order to help put his players in the right frame of mind Clough put a crate of beer on to the coach, encouraging them to have a drink on the journey to Benfica's ground. In his short pre-match team-talk he simply told the players to go out and enjoy the game; they were better than Benfica and all they had to do was prove it. The Derby players took Clough at his word and, in front of a crowd of 75,000 spectators, defended stoutly as Benfica launched wave after wave of attacks. The disciplined defensive display, with Hennessey at its heart, was rewarded with a clean sheet and Derby went through to the last eight of the competition.

• •

There was a slight look of shock among some of the Ajax players following Derby's equaliser; the second half clearly wasn't going to be the procession that they had expected it to be. The next few minutes of the game were scrappy, with Neeskens trying to win the ball for his side at every opportunity and Gemmill and McGovern being just as determined to get it back. Cruyff, meanwhile, was a flurry of activity, directing his team-mates this way and that, while Clough barked out his orders from the touchline. The game swung delicately in the balance and they both knew it.

Derby slowly edged their way up the pitch and the Ajax defence, wary of their offside trap being sprung again, retreated backwards, defending their goal with players rather than with space. Hector, close to the edge of the right-hand side of the penalty area, attempted to break through the defence but Krol, Blankenburg and Hulshoff were soon all around him. The ball was taken from his feet but only cleared as far as Gemmill, who then proceeded on a run which would later be viewed as the defining moment of his career.

First he skipped over a lunging tackle from the German defender before side-stepping a challenge from Krol. Hulshoff still barred his entrance to the penalty area but Gemmill was not to be denied, slipping the ball between the large bearded Dutchman and Hector who was trying to help out but was quickly becoming surplus to requirements. Stuy raced off his line to intercept Gemmill but he was too slow, only being able to watch as the ball was lofted over his diving body before nestling in the back of the net. Derby were in dreamland now!

• •

Ajax's route to the quarter-finals was much less arduous than that navigated by Derby. As holders of the trophy they were given a bye from the first round and then weren't remotely troubled by their second-round opponents, CSKA Sofia. Kovács's side won the away leg in Bulgaria 3-1 and followed that by winning the home match 3-0.

The draw for the quarter-final, however, presented the Dutch champions with a much tougher proposition in the shape of the continent's new rising force, Bayern Munich. Their team contained six players that had been in the West Germany side that had won the European Championship a year earlier and would go on to win the World Cup a year later, including the imposing goalkeeper Sepp Maier, the imperious Franz Beckenbauer and prolific striker Gerd Müller.

The first leg of the quarter-final was played in Amsterdam and Kovács gave a full European Cup debut to a young forward called Johnny Rep. He had burst on to the scene a year earlier when he scored two goals in Ajax's 3-0 victory over the Argentinean side, Independiente, in the final of the World Club Championship. The second of his goals was the most impressive, with Rep starting a run from the halfway line, collecting a pass from Cruyff and then rounding the goalkeeper at full speed, before pushing the ball into the net.

Rep had joined Ajax's youth academy at the age of 16 from a second division club and soon became the pin-up boy of Dutch football. His handsome features, long blond hair and prodigious talent even led to him being nicknamed 'Goldenballs' by one of his team-mates. Rep was confident enough in his own talents not to be cowed by the older, more experienced players and, despite their frequent clashes, it was probably on Cruyff's recommendation that Kovács finally put him in the first team on a regular basis.

The clash between Ajax and Bayern Munich was so keenly anticipated that a group of English football managers chartered a plane to Amsterdam to go and see it, and they certainly wouldn't have been disappointed with what they saw. The West Germans managed to hold out until half-time but were then destroyed by an irresistible display of 'Total Football' in the second period. Kovács's side scored three times in just over a quarter of an hour of play and thus pretty well ended any hopes the Germans had of progressing in the competition. The first goal came after their goalkeeper, the normally reliable Sepp Maier, failed to hold a shot from outside the penalty area and Arie Haan kicked home the rebound. Gerrie Mühren then scored with a sumptuous volley, before Haan got his second with a looping header from a corner. Again, Maier was at fault as he had come rushing off his line to try and catch the ball but had got nowhere near it.

Johan Cruyff eclipsed Franz Beckenbauer with a magisterial performance and was rewarded with a goal just before the end of the match when he headed the ball into the net. The Germans complained that Müller hadn't been fully fit but, in truth, they had been well and truly beaten. Maier was so disappointed by the result and his own performance that he got out of bed during the night and threw his clothes from the hotel window into the canal below. The Germans restored some pride in the second leg with a 2-1 victory, but it was too little too late.

Johan Cruyff didn't play in that game, with his non-appearance being attributed to a knee injury. Some of the Ajax players weren't convinced about the reason for Cruyff's absence and, in a hint of troubles to come, began to talk among themselves about disposing of him as captain.

There was a four-month gap between Derby's victory over Benfica and their quarter-final tie. During that period Derby's league form improved markedly, with the club climbing from 16th to sixth place in the table. Clough's side had received a kind draw in the quarter-finals, avoiding not only Ajax and Bayern Munich but also Dynamo Kiev, Juventus and Real Madrid. Their opponents were the Czech champions Spartak Trnava, who had played only two games in the competition after receiving a bye in the first round. Nevertheless, it would still have been a mistake for Derby to have underestimated them. The Czech side hadn't lost a league game at home in seven years and had won the national title four times in the previous five seasons. That had given the club repeated exposure to the European Cup and they had taken good advantage of the opportunity, reaching the semi-finals four years previously.

For the first time in the competition, Derby had to play their first leg abroad. They also lost for the first time as well, with a goal for the Czech side shortly before half-time giving them the victory. Clough wasn't too disheartened with the result, however, as he was confident that his side could reverse the deficit back at the Baseball Ground. His faith in his players was vindicated with Hector scoring either side of half-time to give Derby an aggregate lead. A nervous finish to the game duly followed as Derby's failure to score in the first leg meant that a single goal from the Czechs would see them win on the away goals rule. While Hector's second goal ultimately proved to be decisive O'Hare's contribution was invaluable, even though he was played out of position in midfield so that both Hector and Davies could be accommodated in the forward line.

There was a one-in-three chance for Ajax and Derby to be paired together in the draw for the semi-finals, but sadly it wasn't to be. The Dutch champions were drawn to play against Real Madrid, while Clough's side had to take on Italian champions Juventus. The first leg, played in Turin, proved to be one of the most controversial matches of Clough's career, and things started to unravel before a ball was even kicked. Clough and Taylor were due to be at a formal dinner in Turin on the night before the game, but when it was time for them to leave Taylor was taken aback to find Clough still wearing his tracksuit and playing cards. The older man voiced his displeasure with Clough's tardiness and a row duly erupted between them in full view of many of the squad. They both returned angrily to their rooms and neither subsequently attended the dinner, no doubt to their hosts' chagrin.

One consequence of this quarrel was that the two men didn't discuss which players they would field against Juventus. When Taylor found out what the team was to be, he was astounded to discover that Clough had selected Tony Parry to play in midfield. Parry had played for Clough and Taylor at

Hartlepool and their principal reason for taking him to Derby was to help their former club through a period of financial difficulty. He had only played four league games for Derby that season and two of those appearances were as a substitute. Clough was well-renowned for making unusual, sometimes eccentric, decisions but selecting Parry for a European Cup semi-final was simply bizarre. Taylor intervened and persuaded him to change the team, with the much more experienced Durban eventually playing instead.

The semi-finals of the European Cup were heady heights for Derby County, and to help them navigate their way through this rather unfamiliar world they hired John Charles, the former Welsh international striker, to act as their ambassador. Charles was a revered figure at Juventus, having scored goals at a prodigious rate for the club a decade earlier, and so was clearly a sound choice. Before the game started, however, Charles twice saw Juventus's German striker Helmut Haller visit the referee's dressing room. The match official was also German and Charles was sufficiently concerned by what he had seen to raise it with the Derby camp.

The visitors initially opted not to make a complaint, but that changed when Taylor saw Haller talking to the referee once more as the players trooped to the dressing rooms at half-time. Spooked by Charles's earlier alert, Taylor suspected that something was amiss and asked to join in their conversation. He was then elbowed in the ribs by Haller and seized by Italian security staff. Taylor feared that he was going to be arrested but was released before the start of the second half, albeit rather shaken and unsettled.

Ironically, the first half of the game had actually gone quite well for Derby. The hosts took the lead with a goal from their veteran Brazilian striker, José Altafini, but Hector scored an equaliser just a minute later. The teams were still level at half-time but the second half was to prove much tougher for the visitors, with Juventus taking control of the tie with two well-taken goals by Causio and Altafini. The disappointment of a 3-1 defeat was compounded by the fact that both McFarland and Gemmill received bookings. They were the only two Derby players who had carried forward a caution from a previous game and these yellow cards meant that they would be suspended for the return leg at the Baseball Ground.

Clough boiled with fury after the game as he was convinced that his team had been on the receiving end of some highly dubious refereeing decisions. He believed that the bookings given to McFarland and Gemmill had been for innocuous challenges, and the contretemps between Taylor, Haller and the referee further fuelled his suspicions that his team had not been treated fairly. When he was approached by Italian journalists after the game Clough told them, via the British journalist Brian Glanville, that he would not talk to 'cheating bastards'. Clough may have been an outspoken figure but he rarely criticised referees and his outburst was clearly borne out of a genuine belief that his club had been duped. Conspiracy theories over that game in Turin have subsequently flourished, but no proof has ever emerged to substantiate Clough's contention that something improper took place.

Notwithstanding Clough's concerns over the conduct of the first leg, Derby still had a potentially valuable away goal to take into their home tie. They attacked incessantly in the first half at the Baseball Ground but the Juventus defence stood firm, with the Italian international goalkeeper Dino Zoff making an excellent save from a Hinton free kick. Derby certainly had their chances, but none were converted and the game remained goalless at half-time. The pivotal moment came in the 57th minute when Derby were awarded a penalty after Hector was fouled. Hinton, normally a reliable penalty-taker, took it but, crushingly, he knocked it wide of the post. If he had scored, then his side would have had over half an hour to get the second goal that would have taken them through on the away goals rule.

Just six minutes later, however, Davies was sent off for head-butting the Juventus centre-half, effectively ending the game as a contest. Trying to break down a disciplined Italian defence with 11 men was hard enough, but with ten it was almost impossible. The match ended, rather predictably, in a 0-0 draw; the referee's whistle finally bringing down the curtain on Derby County's grand European adventure.

The other semi-final between Ajax and Real Madrid promised much more than it eventually delivered. On paper, it was a mouth-watering clash between the reigning champions and the club that had won the European Cup more times than any other. The Dutch side had come a long way since they were knocked out of the competition by the Spanish aristocrats six years previously, and it was soon clear that Madrid's glory days were well behind them. Kovács's team won the home tie 2-1, with Barry Hulshoff volleying the ball home after the Madrid defence had failed to clear it from their penalty area and Ruud Krol scoring from a well-worked free kick routine. The visitors did manage to get a goal back late in the game, but all it did in the end was give them false hope that they could overturn the deficit back at their intimidating Bernabéu Stadium.

Real Madrid's away goal meant that they only needed a 1-0 win in order to reach the final. They worked hard to get it, putting the Ajax defence under heavy pressure, but Heinz Stuy made some fine saves and the game remained goalless until early in the second half. When the goal finally came, however, the Dutch got it. Gerrie Mühren scored with a shot from outside the penalty area, which was deflected past the goalkeeper by one of the Madrid defenders.

His goal might not have been particularly special but what he did shortly afterwards was. Mühren received a crossfield pass from Suurbier, brought the ball immediately under control with his left foot and then proceeded to juggle it between his feet as he waited to play it into the path of the advancing Krol. The Spanish crowd rose to applaud the skill but his team-mate Hulshoff was not impressed. He was fearful of retribution from the Madrid players for the impudent gesture and, indeed, some of the Dutch players did start to get knocked about as a result. It may have only been a brief moment of skill, but it was emblematic of the fact that Ajax were now the masters of Europe, just as Madrid had been in the 1950s.

Ajax duly reached the European Cup Final for the third year in succession and faced Italian opposition once again. The venue for the game was Belgrade and its proximity to Italy meant the crowd was composed largely of Juventus fans, though the fact that it was almost an away fixture for Ajax had little impact on the way that they played. The Dutch side attacked from the start and took the lead after only five minutes. The goal came after Johnny Rep ran to meet a cross from Blankenburg, outjumped his Italian marker and then sent a looping header past the keeper into the corner of the net. Juventus tried to get back into the match, but their play was too cautious to trouble the Ajax defence. It seemed that they were too afraid of being thrashed by Ajax, as Bayern Munich had been, and the conceding of an early goal simply exacerbated those fears.

Ajax's response to Juventus's lack of ambition was simply to slow down the pace of the game and maintain possession of the ball. This may have limited the opportunity for Juventus to build any attacks, but it made for a dull game. The match briefly threatened to burst into life when Juventus striker José Altafini ran on to a pass from midfield and bore down on goal with only the Ajax keeper to beat. Rep, who clearly wanted to make sure that his header was the winning goal, dashed back all the way to his own penalty area and made a lunging tackle on Altafini to prevent him from getting a good shot on goal.

Ajax held on to their slender lead for the remainder of the game and so became the first club since Real Madrid to win three successive European Cups, being allowed to keep the trophy as a result. The Ajax fans, however, were more disappointed than jubilant, with the standard of their team's performance being well below the standard that they had come to expect.

It wasn't obvious at the time, but Ajax's victory over Juventus was the last act of a great team. Discontent had been brewing among the players for some time and the team, having won everything several times over, simply had nothing left to achieve. Success had become so habitual that after receiving the European Cup in Belgrade some of the players didn't even bother joining in the lap of honour. Kovács left the club after the victory over Juventus and the new manager, George Knobel, soon found himself without the talismanic Cruyff.

During pre-season training the Ajax players went through the usual ritual of voting on who was to be captain for the forthcoming campaign. Johan Cruyff, who had led the team to victory over Juventus, put his name forward, but so did Piet Keizer. Cruyff hadn't seen the challenge coming and didn't expect to be deposed, but he duly was. It was a perfect *coup d'état*. A stunned and upset Cruyff immediately rang his father-in-law, who acted as his agent, and told him that he wanted to leave Ajax.

The Dutch maestro played only twice more for the club and was soon on his way to Barcelona, where he was reunited with his mentor, Rinus Michels. In the end, Johan Cruyff's departure from Ajax was probably inevitable. The Biblical story of Joseph told how he incurred the wrath of his brothers for being his father's favourite son, and the tale was repeated in modern-day Amsterdam. Cruyff's team-mates became jealous of the praise and attention that was garnered on him and, just as Joseph's brothers had done, they turned angrily on him. They would soon come to regret doing so, however, as Ajax's prolonged period of success swiftly came to an end without Cruyff in the side.

Ajax lost their league title the following season and their three-year reign in Europe came to an ignominious end when they lost their opening tie to CSKA Sofia, a team that they had beaten easily just a year earlier. Knobel was sacked after only a season in charge, and then the great Ajax side of the early 1970s started to disintegrate. Ajax could have dominated European football for the remainder of the decade, but what had taken many years to put together was soon destroyed. Neeskens followed Cruyff to Barcelona, Keizer retired and then Blankenburg, Haan, Mühren and Rep all left the club. An era was over, but at least the Ajax fans had the memories of the finest club side that the Netherlands has ever produced, and perhaps ever will.

· ·

Back in Derby the fans could barely believe what they were seeing. It hadn't seemed possible at half-time that their side could get back into the game but not only had they done that, they had even taken the lead! Their second half resurgence immediately brought back memories of the 2-0 defeat of Juventus in the semi-finals; Hinton's converted 56th-minute penalty and a spectacular late strike from Hector. They had come from behind to win once before; could they really do it again?

Sadly, Derby's scarcely plausible dreams of glory lasted for only three short minutes. The Ajax players had been taken aback by the Derby revival but it wasn't enough to destroy their resolve; they had faced down tough challenges before and they weren't going to be overwhelmed by this one. Krol picked up the ball midway inside his own half of the pitch and was surprised to see how far he was allowed to advance without being confronted. He made his way into the centre circle and, spotting Rep free on his right, played a square ball into his path. Krol kept moving forward and soon received the ball back from the young striker. Rep also maintained his run and, 40 yards from goal, collected the ball back from Krol for a second time.

The centre of the Derby midfield, for so long an almost impenetrable barrier, suddenly opened up, seemingly taken unawares by Krol's run from defence. Rep advanced with the ball and, from the corner of his eye, spotted Gemmill belatedly making his way towards him. Todd and McFarland, still adroitly patrolling the edge of the penalty area, were too strong an obstruction to attempt to run through and so, 25 yards from goal, Rep decided to hit the ball for all he was worth. He connected with it sweetly, sending it rocketing towards the goal, and there was little Boulton could do to stop it. Relieved Ajax players were soon all around him, with even the hard-to-please Cruyff slapping him hard on the back in congratulation. Now all they needed to do was get the winner.

. . . .

Ajax's fall from grace after their 1973 European Cup triumph was echoed a few hundred miles north in Derby. Clough's side had only three league games left to play after their exit from the European Cup and were still in with a chance of qualifying for the UEFA Cup. They showed their keenness to compete in Europe again by winning all three matches, scoring nine goals in the process and conceding only one. That lifted them into seventh place in the table and a place in the UEFA Cup was almost within their grasp.

It all hinged on the outcome of the FA Cup Final and European Cup Winners' Cup Final, both of which Leeds United were competing in. Victory in either competition would result in Leeds qualifying for the following season's Cup Winners' Cup, and thus relinquishing to Derby the place they had obtained in the UEFA Cup by virtue of finishing third in the league. Don Revie's team had long been a thorn in Clough's side and, even in defeat, conspired to hinder him once more, losing the FA Cup Final to Second Division underdogs

Sunderland before being defeated by AC Milan in the Cup Winners' Cup Final.

Clough's side started the following league season promisingly, winning six and drawing three of their first 12 matches. That lifted them to third place and another successful campaign seemed to be on the cards but, behind the scenes, there was serious trouble at the heart of the club.

Clough had initially enjoyed a good relationship with Derby's chairman, Sam Longson. The self-made millionaire had treated Clough well, often lending him his Mercedes, and the young manager reciprocated by introducing the grateful chairman to famous footballers such as Bobby Moore. Over time, however, a rift developed between the two men which eventually became a chasm.

Clough enraged Longson by the way in which he conducted some transfers, such as when he acquired Colin Todd without agreeing the fee with his chairman beforehand. That was bad enough, but what really caused terminal damage to their relationship was Clough's increasingly outspoken behaviour in public. One example was when Clough was the guest speaker for Yorkshire Television's Sports Personality of the Year award. The prize was given to the Leeds midfielder Peter Lorimer and, rather than complimenting the winner, Clough launched into a tirade of criticism of him and of the club that he played for.

Longson was asked by leading figures in the game to rein in his young manager, but was simply unable to do so. Clough clearly revelled in his reputation for being outspoken and had no intention of curbing his tongue just to appease his long-suffering boss. Longson eventually tired of Clough's excesses and, if only for the sake of his own self-esteem, felt impelled to prove who really ran the club. He started to issue instructions that he knew would rile Clough, such as requiring his newspaper articles to be vetted by the board before they reached the press as well as obtaining their blessing before appearing on television.

Longson even ordered that Clough's drinks cabinet be locked which, given his later, much-publicised, drinking problems, could only have enraged the manager.

Clough fell into the trap and argued bitterly with Longson over the restrictions placed on his dealings with the media. When Longson refused to budge, Clough resigned and Taylor loyally followed him. The two men believed that the board would not accept their resignations, given how much success they had brought to the club, but that proved to be a dreadful miscalculation. Longson was not the only member of the board who was tired of Clough's antics and so, despite what he had done for the club, his bluff was called. The resignations were accepted and, despite a high-profile campaign by Derby supporters to get them reinstated, Clough and Taylor were left looking for alternative employment.

Clough's departure from Derby came less than two months after Cruyff played his last game for Ajax. The stars that would have brought them together had almost aligned, but their paths then diverged widely, with Cruyff heading off to Spain while Clough embarked on a short, ill-fated sojourn at Brighton and Hove Albion.

The two men were destined never to meet within the confines of a football pitch, though they did once share a television studio, both being pundits on an ITV panel for the 1978 World Cup. That is scant consolation, however, for those of us who wanted to see a clash between two of the most dominant personalities in 1970s football. Cruyff's Ajax and Clough's Derby both found success, but with radically different approaches to the game. We'll never know who would have triumphed had they met in Belgrade, but one's thing for certain; it definitely wouldn't have been dull.

••

As the match wore on Ajax were clearly in the ascendency. Derby's inability to hold on to the lead for more than three minutes had been a grievous blow, with a crucial sliver of their self-belief leaking away when Rep's blistering shot crashed into the back of the net. What was also becoming evident was that the Ajax players were looking far less tired than their opponents. The oppressive conditions were the same for both sides but Ajax were undoubtedly coping with them better. Whether it was due to Ajax having played 12 fewer games than Derby that season, or to the hard training that Michels had put them through all those years earlier, they were clearly in better condition for times like these.

Clough's side laboured as the minutes ticked away to the end of normal time, clearly longing for the rest that the referee's whistle would bring. They were managing to keep Ajax at bay for the time being, but doing so for another 30 minutes of extra time appeared to be well beyond them.

Peter Taylor could see what was coming and he jumped to his feet, gesticulating feverishly at Archie Gemmill. The diminutive Scotsman was one of the few Derby players that weren't out on their feet and Taylor knew that he had at least one lung-bursting run left in his legs. Gemmill, who was doing his best to help shield the Derby penalty area from Ajax attacks, was therefore amazed to see Taylor directing him towards the centre circle.

The reason for Taylor's counter-intuitive ploy became clear when Todd managed to prise the ball away from Keizer's feet, clearing it hastily up the pitch with as much height and distance as he could muster.

Roger Davies had been brought on as a substitute for the exhausted O'Hare a few minutes earlier and he made a bee line for Todd's clearance, jumping above Krol and flicking the ball into open space just inside the Ajax half of the pitch. Gemmill had anticipated the header and he eagerly latched on to the ball, hurdling over a rushed challenge from Blankenburg before bearing down on the Ajax goal. The back-pedalling

Hulshoff was the last line of defence and it soon became evident what he would have to do.

The most important thing was to stop Gemmill before he reached the penalty area but his pace caught out the bearded Dutchman, whose desperate challenge took place a few inches further on than he had intended. Hulshoff lunged at the ball but it just escaped his reach, his outstretched foot connecting instead with Gemmill's ankle. The velocity at which the Scotsman was travelling inevitably resulted in him crashing to the floor, his body thudding into the turf near the penalty spot.

The Yugoslavian referee, who had struggled to keep up with the speed of Gemmill's run, was hardly best placed to see exactly where the foul had taken place. To his credit he acknowledged this by trotting towards the linesman to ascertain what he had seen. Their discussion was short, but decisive; its outcome clear when the referee pointed his finger towards the penalty spot. He was immediately surrounded by incensed Dutchmen, not only angry about the decision he had reached but also because Derby had been given an opportunity to escape from the stranglehold that Ajax had on the game. Cruyff led the protests but, despite their eloquence and passion, they were always destined to be in vain.

There was no discussion among the Derby players as to who would take the penalty kick. It was Alan Hinton's job, pure and simple. The curly-haired winger had turned round the semi-final against Juventus with a converted penalty and now he had the opportunity to win the European Cup with another 12-yard strike. Clough and Taylor would later say that they never doubted he would score, but those that saw their faces as he stepped up to the ball didn't witness any such certainty. Hinton's kick was firm but Stuy had correctly read the flight of the ball, diving energetically as it flew towards the left-hand side of his goal. His fingertips connected with the ball but, crucially, not his palm; the force of the shot taking the ball into the back of the net.

As the delirious Derby players celebrated Cruyff ran into the net and retrieved the ball, carrying it swiftly back to the centre circle. Theoretically there was still time for Ajax to get an equaliser but Derby were re-energised by their reprieve and they defended stoutly for the few remaining minutes. Todd worked hard to stop the ball from reaching Cruyff, Webster kept Keizer on a short leash and McFarland was, quite simply, immense. He won every header in the air, every tackle on the floor and everything in between. Perhaps extra time wouldn't have been such a trial, after all.

The final whistle was greeted with jubilation by the Derby players and with disbelief by the Dutch. They simply hadn't expected to have been troubled by the English team, let alone beaten. The pundits who had confidently predicted an Ajax victory did their best to cover up their error, referring persistently instead to how capricious football can be. Ignoring his celebrating players, Brian Clough left the touchline and walked across the pitch, making his way towards the despondent Ajax captain. Seeing Clough approach, Cruyff lifted his head and stretched out his hand to his adversary. Clough shook his hand warmly and then, to Cruyff's utter bemusement, leant forward and kissed him on the cheek. He'd heard that this English manager was a little unorthodox, but kissing him? What was he thinking? If nothing else, it certainly made the Derby players laugh; Cloughie, what would he do next?

4
The Battle of Britain

European Cup Final, Olympic Stadium, Rome, 30 May 1984

Liverpool v Dundee United

Liverpool	**Dundee United**
Bruce Grobbelaar	Hamish McAlpine
Alan Kennedy	Maurice Malpas
Alan Hansen	Paul Hegarty (captain)
Mark Lawrenson	David Narey
Phil Neal	Richard Gough
Ronnie Whelan	Eamonn Bannon
Graeme Souness (captain)	Billy Kirkwood
Sammy Lee	Derek Stark
Craig Johnston	Ralph Milne
Kenny Dalglish	Paul Sturrock
Ian Rush	Davie Dodds

Referee: Erik Fredriksson (Sweden)

The deep lines on Joe Fagan's face seemed even more pronounced beneath the fierce glare of the floodlights, the worries in his mind clearly etched into his skin. His Liverpool side were not just expected to win this final, they were supposed to walk it; crushing the Scottish underdogs beneath their mighty boots. His team didn't just play in a different league to Dundee United; they existed in a different world. Their average home gates were three times the size of United's and they had finances to match, enabling them to take their pick of the country's best players and not having to rely on a fickle stream of homegrown talent. Fagan didn't envy his opposite number in that regard. Apparently, they even had a part-time player in their side – in a European Cup Final!

It may have been a clash between the haves and have-nots of British football but the favourites weren't guaranteed a victory. Fagan knew all too well that football wasn't that predictable. The previous year Aberdeen had beaten the mighty Real Madrid in the final of the European Cup Winners' Cup and who'd seen that coming? Liverpool had put in a few dubious performances that season against lesser teams and Fagan hoped against hope that he wasn't going to have to sit through that again. He looked at the United players as they waited for the kick-off and reflected that not one of them would get into the Liverpool side, apart from one of their centre-halves, perhaps. Yes, they should win, but something in his bones told him that it was going to be a long night.

Meanwhile, the television and radio commentators in the stadium were in overdrive, remarking proudly that this was the greatest night in the history of British football. The first European Cup Final between English and Scottish sides was certainly historic, but it was part of a much wider narrative of British success in European competitions. English teams had won six of the previous seven European Cups and that season, for the first and only time, the six semi-finals in the European

Cup, European Cup Winners' Cup and UEFA Cup all featured a British side. Aberdeen and Manchester United both reached the semi-finals of the European Cup Winners' Cup while Tottenham Hotspur and Nottingham Forest reached the same stage in the UEFA Cup, with Spurs winning the trophy a week earlier. And now, here in the Eternal City, two very different worlds were about to collide.

. . . . , ...

The 1970s was a momentous decade for Dundee United and Liverpool, witnessing the emergence of the Tayside club as a genuine contender in Scottish football and the transformation of the Merseysiders from a domestic force into a European powerhouse. Bill Shankly was still in charge at the start of the decade, winning the league title and UEFA Cup in 1973 and the FA Cup in 1974 before handing over the reins to his long-standing partner, Bob Paisley, for the start of the 1974/75 season. Shankly had won almost everything there was to win but the ultimate prize – the European Cup – had remained frustratingly out of reach. It was left to his successor to finally guide Liverpool to the trophy, with a 3-1 victory over Borussia Mönchengladbach in Rome in 1977.

The avuncular Paisley may have secured a famous triumph, but had done so with a team largely inherited from Shankly. He needed to build his own side and, in an inspired eight-month period between May 1977 and January 1978, recruited three Scottish players that went on to form the spine of the Liverpool team for the next six years. The first to arrive at the club was the youngest and most unheralded of the three players: Alan Hansen. Back then Liverpool often used to buy players near the end of the financial year to reduce their profits and, hence, their tax liabilities. The nature of the transaction gave Paisley the freedom to take a chance on players that had not proved themselves at the top level, as even if he got it wrong the club still saved some money on its tax bill. The £100,000 that Paisley paid to Partick Thistle for the 21-year-old Hansen, therefore, proved to be one of the wisest acts of tax avoidance in the club's history.

One of the key reasons for Liverpool's success under Paisley was his desire to field central defenders who were comfortable with the ball at their feet. The history of the British game is replete with centre-halves that are built like tanks, fight like lions and play the game with little thought of their safety or those around them. Paisley was well aware of the virtues of that type of player, but he wanted someone who could bring the ball out of defence and build intelligent attacking moves and the elegant Hansen fitted the bill perfectly. The Scot was at his best when running out quickly from defence with the ball at his feet, building precise attacks rather than just launching the ball up the pitch in the general direction of the forwards.

It is fair to say that Hansen wasn't an obvious choice for a centre-half. He didn't have the muscular build of those that frequented that position, was not particularly adept at tackling and was hardly renowned for winning aerial challenges. Hansen's strength as a defender, however, lay in his ability to read the game and anticipate what was going to happen. He aimed to win the ball by intercepting it, rather than by hurling himself at an opponent, and consequently was never the type of player that would come back into the dressing room caked in mud from throwing himself around the pitch. His desire to stay on his feet as much as possible helped him to avoid the type of injuries that can be incurred by steaming into tackles and also meant that he rarely got on the wrong side of referees. Hansen was never sent off in his career and bookings were also uncommon; a rare record among centre-halves.

The next Scot to arrive was Celtic striker Kenny Dalglish, an acquisition forced on Paisley by the departure of Kevin Keegan to SV Hamburg. The much-loved Keegan was seemingly irreplaceable but Dalglish eventually went on to eclipse his predecessor; his superior technical skills ultimately making him a more effective force than the all-action Keegan. Dalglish had a great natural awareness of what was going on around him and an acute ability to see options for attacking moves that most other players would never notice. His legs may not have been all that quick but that deficiency was more than compensated for by his speed of thought, which enabled him to leave defenders for dead before they realised what he was up to.

The diminutive Glaswegian was also a courageous player. He spent a lot of his time on the pitch with his back to defenders and, aided by a low centre of gravity and great natural balance, would position himself so that he would bounce off challenges from more heavily built defenders. Dalglish went on to become one of the most decorated players in the history of the British game, collecting at least one winners' medal in each of the 13 seasons between 1971/72 and 1983/84.

The final Scot to be recruited by Paisley was midfield anchor Graeme Souness. His career started with Tottenham Hotspur but he found it difficult to settle in London and, after many fallings-out with the Spurs hierarchy, he was transferred to Middlesbrough. Under the tutelage of Jack Charlton he acquired the self-discipline needed to make the most of his natural talents and his strong performances persuaded Paisley to pay a record fee to take him to Merseyside. His value to the Liverpool side was akin to that of an all-rounder to a cricket team; some midfielders are ferocious tacklers and some are wonderful passers of the ball, but it is a rare creature that can excel at both. The irascible Souness did. If opposing teams wanted to play football then he would take them on that level, but if they wanted a battle then he was up for that as well. His combative approach did cause him problems early in his career but his disciplinary record improved over time and, though he still collected plenty of bookings, was never sent off while playing for Liverpool.

TEAM URUGUAYO

1. Enrique Ballesteros. - 2. José Nazzasi. - 3. Ernesto Mascheroni. - 4. José L. Andrade.
5. Lorenzo Fernández. - 6. Alvaro Gestido. - 7. Pablo Dorado. - 8. Héctor Scarone.
9. Héctor Castro. - 10. Pedro Cea. - 11. Santos Iriarte.

The Uruguay 1930 World Cup-winning team, lined up in their standard 2-3-5 formation

The long tradition of Scots invading the Wembley pitch started here. Jubilant fans congratulate Jimmy McMullan after the 5-1 thrashing of England in 1928

Italy players line up before their 1-0 defeat to North Korea at the 1966 World Cup. They'd soon become acquainted with a lot more fruit

Honour restored. Italian captain Giacinto Facchetti lifts the Henri Delaunay Cup after his side's 2-0 victory over Yugoslavia in 1968

Well done Bobby! Roger Hunt congratulates Bobby Charlton, England's goalscorer in the 1-0 defeat of Spain in the first leg of their 1968 European Championship quarter-final

Clough and Cruyff together at last, though sadly not within the confines of a football stadium. Not sure what Elton John is doing there

Joy unconfined. Graeme Souness and Michael Robinson celebrate after Liverpool's victory over Roma in the 1984 European Cup Final

Ee aye addio, we won the cup! Joe Fagan relaxes with the trophy after Liverpool's 1984 European Cup triumph over Roma

Jim McLean, instigator of the Tannadice revolution

Are you sure, ref? Pedro Troglio clearly believes that the dismissal of his team-mate, Gustavo Dezotti, in the 1990 World Cup final is a little harsh

Inches away. Chris Waddle's shot beats the West German goalkeeper in the 1990 World Cup semi-final but then cannons back off the post

Don't Cry for Me Argentina. Terry Butcher consoles Paul Gascoigne after England fail to reach the 1990 World Cup Final against Argentina

Der General, *Ottmar Hitzfeld is lifted up by his players after Bayern Munich's 2001 UEFA Champions League triumph over Valencia*

Out on their feet: Danny Mills and Rio Ferdinand try to take in Leeds' Champions League semi-final defeat to Valencia

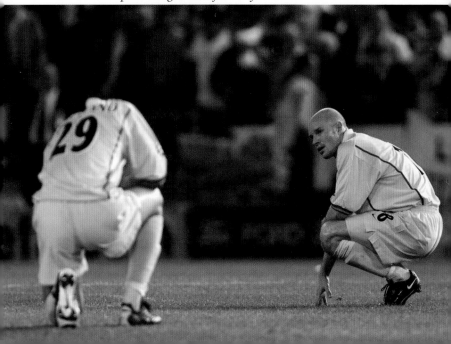

Souness went on to become the classic working class hero, escaping from a post-war prefab in Edinburgh to become captain of the best football club in Britain. He soon developed a penchant for the better things in life, whether it was clothes, drinks or cars, and duly became known as 'Champagne Charlie'. Indeed, when he moved to Liverpool he initially stayed in a hotel and ran up a £200 bar bill in his first fortnight there, which was no mean feat in 1978. Souness was usually deployed as a shield in front of the defence, protecting them from strikers that dropped back into midfield in an attempt to draw the Liverpool defenders out of position. He had an excellent first touch and a fierce shot, the only weaknesses in his game being his relative lack of pace and rather average ability in the air. Perhaps the greatest tribute that can be paid to Souness is that, after leaving in 1984 to play in Italy, he was never satisfactorily replaced in the Liverpool midfield until Steven Gerrard came along 15 years later.

Bob Paisley's new-look Liverpool side was an unqualified success. They retained the European Cup in 1978, beating FC Bruges at Wembley courtesy of a Dalglish goal, and also went unbeaten in 85 home games between 1978 and 1981. During that spell Liverpool won the 1978/79 league title with a record-breaking 68 points from a maximum possible of 84, conceding only 16 goals. That side is often considered to have been the finest in the club's history and it was nearly all of Paisley's making. He had many gifts as a manager but probably chief among them was his shrewd judgement when it came to acquiring players. Taking over from the outspoken Shankly was never going to be a simple task, but the modest Geordie somehow managed to make it look relatively easy.

• •

Those who had expected a blood-and-thunder cup final, full of passion and fury, were soon disabused of such a foolish notion. If the final had been between any other two British sides then that may have been the case, but Dundee United and Liverpool were not cast in that mould. There were plenty of teams back home that would launch the ball forward at the earliest opportunity, thudding 40-yard passes high into the air with the vague hope that it would land somewhere near one of their own players. These two British teams, however, treated the ball with respect, caressing it between one another with care and trying their utmost not to lose possession of it. This more cerebral approach may have appealed to the purists in the crowd, but among the watching millions back in Britain there was much shifting in seats and drumming of fingers on armrests.

It was Dundee United's defenders that came in for most criticism from the bored neutrals, with their almost endless sideways passes seemingly designed to send people to sleep in their armchairs. They weren't doing this through fear or from lack of imagination, however; it was actually part of a carefully crafted strategy to draw Liverpool forward and so create space on the pitch that the Dundee United strikers could attack. The ploy may well have fooled many British sides but Liverpool had come across these tactics before when playing on the continent and they refused to take the bait, stubbornly maintaining their deep back-line.

There was a real danger that this much-anticipated European Cup Final would turn out to be a damp squib. The vast Olympic Stadium was nowhere near full, with local fans shunning what they expected to be a rather unsophisticated match between two well-organised, athletic British sides. Even the previously enthusiastic commentators were starting to wonder just when this match would spark into life. The only real entertainment came from the two opposing sets of spectators, with the red-shirted Liverpool supporters and tangerine-clad Dundee United fans competing to be heard on the television sets back home. The Liverpool fans may have heavily outnumbered their Scottish counterparts but Dundee United, underdogs on the terraces and out on the pitch, were putting up a pretty spirited fight.

• •

There are some football managers who are so successful that their personal record of achievement towers over the history of the club that they won trophies for. Brian Clough, with his two successive European Cup triumphs at Nottingham Forest, is one example, as is Don Revie who had an unrivalled run of triumphs at Leeds United. Jim McLean is another such manager. Dundee United had never won a major trophy when he took over in 1971, but since then the club has won one league title, two Scottish Cups and two Scottish League Cups. McLean was the manager for three of those five triumphs and chairman for a fourth. There have been a number of men that have had a significant impact on Dundee United's fortunes over the years, but none more so than McLean.

Dundee United were formed in 1909 and spent almost all of their first half-century of existence in the Scottish Second Division. There was precious little for their fans to celebrate in those 50 years and there were several occasions when the club hovered on the brink of extinction. Dundee United ended the 1958/59 season two places from the bottom of the Second Division, ranked 35th out of Scotland's 37 league clubs. An average of less than 3,000 spectators attended their home games and even the most optimistic of those fans would not have dared hope for anything more than a decent run in the Scottish Cup.

Yet, 25 years later, Dundee United were able to count themselves as one of the four best teams in Europe. It was an incredible reversal of fortunes and its roots can be traced back to the appointment of Jerry Kerr as manager in the summer of 1959. Kerr led Dundee United to promotion in his first season in charge and over the next decade made them into a respected force in Division One. In 1966 they even defeated the mighty

Barcelona in the first round of the Fairs Cup, winning not only at home but also away at the intimidating Nou Camp stadium.

Kerr was undoubtedly a fine manager but he also had financial resources at his disposal that his predecessors could only have dreamt of. Prior to his appointment the club's finances were in a precarious state and so the Dundee United Sportsmen's Club was established to generate much-needed funds. They decided to set up Taypools, a weekly pools competition modelled on a scheme run successfully by Warwickshire County Cricket Club. It caught the imagination of the city's residents to such an extent that, by 1964, over 90,000 entries were made a week; a huge figure considering that Dundee's population at the time numbered around 190,000. The sizeable funds generated by Taypools were donated to the club so that it could improve its rather ramshackle ground and Kerr was also able to acquire a fine squad of players. Attendances increased as the team became more successful and the club's bank balance swelled in turn. Far exceeding the expectations of its founders, Taypools turned out to be the spark that lit the fire. It gave Dundee United a sound financial base on which success on the pitch could be built and, when McLean took over from Jerry Kerr in 1971, the club finally had a man who could deliver it.

McLean had spent his playing days as a journeyman inside-forward, plying his trade for Hamilton Academical, Clyde, Dundee FC and Kilmarnock. After his career ended he accepted an offer to become the coach at Dundee FC and soon made his presence felt, improving the team's fitness to such an extent that he attracted the attentions of neighbouring Dundee United who invited him to apply for the manager's post when Kerr stepped down. He impressed them sufficiently at the interview to be offered the job and, after only 18 months as coach at Dundee FC, he crossed the 200 yards that separates Dens Park from Tannadice.

The man Dundee United appointed could fairly be described as an authoritarian, single-minded, perfectionist. To say that he had high standards is putting it mildly; he was once so dissatisfied with the second half performance in a 6-1 crushing of Motherwell (they had been 5-0 up at half-time) that he withheld some of the team's bonus for failing to entertain the crowd. Rarely seen with a smile on his face, McLean was the type of man who was as hard on himself as he was demanding of his players. No matter what the result was, or how good the performance had been, McLean always saw what could have been done better and never hesitated to tell his players where they had gone wrong. He was never a man to hide his feelings and it was not only his players who felt his wrath. He often vented his spleen at match officials, once being so demonstrative that he was banned from the touchline for an entire year as a consequence.

One of McLean's key priorities was the maintenance of discipline at the club. He would frequently fine players to keep them in line and didn't restrict the punishment to common offences, such as arriving late for training or earning cautions for dissent. McLean was also known to fine players for minor misdemeanours, such as not shaving before a game, turning up with dirty boots or having hair that he judged to be too long. McLean always researched a player's character before signing him to ensure that he didn't recruit disruptive personalities that would upset or disturb the culture that he had patiently established. The consequence of this rigour was a squad of players that, most of the time, knew how to conduct themselves both on and off the pitch.

McLean's strategy for lifting Dundee United into the upper echelons of Scottish football was based on recruiting and developing talented young players. Despite the healthy injection of funds from Taypools the club still didn't have sufficient money to sign the best players in Scotland. That meant that the only realistic option available to McLean was to grow his own talent. Financing a youth development programme on the scale that McLean needed was expensive, so the manager was fortunate in having a board of directors that were prepared to make the investment and then wait patiently for the results.

The greatest drawback to McLean's approach was the risk of larger, wealthier clubs enticing his young players away once they had established themselves. McLean learnt this lesson the hard way after losing Andy Gray to Aston Villa in 1975 for the rather paltry sum of £110,000. Four years later the Birmingham club sold the future Sky Sports pundit to their local rivals, Wolverhampton Wanderers, for a then-British record fee of £1.5m. To counter this threat McLean and the Dundee United board came up with a novel solution: they would reward players that were prepared to commit themselves to the club for the long term by enrolling them in a generous pension scheme that would help sustain them after their playing careers came to an end. The plan had the desired effect, persuading a number of key players to sign long-term deals with the club.

One such player was central defender David Narey, who was probably the most successful product of McLean's youth development programme. Narey made his debut in 1973 at the age of 17, becoming a regular in the side the following year. He went on to play for the club for a further 20 years, making 866 appearances in total, a club record that will probably never be beaten. Narey was quick, timed his tackles impeccably and read the game well. He could also distribute the ball accurately, not being one of those central defenders that treated the ball as if it was a hot coal when it reached their feet. Narey had a naturally calm persona and, on occasions, could even come across as being a little blasé. McLean once commented that if Narey was running against the club's fastest players he would probably beat them narrowly, but if he was running against the slowest would still only win by the same distance!

Narey went on to become the first Dundee United player to represent Scotland, making his debut in 1977. The high point of his international career came in a game against Brazil at the 1982 World Cup, when he opened the scoring with a memorable strike from the edge of the penalty area that was the equal of anything the South Americans could do.

McLean paired Narey in the centre of defence with another Dundee United legend, Paul Hegarty. He started his career as a striker and was signed by McLean from Hamilton Academical in 1974 after having scored regularly for the South Lanarkshire club. Hegarty found goals harder to come by when he moved up a division to play for Dundee United, lacking the vital half a yard of pace that was needed to be a success at that level. Rather than giving up on Hegarty, McLean decided to play him in central defence in a friendly against Everton. The experiment turned out to be a success and McLean and Hegarty never looked back.

Despite being a few inches shorter than Narey, Hegarty was stronger than his defensive partner in the air and his aggressive style also complemented Narey's more measured approach. Narey and Hegarty's central defensive partnership went on to last for more than a decade and became the pivot around which McLean built the rest of his side.

Playing behind Narey and Hegarty was the only player not to have been recruited by McLean; a goalkeeper with an unmistakably Scottish name: Hamish McAlpine. He became first-choice goalkeeper in 1971 and missed only a handful of league games over the following 15 years. McAlpine was a natural athlete who excelled at cricket and was good enough to have become a professional golfer, had football not been his first love. What enabled him to be such an accomplished sportsman were his superb hand-eye co-ordination and great reflexes, which he used to great effect on many occasions.

McAlpine may have been a fine goalkeeper but, like many of his ilk, he was really just a frustrated outfield player. He hated doing specialist goalkeeping training and often insisted on not playing in goal in practice matches. Given his predilection for playing outfield it was hardly a surprise that he would often leave his penalty area during games to tackle forwards or head the ball away. Indeed, he was so comfortable with the ball at his feet that for a while he even became the team's designated penalty taker, scoring three times from the spot before McLean decided to give the job to someone else.

McAlpine played the game with a smile on his face and developed a great rapport with the fans behind his goal, often conducting them in song or giving them a little dance to amuse them. It would be a mistake, however, to simply dismiss McAlpine as being no more than a court jester. He knew his own mind and would stand his ground if he needed to. Indeed, he once had a huge row with McLean about how best to defend a corner that became so vociferous the manager decided to restore his authority by sending the goalkeeper home, which was no petty gesture given that Dundee United were on an end-of-season tour in Japan at the time!

One of McLean's first challenges as manager was the seemingly mundane task of making his club the best in Dundee, with United having lived in the shadow of Dundee FC for almost their entire existence. It wasn't until Kerr's initial season in Division One in 1960/61 that United finished higher in the league than their neighbours for the first time and, even then, it was only by one place and one point. Dundee FC responded to that imposition by embarking on the most successful period of their history, winning the league title the following season and then reaching the semi-finals of the European Cup a year later.

The two clubs tussled for supremacy over the next decade before the decisive moment came in McLean's fifth year at the club. Both clubs were battling to stay in the Scottish Premier Division and, on the last day of the season, United managed to secure an away draw at Glasgow Rangers (despite McAlpine hitting the post with a penalty).

That meant that they finished level on points with Dundee FC, who were subsequently relegated because of their inferior goal difference. The margin between the two clubs at that point in time may have been fractional but their respective futures were about to diverge widely; United going on to have great success under McLean while Dundee FC almost sank without trace.

McLean continued to develop talented young players, one of whom was full-back Ray Stewart. He intended Stewart to be another long-term fixture in his side, but thought again when West Ham United made an offer of £400,000 for his services. It was twice McLean's own valuation of the player and a lot of money for a largely unproven 19-year-old. McLean quickly accepted the offer and spent part of the windfall on acquiring Eamonn Bannon from Chelsea for £165,000, a Scottish club record at the time. Bannon started his career at his hometown club Heart of Midlothian, before a short, unhappy spell in London was brought to an end when McLean saw the opportunity to bring him back to Scotland. Bannon had tremendous stamina and used it to great effect on the left-hand side of midfield, either racing back to help to shield the defence from attack or sprinting up to the opposite byline to send crosses into the penalty area.

McLean's investment in Bannon was soon recouped. Within a couple of months of the midfielder joining the club Dundee United reached the 1979 League Cup Final against Aberdeen, which turned out to be one of the turning points in the history of Scottish football.

The domestic game had been dominated for decades by the 'Old Firm' of Celtic and Rangers, but now a 'New Firm' was rising to challenge them. Prior to the 1979/80 season the two Glasgow giants had won three-quarters of the post-war league titles, 70 per cent of the Scottish Cups and over half of the Scottish League Cups. Yet, for a few years in the 1980s, the 'big two' became the 'big four' as Alex Ferguson's Aberdeen and Jim McLean's Dundee United elbowed their way on to the top table. In the seven seasons between 1979/80 and 1985/86 the upstarts from Scotland's east coast won four league titles, four Scottish Cups and three League Cups between them; a total of 11 trophies to trump the ten won by Celtic and Rangers.

Unfortunately for such a pivotal game the 1979 League Cup Final, played at a Hampden Park that was only a third full, turned out to be a dismal affair. The score was 0-0 after 90 minutes and even extra time didn't result in a goal being scored. A replay was scheduled for four days later and the venue was switched to Dens Park, home of local rivals Dundee FC. The change of location was supported by both clubs and their fans responded by filling the stadium. Ferguson kept the same side that had dominated the first game while McLean decided to shuffle his pack. This time it was Dundee United that dictated proceedings, running out clear 3-0 winners. It was the first ever trophy won by Dundee United and a personal triumph for McLean who, after eight years of hard work, finally saw his methods bear fruit.

• •

The fact that both Dundee United and Liverpool had reached the 1984 European Cup Final was portrayed in the media as a great success for British football but, in truth, it was Scotland's finest hour. Almost two-thirds of the players that started the game were Scottish and it was Liverpool's northern contingent that was doing most to bring the game alive. The elegant Hansen was the fulcrum of Liverpool's attacking moves, bringing the ball out of defence with grace and composure, while Souness was the game's dominant figure in midfield, stroking passes around with ease and daring anyone to come and tackle him. The real class act on the pitch, however, was the diminutive Dalglish. He drifted between midfield and attack, pulling David Narey out of position while repeatedly attempting to split the Dundee United defence wide open with slide-rule passes. He hadn't fashioned a killer move yet, but it was becoming increasingly clear that it was only a matter of time before he would.

As the first half wore towards a close Jim McLean started to reflect on his side's performance in advance of his half-time team-talk. It hadn't been a bad display as far as he was concerned, but he knew that his players could do better. He could see how wary they were of Liverpool and that caution was inevitably reflecting itself in their play. The English side were becoming increasingly dominant and it was therefore with some relief that McLean saw Narey dispossess Dalglish with a clinical tackle. The Dundee United player came out of the challenge with the ball at his feet and immediately knocked a 20-yard cross-field pass to Bannon on the left wing. Bannon collected the ball and then cut inside to run at the heart of the Liverpool defence, evading a tackle before being sent tumbling to the floor by Souness.

The Liverpool captain felt that it was a fair challenge, so he was a little disappointed to hear the Swedish referee blow his whistle for a free kick. The offence had taken place around ten yards outside the penalty area and McLean instinctively tensed his body, sensing that this was a real opportunity for his team to score against the run of play. He had practised routines with his players for a free kick in this area of the pitch almost endlessly and so watched breathlessly as they automatically took up their allotted positions. Narey placed the ball at his feet, watching the Liverpool defensive wall warily to see if they advanced while the referee's back was turned. Once he was satisfied that they were far enough away Narey flicked the ball back towards Bannon, who was racing in with the clear intention of slamming the ball at goal.

The wall immediately broke as the Liverpool players came rushing forward in an attempt to get their bodies in the way of the expected shot, but Bannon had no plans to shoot. As he reached the ball he came to a shuddering halt, scooping it up and lofting it over the heads of the shocked Liverpool players. The Dundee United captain, Paul Hegarty, came running in and his head connected sweetly with the ball, sending it cleanly past Grobbelaar's despairing dive. Joe Fagan was now a very worried man.

• •

Bob Paisley's Liverpool started the 1980s as they had ended the previous decade, winning the 1979/80 First Division title and then another European Cup in 1981 with a 1-0 victory over Real Madrid. The winning goal was scored by the side's left-back, Alan Kennedy, who was another of Paisley's 1978 acquisitions, having first caught his eye with an impressive performance in Newcastle United's FA Cup Final defeat to Liverpool four years earlier. Kennedy's greatest asset was his pace and he used it to great effect when attacking on the overlap or chasing down opposition wingers. There were more technically proficient players in the Liverpool side but no one could ever doubt Kennedy's commitment or his ability to do something impulsive and unexpected. Indeed, his goal against Real Madrid came after he ran at their defence late in the game, catching them unawares.

Playing on the opposite side of the defence in that victory was Paisley's first signing as Liverpool manager, Phil Neal. He had been offered the chance to sign for Bill Nicholson's Tottenham Hotspur when he was a schoolboy but stayed on at school to get his 'O' levels, lest he should not make the grade in professional football. Neal joined his local side, Northampton Town, instead and spent six seasons with them before getting the chance of a lifetime with Liverpool.

Neal repaid Paisley's faith in him handsomely, becoming one of the club's most decorated and dependable players. In the ten seasons between 1975/76 and 1984/85 Neal missed just one out of 420 league games, once even playing with a broken toe, so keen was he to keep his place in the side. While Neal wasn't a particularly spectacular player he rarely put a foot wrong and his ice-cold demeanour made him a steadying influence on the side, also serving him well when taking penalties which he did effectively for many years. Neal went on to become one of the most successful English players of all time, winning an incredible four European Cups, eight championships, four League Cups and one UEFA Cup, with only the FA Cup eluding his grasp.

The Liverpool side that beat Real Madrid included several players that were nearing the end of their careers, so Paisley brought in a number of new faces for the 1981/82 season. One of them was the sometimes eccentric, occasionally brilliant, but always entertaining, Zimbabwean goalkeeper, Bruce Grobbelaar. He was signed from Canadian side Vancouver Whitecaps in March 1981, having been spotted while playing on loan for Crewe Alexandra. Paisley originally intended to play him in the reserves until he was ready to take over from England keeper and Anfield legend Ray Clemence. Grobbelaar wasn't the quiet, retiring type and he warned Clemence that he would soon have his place in the team. Clemence had been the first-choice goalkeeper at Anfield for over a decade but saw enough of Grobbelaar's performances in the reserves to see that there was substance behind the Zimbabwean's boasts. The unnerved Clemence didn't even wait for the new season to start, asking Paisley for a transfer and subsequently moving to Tottenham Hotspur.

Clemence's abrupt departure meant that Paisley had no option other than to throw Grobbelaar in at the deep end. The Zimbabwean was not really ready to play top-flight football and his inexperience soon became apparent. His performances came under criticism from all quarters, including concerned coaching staff, frustrated team-mates, impatient fans and a hostile media that nicknamed him the 'Clown Prince'. Weaker characters would have sunk under the pressure but Grobbelaar was clearly made of sterner stuff. He had already lived a full life before arriving at Anfield, having fought in the Bush War in Zimbabwe for two years while completing his National Service.

Like Hamish McAlpine, Grobbelaar was a natural athlete and could have made a living from a number of different sports. He was an accomplished cricketer, a fine baseball player and a particularly strong swimmer. The Zimbabwean opted for football and never looked back, making best use of his impressive physique and great agility. Grobbelaar was a fearless goalkeeper, being prepared to throw himself into the thick of the action regardless of the consequences that could follow. One of the distinctive aspects of his game was his willingness to come a long way off his line to try and win the ball when it was crossed into the penalty area. He would rarely warn his team-mates that he was coming, and if they made the mistake of getting into his path he would simply shove them out of the way. Grobbelaar sometimes found it difficult to keep his concentration throughout a game, especially when he had little to do because Liverpool were playing so well, and so would often entertain the crowd by talking to them or swinging on the bar.

Another player who joined the club in the summer of 1981 was the elegant Republic of Ireland defender and future media pundit, Mark Lawrenson. Paisley didn't really need to strengthen the Liverpool defence at the time but was wary of the impact that Lawrenson would make if he joined one of their rivals. He therefore decided to pay a club record fee in order to deny them his services. Lawrenson was principally a centre-half but was versatile enough to play in a number of different positions. That enabled Paisley to play him at left-back, and even in midfield, until the opportunity arose to partner him with Hansen in the centre of the defence. When Lawrenson finally got the chance to play in his preferred position he soon made it his own, making good use of his pace and ability to win the ball cleanly in a tackle.

Paisley opted to refresh his midfield by giving a chance to Ronnie Whelan, who had been at Liverpool since being signed in 1979 from Dublin side Home Farm shortly before his 18th birthday. The Irishman didn't excel at any one aspect of the game but was competent in all of them, thus making him an extremely reliable and effective professional footballer. He needed only one touch of the ball in order to control it, played equally well with either foot, would make hard tackles when they were needed and also contributed his fair share of goals from midfield.

Another youngster who made his breakthrough in the 1981/82 season was Welsh striker Ian Rush. He was signed from Chester City in 1980 for quite a considerable sum, even though he was still only 18 years old. Rush was initially overawed at being at the most successful club in the land and struggled to impress his new team-mates, many of whom concluded that the youngster would not make the grade at Anfield. Rush persevered, however, and when he started to act on Paisley's advice to be more selfish when in sight of the opposition goal, the goals soon started to flow.

One of the key reasons for Rush's emergence as one of the best strikers in Europe was his partnership with Kenny Dalglish. The diminutive Scotsman was the ideal foil for Rush, holding the ball up when it was passed forward and then playing it into his teammate's path. Rush's principal asset was his pace and he was at his most effective when chasing balls played over or through the defence by Dalglish. The two players' respective skills dovetailed perfectly, with Rush playing the best football of his career alongside Dalglish. Rush went on to score 346 goals in 660 appearances for Liverpool; a ratio of more than one goal for every two games played. His value to the club was such that, in a run of 145 matches between 1980 and 1987, Liverpool never lost when he scored.

Paisley's rejuvenated side continued to dominate English football, overcoming a poor start to the 1981/82 season to win the league title as well as the League Cup. They then repeated those two triumphs in 1982/83, which was a fitting end to Paisley's final season in charge at the club. Liverpool finished 11 points ahead of second-placed Watford in the league, though the gap should really have been even greater than that. The title was secured well before the end of the season and, with the job done, the side's form collapsed with Liverpool drawing two and losing five of their final seven league matches. It was a slightly disappointing end to Paisley's reign but, perhaps understandably, the players struggled to motivate themselves for games that they no longer needed to win.

Paisley communicated his wish to retire to Liverpool's board of directors well in advance of his departure, which meant that they had plenty of time to consider the appointment of his successor. They wisely recognised that the principal reason for the club's long run of triumphs was the continuity and stability that had been in place since Shankly's appointment as manager nearly a quarter of a century earlier. When the Scotsman arrived at the club Bob Paisley and Joe Fagan were part of the coaching staff and, in a decision that was to shape the future of the club for decades, he decided to keep both of them on. Paisley was the first of the two men to step into Shankly's shoes and then, on 1 July 1983, the craggy-faced Fagan became the second.

If there was one symbol of the continuity that had brought decades of success to Liverpool, then it was the club's infamous 'boot room'. The room itself was an unassuming place, just being a small area near the dressing room where boots and other football paraphernalia were kept. However, in the 1970s and 1980s it became a mythical, fabled place in which Liverpool's domination of European football was plotted.

It was Fagan who initiated the practice of using the room to hold post-match discussions among the coaching staff, picking over and analysing the side's victories and defeats. The boot room, therefore, became a mechanism for ensuring continuous improvement; a way of making certain that the club never became complacent or gave other teams the chance to catch up. Indeed, it was somewhat fitting that it was the boot room that hosted these discussions, given that their principal purpose was to keep Liverpool one step ahead of the opposition.

. . . .

Joe Fagan was not a happy man at half-time, as his players found out as soon as they arrived in the dressing room. They may have had more possession of the ball but they had failed to do anything purposeful with it, and having conceded a goal made that failure even more galling for Fagan. The nature of that goal was also a sore point with Fagan, who told his players in no uncertain terms that they were fools to have been mugged by such a simple free-kick routine. He demanded a swift improvement in the second half and there were none brave enough in the dressing room to suggest that they had simply been unlucky. Souness may have been one of the best players on the pitch in the first half but he knew that Fagan needed his captain's support and so he echoed his words, telling his team-mates through gritted teeth that failure simply wasn't an option.

The two teams took to the pitch for the second half and, just as at the start of the first period, there was little to choose between them initially. Liverpool's play was noticeably more determined, but they found themselves up against a Dundee United side whose confidence had been buoyed by their late first half goal. Bannon was being particularly effective on the left flank, occupying Neal with his offensive runs and preventing the Liverpool full-back from getting forward. The Dundee United defence also continued to keep the Liverpool strikers in check, with Hegarty getting the better of Rush in the air and Narey preventing Dalglish from getting hold of the ball in dangerous positions.

Jim McLean was quietly pleased with how his team were playing, but his good mood was not destined to last for long. A dozen minutes into the second half Bannon picked the ball up near the halfway line and advanced towards the rapidly retreating Neal. He ran close to him and skipped past his hasty challenge but Lawrenson was on the scene almost immediately, sliding in with a tackle that took the ball cleanly from Bannon's feet and into the path of Sammy Lee, the only native Liverpudlian in the side. Lee scurried off with the ball, making a beeline for Narey who had no choice other than to try to deal with the red-haired midfielder, even though that meant letting Dalglish out of his sight. Narey tried to dispossess Lee, but he quickly flicked the ball sideways to Souness who threaded it forward to the unmarked Dalglish. With the ball at his feet and with space in front of him for the first time in the match, Dalglish advanced purposefully at the United goal. Hegarty came out to meet him but, before he could get there, the ball was switched into the path of Rush who, from just inside the penalty area, swept the ball low past McAlpine's outstretched palm. Even Joe Fagan afforded himself a slight smile.

• •

Dundee United's long-suffering fans may have had to wait for 70 years to see the club win their first trophy, but they didn't have to wait too long before seeing them win another. McLean's side fought their way to a second consecutive League Cup Final in 1980 and, in a triumph for the city, their opponents were fierce local rivals Dundee FC. The Scottish League wisely opted to play the final in Dundee and, following a coin toss, Dens Park was selected as the venue. Not only was the location the same as in the previous year but the scoreline was identical as well, with United winning 3-0.

The goalscorers in that final were the team's two strikers: Paul Sturrock and Davie Dodds. The slender Sturrock was adept at dragging defenders out of position and performed a vital role in the team by linking midfield and attack. He went on to become Dundee United's second-highest goalscorer of all time and, unsurprisingly, was the regular subject of enquiries from other clubs. Celtic and Manchester United, among others, tried to sign him but McLean would never entertain disposing of one of his crown jewels. Sturrock was capped 20 times for Scotland, a total that would have been much higher if his main rival for a place in the team hadn't been Kenny Dalglish. Nevertheless, Sturrock still became the first Dundee United player to score for the national side and played in the 1986 World Cup finals in Mexico when Dalglish was injured.

Sturrock's striking partner was the lanky target man, Davie Dodds. He was the more aggressive of the two players and he used his ample stamina to take on thankless tasks for the team, such as closing down full-backs and preventing them from attacking down the flanks. Dodds was at his most effective in the six-yard area and his knack for getting into good goalscoring positions enabled him to become the club's third-highest goalscorer of all time. Indeed, the fact that he only scored 20 fewer goals than Sturrock, but played over 200 fewer games, testifies to just what a prodigious scorer he was.

Often playing behind Dodds and Sturrock were central midfielders Billy Kirkwood and Derek Stark, probably the two most unsung players in McLean's side. Kirkwood was originally a striker, even being the club's joint-top goalscorer one season, before McLean came to the view that his best position was in midfield. He was a versatile player, managing to appear in every outfield position during his time at the club. Kirkwood rarely gave the ball away, and was much appreciated by his team-mates as a consequence, though his workmanlike style rarely drew plaudits from the crowd.

Derek Stark was initially a part-time player, almost leaving football to become a police officer, before finally taking the plunge and devoting himself to the game. He became the hardest-working player in McLean's team, specialising in tackles that made even his fellow professionals wince. Sadly, Stark's career ended at the age of only 26 after falling victim to a knee injury that just wouldn't heal. He duly left the game to start a new career with the Fife Constabulary.

The 1980/81 season also saw the debut of another of McLean's tyros; Richard Gough. Born to a Scottish father and Swedish mother, Gough was raised in South Africa before coming to Scotland as a teenager to try and make a living from football. He failed a two-week trial with Rangers but made enough of an impact on McLean for Dundee United to sign him. He played him as a right-back, but it was as an uncompromising central defender that Gough was to find most success during his career. After serving his apprenticeship in Dundee, Gough spent a year with Tottenham Hotspur before returning to the club that had rejected him seven years earlier: Glasgow Rangers. He was reunited there with Walter Smith, who had been his coach and mentor at Tannadice and was now assistant manager at Ibrox. Smith later became Rangers' manager and the two men enjoyed an incredibly successful spell together, with Gough winning nine consecutive league titles, three Scottish Cups and six League Cups.

Dundee United managed to reach two further cup finals in 1981 but were beaten both times by Glasgow Rangers; a 4-1 defeat in the Scottish Cup being followed by a 2-1 defeat in the League Cup. Dundee United's goal in the second of these two finals was scored by Ralph Milne, the side's right-midfielder and, arguably, most enigmatic figure. His story is the all-too-familiar tale of a great talent that failed to fulfil its potential. He had the ability to have graced the World Cup finals but, in the end, was never even capped by his country. Milne's greatest gift was his ability to run at defenders at pace, quite literally putting them on to the back foot, before delivering accurate crosses or striking at goal. Milne had the flair to open up the tightest of defences and, despite playing on the wing, scored many goals for the team. Indeed, many of his strikes were stunning, including blistering shots from long range and delicate lobs over ill-placed goalkeepers.

Milne was one of McLean's key players when Dundee United stormed the football world in the early 1980s but his form started to fade in the years that followed. His burgeoning natural talent was blunted by his involvement in the heavy-drinking culture that blighted football at that time and, as his performances started to falter, he was barracked by supporters and his confidence declined as a result. Milne had a volatile relationship with McLean, who became increasingly frustrated that such a talented player had so little of the application and drive that characterised players such as Dodds, Hegarty and Sturrock. McLean eventually lost patience with Milne and cast him out of the club, with uneventful spells with Charlton Athletic and Bristol City following. To Milne's great surprise he was then thrown a lifeline by Alex Ferguson, who was in the early years of his long reign at Manchester United. Sadly, Milne failed to make much of an impression at Old Trafford and slowly drifted out of football, dying in 2015 at the age of only 54 following liver problems.

The 1981/82 season may have ended trophyless for Dundee United but it did witness the debut of another player who would become a club legend: Maurice Malpas. He spent the first few years of his career combining football with his studies for a degree in electrical engineering and so had to train in the evenings, meaning that he often only met up with his team-mates on matchdays. Malpas continued with that arrangement for several seasons, becoming the last part-time player to appear for Scotland when he made his international debut against France in 1984. Playing at left-back, Malpas was a consistently strong performer who read the game well and was rarely caught out of position. His career with Dundee United lasted for almost 20 years, with only David Narey making more appearances for the club. Malpas did, however, become Dundee United's most capped player of all time, making 55 appearances for Scotland as well as playing in two World Cups.

McLean's stature, both within the club and within football in general, continued to rise as United became more successful. In 1982 he was invited to join the club's board of directors and also went to the World Cup with Scotland as assistant manager to Jock Stein. Working with the legendary ex-Celtic boss was a superb opportunity for McLean and it also gave him the opportunity to see the nation's best players at close quarters. McLean was pleased to see that the two Dundee United players in the squad, Narey and Sturrock, could hold their own in such esteemed company and duly returned from the World Cup confident that he had the personnel needed to mount a credible challenge for the league title.

Dundee United started the 1982/83 league season well, winning five of their first nine matches and drawing four. They scored 17 goals in those games, including a 6-0 thrashing of Morton, while the defence was breached only three times. That lifted the club up to second place in the table but a 5-1 thrashing away to Aberdeen brought that good run to an end. McLean's players reacted positively to that disappointment by winning their next seven games, scoring 25 goals in the process and conceding only three. That sequence of games included a seven-goal hammering of Kilmarnock and a 5-0 pasting of Motherwell. Once again it was Aberdeen, however, who brought them back down to earth, with Alex Ferguson's men beating them 3-0 at Tannadice.

As the league season entered its final quarter Dundee United faced a series of key matches in their push for the title. In mid-March, they travelled to Aberdeen, who were three points ahead of them in the table and had scored eight goals against United in their previous two contests. A further victory for the home side would, in all likelihood, lift them out of United's reach and spell the end of McLean's league title aspirations for yet another season. The hero and villain of the game turned out to be Ralph Milne, who scored twice within a five-minute spell during the first half but then got himself sent off in the second half for kicking out at an Aberdeen defender after being hauled down. The Dons had got a goal back by the time of Milne's dismissal and so his team-mates had to battle hard to hold on to the victory.

Celtic were also in close contention for the title and the two sides had to play each other twice within the space of a fortnight. The first match was at Celtic Park and the Glasgow side won it 2-0. A brace of victories over Dundee United would have given Celtic an almost insurmountable lead in the table and so it was essential that McLean's men emerged victorious in the rematch. This time it was Gough who lost his composure and got sent off, leaving his side to try and hold on to their 2-1 lead. Celtic managed to force an equaliser and it looked as if it was all over for the ten men but, with just six minutes of the game remaining, Milne came to the rescue with a superb shot to give Dundee United a much-needed win.

That victory lifted United to within a point of Celtic and there were good grounds for optimism, given that they faced a relatively simple run-in. McLean's side disposed of Kilmarnock with a 4-0 scoreline while Aberdeen did them a huge favour by beating Celtic, meaning that for the first time that season McLean's side topped the table.

Next up was an away fixture at Morton and, with so much at stake, the United board decided to dip into their reserves and subsidise the cost of the trip for the club's fans. So many of them took up the offer that it effectively became a home match, with the United fans heavily outnumbering their hosts. Buoyed by the travelling support, United cantered to a 4-0 victory, not even being troubled by Paul Hegarty having to go in goal when the injured Hamish McAlpine was unable to continue.

United's strong run of form continued against Motherwell, with the Tangerines registering a third successive 4-0 win. That victory meant that another in their final game of the season would give them the title. Should they fail to do so, however, Celtic and Aberdeen were both poised to snatch it from their grasp. The title race in 1982/83 was the closest in Scottish league history, with just one point separating the three leading sides, each of whom could win the trophy if results went their way. Indeed, Dundee United and Celtic's records were so similar that if United's final league game finished 0-0 and Celtic won 2-0 they would both end the season with a matching number of points, goals scored and goals conceded, meaning a play-off match would be needed.

If the prospect of being league champions for the first time in the club's history wasn't tantalising enough, United's opponents in their final game were Dundee. Unsurprisingly, the game at Dens Park was a sell-out and McLean's side wasted no time in imposing themselves. Only four minutes had been played when Milne collected the ball just outside the centre circle and raced towards the penalty area. He saw that the Dundee goalkeeper was too far off his line and chipped the ball over him with inch-perfect precision. Too often great occasions are not graced by great goals, but that was arguably the finest goal that Milne ever scored in his career.

Only seven minutes later McLean's side were awarded a penalty when Narey was bundled over as he dashed towards goal. Bannon took the kick and the visiting supporters watched in horror as it was parried easily by the Dundee goalkeeper. Before their hearts had time to sink, however, Bannon latched on to the rebound and fired it past the prostrate goalkeeper.

McLean's side were 2-0 up within 11 minutes and, regardless of what was happening in Glasgow and Aberdeen, it looked almost certain that the league title was coming to the city of Dundee for only the second time in nearly 100 years. Then, just before the half-hour mark, the home side scored to secure a foothold in the game.

The United players found out at half-time that Celtic were losing 2-0 so approached the second half cautiously, trying to hold on to their narrow lead rather than push on for a third goal. That made for a nervous, cagey game and it almost proved calamitous as Celtic fought back strongly, eventually running out 4-2 winners. However, after enduring what must have seemed to have been an eternity, the United supporters were able to erupt in joyous celebration when the referee finally blew his whistle to bring the derby to an end. McLean and his men had achieved something truly magnificent and there were few in Scotland mean enough to begrudge them their long-overdue triumph.

. . . .

Liverpool's equalising goal proved to be the trigger for half an hour of scintillating play which showed British football at its best. Skill and dexterity with the ball was allied with sheer physical effort to produce open football that flowed from one end of the pitch to the other, delighting the commentators and galvanising even the most disillusioned of armchair fans. The Dundee United forward line was particularly impressive, with

Sturrock engaged in an engrossing duel with Lawrenson and the aggressive Dodds giving Hansen a hard time, especially when balls were played up to him in the air. The deliverer of many of those crosses was Ralph Milne, who was gradually getting the better of Alan Kennedy, wearing the older man down with his dynamic, well-directed runs down the right wing.

The football may have been getting tastier, but so were the tackles. Ronnie Whelan had begun to make a number of purposeful runs down the left wing and Gough opted to counter them with some robust challenges, one of which sent the Irishman sprawling on to the athletics track that circled the pitch. The referee had waved play on after the earlier tackles, but was not prepared to let Gough's latest effort go unpunished, brandishing the yellow card at the suitably chastened Scotsman. Davie Dodds was also unsparing in his battle with Alan Hansen, causing the normally unflappable centre-half to look more than a little flustered. Indeed, Dodds came close to giving Dundee United the lead once more, rising above Hansen to send a header curling towards the top corner of the goal and forcing a splendid save out of Grobbelaar.

McLean's side certainly had their chances but, with barely a quarter of an hour left to play, they had to rue not converting any of them. Liverpool's attack started when Hansen brought the ball out of defence, nimbly side-stepping a challenge from Kirkwood before slipping it into Souness's path. The Liverpool captain advanced swiftly with the ball and, 20 yards from goal, he flicked it to Dalglish, who shielded it from Narey before looking up to see what his options were. Souness had continued his run and, without having to break stride, he soon found the ball back in front of him. It bounced invitingly off the slick turf and Souness smashed it for all he was worth, sending it screaming past McAlpine and into the back of the net. The Scots had outdone the Scots; an irony not lost on the bitterly disappointed Dundee United fans behind the breached goal.

• •

Joe Fagan never really wanted to be the manager of Liverpool Football Club. He knew all too well what a lonely job it could be but, despite having never managed a league club before and being 62 years of age, he still reluctantly took on the biggest task of his entire career. Fagan was, by nature, a loyal man and had been a devoted servant to the club for 25 years. He knew that if he did not accept the job that had been offered to him he was effectively forcing the club to take on an outsider. Unable to bear the thought of all that he had helped to build being torn down in front of his eyes, Fagan gritted his teeth and accepted the job. He may have taken over a great squad from Paisley but that didn't make his job easy. In fact, the opposite was true. Fagan had also inherited sky-high expectations from Liverpool fans who were accustomed to winning trophies every season and for whom failure to win another league title, at least, would surely presage a crisis.

Fagan had been a centre-half during his playing days, though not a particularly noteworthy one. His career had barely begun when war broke out in 1939 and he lost a significant portion of it to the conflict. Fagan returned to Manchester City after the fighting ended and helped them to win the Second Division title in 1947; the only honour he won as a player. He was determined to stay in the game as his career came to an end, taking on a succession of player-manager and coaching roles in a bid to avoid doing a 'real job'. His efforts at unfashionable places such as Rochdale and Nelson enhanced his reputation, and when he was offered a role on the coaching staff at Liverpool the native Scouser accepted with alacrity. Fagan started working alongside Bob Paisley, who was the first-team trainer at the time, and the rapport that he built up with him sustained their relationship for the next quarter of a century. Bill Shankly was recruited as the club's new manager a little over a year later and, together, the three men slowly transformed Liverpool into one of the greatest clubs in the world.

Fagan was a humble, honest, approachable character whose warm, charming nature led to the players nicknaming him 'Uncle Joe'. He was one of life's natural peacekeepers and had often acted as a mediator between Shankly, Paisley and the players, quietly resolving differences before they became dilemmas. Fagan rarely lost his temper with under-performing players; normally getting his message across with a few quiet words rather than by throwing teacups. Yet, when he was riled, he would become a force to be reckoned with; his selective use of intemperate outbursts being so much more effective because they happened so infrequently. An excellent man-manager, Fagan instinctively knew when players needed to have their confidence built or their feet kept on the ground and consequently was a figure within the club that commanded respect.

Fagan had formed a strong bond with Graeme Souness during his years as the assistant manager and this paid great dividends when he took over as manager. Souness wasn't quite the finished article when he arrived at Liverpool; his off-field activities left a lot to be desired and his tendency to make rash challenges resulted in him incurring more bookings than he should. It was Fagan who had taken him to task, helping him to curb his wilder instincts to such an extent that he was now the team captain. Souness acknowledged and appreciated what Fagan had done for him and consequently had genuine affection for him. Prior to the start of Fagan's first season in charge Souness met with his team-mates and stressed how important it was for them to play well for their new manager, thus ensuring that the dressing room was behind him before a ball had even been kicked.

Paisley may have bequeathed a strong squad of players to Fagan, but the new manager was acutely aware that he would have to keep improving it if Liverpool were to maintain their position as the best side in the country. His initial forays into the transfer market, however, were not as successful as he had hoped. His targets were Charlie Nicholas, a Scottish striker who scored an incredible 48 goals for Celtic in the previous season, and Michael Laudrup, a young Danish forward of whom great things were expected. Fellow Scots like Dalglish urged Nicholas to sign for Liverpool but he opted to join Arsenal instead, wary of the scale of the task of being Kenny Dalglish's long-term replacement. Laudrup was prepared to join the club but his contractual demands were not acceptable to the board so he ended up signing for Italian giants Juventus. Fagan may have been frustrated in his search for a new striker, but he was not to be denied; signing Irish international Michael Robinson shortly before the start of the new season.

Robinson needed little persuading to join the reigning league champions. His club, Brighton and Hove Albion, had just been relegated to the Second Division and he was so keen to play for Liverpool that contract negotiations with Fagan were concluded within ten minutes. Robinson's career had started at Preston North End, where he had made enough of an impression for Manchester City to pay a hefty transfer fee for him. The Irish striker seemed destined for stardom but he failed to settle at Maine Road and was sold to Brighton a year later. Robinson slowly rebuilt his career on the south coast and helped Brighton to reach the FA Cup Final in 1983, knocking out Liverpool at Anfield on the way. That must clearly have had an influence on Fagan who signed him for Liverpool a few months later, though for only a third of the fee that Manchester City had paid for him four years earlier.

Robinson was a strong, industrious forward, but he never became a prolific goalscorer and that eventually proved to be his downfall at Anfield. He went straight into the first team, making his debut in Liverpool's 2-0 defeat to Manchester United in the Charity Shield at Wembley. Robinson not only failed to score in that match but also in his next eight games for the club.

Indeed, it wasn't until Liverpool started their European Cup campaign that he finally managed to get his name on the scoresheet. Liverpool's first-round opponents were Danish champions Odense. It looked, at first glance, to be a fairly kind draw as Fagan's side were taking on part-time players from a country that had never really made much of an impression on the competition. Danish football, however, was on the rise. The national side were in the process of qualifying for the 1984 European Championship finals ahead of England and would go on to perform admirably in that tournament, losing in the semi-finals to Spain on penalties.

The first leg was played in Denmark and Dalglish scored the only goal of the game to take a valuable lead back to Anfield. The second leg proved to be a much more straightforward affair with Liverpool running out 5-0 winners. Dalglish scored twice to secure the British record for the most goals scored in the European Cup, beating the previous total set by Denis Law, and a much-relieved Robinson also scored twice. Shortly after the victory over Odense, Liverpool travelled to play West Ham, who were top of the table after winning their opening five games of the season. Liverpool swept them aside 3-1, with Robinson scoring all three. It appeared that he had put his initial problems behind him, but his first-team appearances gradually became more sporadic as Fagan slowly tired of his inability to score on a regular basis.

Dundee United had one of the easiest possible draws for their first-round European Cup tie, being paired with Maltese side Hamrun Spartans. Liverpool may have had many years of experience in European competitions but it would be a mistake to assume that McLean's side were novices in this regard. Dundee United had participated in either the UEFA Cup or European Cup Winners' Cup for eight of the nine seasons prior to 1983/84 and had built up an invaluable understanding of how to approach games against continental sides. That experience helped them to reach the quarter-finals of the UEFA Cup in both 1981/82 and 1982/83, with McLean's side claiming some notable scalps on the way. They beat Monaco 5-2 away from home and also thrashed Borussia Mönchengladbach, twice winners of the trophy, 5-0.

Predictably, Hamrun Spartans were not much of an obstacle for McLean's side. The first match was played on a barren, deeply rutted pitch but Dundee United still ran out easy 3-0 winners, going on to win the return fixture by the same scoreline. The game was marred, however, by an injury to Sturrock which was serious enough to keep him out of United's second-round tie against Belgian champions Standard Liège. The Belgian side presented McLean and his men with a much tougher challenge, with the previous season's European Cup Winners' Cup finalists being managed by the talented Raymond Goethals who later guided Marseilles to European Cup glory. He had assembled a fine squad of players at Standard Liège, including the West German striker Horst Hrubesch who scored both goals in his nation's victory in the final of the 1980 European Championships.

McLean's side had previously played Standard Liège in the first round of the 1978/79 UEFA Cup, losing the away match 1-0 and then only managing a 0-0 draw back at Tannadice. The draw for their latest encounter required them to play the first leg in Liège again and, this time, McLean was determined that his side would not return to Dundee with a deficit to overturn. He duly instructed his players to defend in depth and they worked hard to control the game, ensuring that it finished goalless.

The second leg back in Dundee proved to be one of the club's finest ever performances, with Ralph Milne once again being the star of the show. Midway through the first half he scored with a diving header before doubling his side's lead just before half-time with a delightful chip over the goalkeeper. The second half was only a few minutes old when Hegarty scored to put the tie beyond the Belgians, rising majestically above their defence to bury Milne's corner past the goalkeeper. Dodds then added another with a trademark goal from within the six-yard area, forcing his way past the Liège defence to get on to the end of Gough's cross. The emphatic victory over Standard Liège immediately raised a few eyebrows and covetous eyes soon started to settle on the source of the Tannadice revolution.

Within a few days of that stunning victory Glasgow Rangers requested permission from United's board to talk to Jim McLean about becoming their new manager. Scotland's most successful ever side had been struggling for a while, not having won the league for five seasons and having been completely out of the running when United won the title. Their first choice was Alex Ferguson, who had recently led Aberdeen to the European Cup Winners' Cup with a victory over the mighty Real Madrid, but he opted to stay at Pittodrie. Rangers therefore turned their attentions to McLean, offering him a financial package way in excess of anything his current employers could afford.

After much soul-searching McLean decided to put his family, who were happily settled in Dundee, first. It was a noble decision as his career would surely have been better served by a move to Glasgow, where he would have had a much greater chance of winning trophies on a regular basis than he would with Dundee United.

While McLean's side were taking on Standard Liège, Liverpool were grappling with the challenge posed by the Basque side, Athletic Bilbao. As well as being champions of one of the most demanding leagues in Europe their team included the infamous 'Butcher of Bilbao', Andoni Goicoechea, who had broken Diego Maradona's ankle in a horrendous tackle earlier that season. Goicoechea didn't commit any atrocities in the first leg at Anfield but he did help to ensure that the Basques left with the goalless draw they had come for, frustrating the hosts with a solid defensive performance. It may have appeared that Bilbao had the upper hand in the tie but Liverpool were far from being out of it. Not only had they prevented the Basques from scoring an invaluable away goal, but they also knew that Bilbao would have to play a more open game in the second leg which would give the visitors more opportunities to score, even if only on the counter-attack.

In between the two matches against Bilbao, Liverpool played a home league game against Luton Town. The fact that Fagan's side won was not particularly remarkable, but Ian Rush's performance was. He scored twice in the first five minutes, had got his hat-trick by half-time and then went on to score two further goals in the second half as Liverpool romped home 6-0. That still wasn't enough, however, for the demanding Souness who urged Rush to push on for a sixth goal. The 1983/84 season proved to be the most prolific of the Welshman's career as he scored an astonishing 47 goals (32 in the league, eight in the League Cup, two in the FA Cup and an invaluable five in the European Cup), duly winning the Golden Boot for being the top scorer in Europe.

Back in the European Cup, Fagan knew that Liverpool would come under great pressure in the away leg so he advised his players to keep possession of the ball and frustrate Bilbao. Souness led the way and was Liverpool's most influential player, later judging it to be one of the finest games that he ever played for the club. Rush was on the receiving end of a number of harsh challenges but he kept his composure and got his revenge halfway through the second half, scoring with a header that bounced off the turf before beating the goalkeeper. The away goal was invaluable as it meant that Bilbao had to score two goals if they were to win the tie. The Basques continued their attacks until the end of the game but Fagan's side stood firm, holding on for a courageous 1-0 victory. The magnitude of Liverpool's triumph was confirmed later that season when Bilbao went on to win the Spanish league and cup double.

• •

Dundee United tried hard to get back into the match, but Liverpool were masters at keeping possession of the ball when they had a lead to defend. McLean's players gamely tried to get hold of the ball, readily chasing every pass and pursuing each lost cause, but it was to no avail. They desperately wanted to give the small band of travelling Dundee United fans something to cheer about; something to ease the 1,200-mile journey back home. Liverpool, however, were not playing ball. They casually knocked the ball around between themselves and made little effort to advance up the pitch, being content to play sideways passes until the referee brought the game to an end.

As well as being dull to watch, Liverpool's tactics also frustrated the opposition enough to provoke a number of fierce tackles; some of which were so robust that the culprits barely seemed to care whether they stayed on the pitch or not. The Liverpool players managed to dodge most of the ferocious challenges but one of them found its mark; Derek Stark crunching into Graeme Souness with a tackle so venomous that it drew audible gasps from the crowd. The Dundee United midfielder was fortunate not to be sent off, escaping with just a booking, but it may have been better for him if he had have been dismissed, for Souness was clearly not a happy man.

There was almost a cruelty in the way in which Liverpool kept the ball, seemingly taunting McLean's side as the minutes ticked away to their inevitable victory. It appeared that it would sour the end of what had been a fine game of football, which is why what happened next was all the more welcome. Hansen played the ball out to Kennedy, who swiftly knocked it back infield to Lee. The pass, however, was slightly under-hit and, within a flash, Milne collected it. He looked up and saw the Liverpool defence arrayed in front of him; a wall of red shirts that would never allow itself to be penetrated this late in the game. Grobbelaar, however, was a couple of yards further ahead of his goal-line than he should have been, so Milne flicked the ball up slightly before lobbing it high into the air. The Zimbabwean goalkeeper immediately realised his error, back-pedalling furiously as the ball reached the top of its arc before descending towards the goal. Grobbelaar threw himself up into the air and thrust his fingers at the ball, brushing it slightly before it, and he, ended up sprawled in the back of the net. Ralph Milne may have been exhausted but few could have guessed as he raced around the pitch in a doomed attempt to evade his jubilant team-mates. He soon disappeared beneath a mass of bodies, while the Liverpool players looked wearily at each other, preparing themselves mentally for another half an hour of football.

. . . .

There was a four-month gap between Liverpool's victory over Athletic Bilbao and their quarter-final tie against Portuguese champions Benfica. Fagan's side used the time well by consolidating their position at the top of the league table, though not everything went their way. They travelled to Coventry City in early December and suffered a rather unexpected 4-0 hiding. It took only 40 seconds for Liverpool to concede the first goal, following a mistake by Grobbelaar, and they were 3-0 down by the break. There were ructions in the dressing room at half-time as manager, coaching staff and players all indulged in a collective orgy of criticism. It was all to no avail, however, as Liverpool let in a further goal in the second half; the first time in over three years they had conceded four goals in a league match. If their rivals hoped that this result foretold a crisis at Anfield, they were to be bitterly disappointed. A week later Fagan's side put the result at Coventry well behind them, thrashing Notts County 5-0 at home.

Liverpool started 1984 three points ahead of second-placed Manchester United, with the two sides meeting on the second day of the new year in an eagerly anticipated clash. The resulting 1-1 draw was a little disappointing for Fagan's side as it was the third time that season that they had failed to beat their local rivals. What truly marred the day, however, was a dreadful injury suffered by Kenny Dalglish. He jumped for the ball with Kevin Moran, later to become the first player to be sent off in an FA Cup Final, and the Irishman's flailing arm caught him in the face. The brave Dalglish wanted to carry on playing but had suffered a fractured cheekbone and was clearly in no state to continue. Dalglish was hospitalised for a while as a result and it would be two long months before he was fit again.

Dalglish's enforced absence coincided with a sequence of disappointing results for Liverpool. They contrived to lose 1-0 at home to Wolverhampton Wanderers, who were rooted to the bottom of the table after only winning three of their opening 22 games, and were then knocked out of the FA Cup by Brighton and Hove Albion, who were lying in mid-table in the Second Division at the time.

Fagan wearily turned his attentions to the League Cup, in which his side had reached the semi-finals. It appeared that Liverpool had landed the plum draw, having avoided Aston Villa and Everton, being paired with Third Division Walsall instead. The semi-finals were played over two legs and, with the first game to be played at Anfield, a decent result would surely make the second match no more than a formality. Walsall had already knocked out Arsenal at Highbury, however, and with Dalglish, Lawrenson and Souness absent through injury the underdogs sensed the chance of an upset.

On an embarrassing night for Fagan's men the plucky Midlanders twice pegged the hosts back, securing a commendable 2-2 draw. Liverpool finally put the minnows in their place a week later though, beating them 2-0 to reach their fourth consecutive League Cup Final.

The first leg of Liverpool's quarter-final against Benfica was at Anfield and the visitors came with the clear intention of frustrating the home side, just as Bilbao had done in the previous round. The Portuguese side were managed by future England coach Sven-Göran Eriksson, who had led Gothenburg to a UEFA Cup triumph in 1982 and Benfica to the runners-up spot in the same competition a year later. His tactics worked perfectly for the first 45 minutes so Fagan decided to take a gamble, bringing Kenny Dalglish on at the start of the second half in place of Michael Robinson. Dalglish was still making his way back from injury and had only played in two reserve games since having broken his cheekbone. The Scotsman didn't let Fagan down, however, with his inventive play stretching the Benfica defence far more than it had been in the first half. The pressure eventually told, with Liverpool's goal coming midway through the second period. Alan Kennedy broke away on the left wing and sent a cross soaring over the Benfica defence that Rush met at the far post, burying his header past the stranded goalkeeper.

Back in Lisbon Liverpool were greeted by over 70,000 hostile spectators who tried to intimidate the players by pelting them with coins and oranges as they warmed up. Fagan knew that the best way to silence the home fans was to score an early goal and he urged his team to attack Benfica right from the start. His players responded to his exhortations, scoring after only nine minutes when Whelan beat the Portuguese goalkeeper with a header that really should have been saved. Fagan decided to play Rush on his own in attack, relying on midfield players running from deep to support him, and the plan worked to perfection; Rush dragging defenders out into wide positions and leaving space for the midfield players to attack into.

Liverpool scored again after just over half an hour to effectively end the tie as a contest, the away goals rule meaning that Benfica had to score four goals if they were to reach the next round. The Portuguese side did get one back during the second half (the first that the Liverpool defence had conceded in the European Cup that season) but it came too late to alter the outcome. As if to emphasise their superiority, Liverpool responded by scoring twice more. The first came from another header by an unmarked Rush following a cross from Dalglish, while the second was scored by Whelan after he ran into the penalty area and placed the ball past the goalkeeper at his near post. Again, the Portuguese goalkeeper should have done better but, by this stage, his failures had become rather academic.

As Liverpool awaited their European Cup semi-final, they had the welcome distraction of a League Cup Final against local rivals Everton. It was the first time that the two clubs had met in a major final and the occasion was greatly anticipated on Merseyside. Unfortunately, the game failed to live up to its billing, with Liverpool being hustled out of their stride by a resurgent Everton side that refused to accept that they were forever destined to live in their neighbour's shadow. The game went into extra time but still finished goalless, with a replay scheduled for three days later in Manchester.

While the rival fans had mingled amicably on the Wembley terraces, there had been an unpleasant spat between Fagan and one of his midfield players, Craig Johnston. The relationship between the two men had never been particularly harmonious, and when Fagan decided to substitute Johnston the latter made an ill-tempered remark that incurred the manager's wrath in front of the watching world. It was an uncomfortable moment but Fagan let it pass, selecting Johnston again for the replay. Liverpool went on to win the game, with Souness scoring the only goal midway through the first half. It was the club's fourth successive League Cup triumph and, having won his first trophy as Liverpool manager, Fagan finally started to step out of his predecessor's shadow.

Joe Fagan's bête noire, Craig Johnston, was another of Bob Paisley's recruits, having been signed from Middlesbrough in 1981. Johnston was a charismatic figure who had been born in South Africa and raised in Australia before coming to England to try and make his way in the professional game. He was a tireless footballer, making use of his prodigious reserves of energy to race around the pitch and never allowing opposing players to rest. Johnston could be an unpredictable player, though, and often exasperated team-mates by not passing the ball to where they thought it was best needed, or trying to do something difficult when a simpler option would have been more effective.

Liverpool may have been on their way to yet another league triumph, but Jim McLean's Dundee United were struggling to defend their crown. Their season started with five consecutive victories, but a sequence of six games in October and November in which they won only once cost them valuable momentum. They never managed to rise above third place in the table for the remainder of the season and the domestic cup competitions offered little respite, with Glasgow Rangers knocking them out of the semi-finals of the League Cup and Aberdeen defeating them in the quarter-finals of the Scottish Cup. Their only remaining chance of winning a trophy that season was the European Cup and their prospects improved markedly when they were handed the best possible tie in the quarter-finals, being drawn against Austrian champions Rapid Vienna. It would be wrong to dismiss their opponents as pushovers, however, as they were good enough to reach the following season's European Cup Winners' Cup Final.

The first leg was played in Vienna and Dundee United did not perform to their usual standards, with the players looking noticeably nervous. McLean's side somehow managed to score against the run of play, however, with a well-struck 25-yard shot by Derek Stark giving them the lead. A sterling display of goalkeeping from McAlpine made an unlikely looking victory a real possibility, but two late goals from the Austrians inflicted on United their first defeat in the European Cup.

McLean's team kicked off the return fixture at Tannadice two weeks later knowing that a 1-0 victory would be sufficient for them to beat the Austrians on the away goals rule, and that's exactly what they proceeded to do. Just over 20 minutes into the game Stark slipped the ball to Dodds who, unmarked just outside the six-yard area, fired his shot high past the goalkeeper. McLean's side didn't deliver the same level of performance as they had against Standard Liège, but they worked hard and duly held out for the single-goal victory that secured their place in the semi-finals.

The other two teams left in the European Cup were Romanian champions Dinamo Bucharest and Italian giants AS Roma. The draw for the semi-finals pitted England against Romania and Scotland against Italy, thus keeping the tantalising prospect of an all-British final alive. It may have appeared that Dinamo Bucharest posed less of a threat than some of the clubs that Fagan's side had faced in the competition that season but there was still good reason for Liverpool to be cautious. The Romanians had already defeated the European Cup holders, SV Hamburg, in the second round and Liverpool's two previous attempts at winning the European Cup had both ended in defeat to unfancied sides from eastern Europe, with CSKA Sofia defeating them in 1982 and Widzew Łódź in 1983.

The first leg was played at Anfield again and, just as the previous two visiting teams in the European Cup had done, the Romanians did their utmost to stop Liverpool from playing. Unlike Bilbao and Benfica, however, they made much greater use of the darker arts of the game in an effort to achieve that end. They kicked the Liverpool players, spat at them, threw punches and, when the opportunity arose, lay on the floor and pretended to be injured. The violence reached a crescendo when Souness, enraged by another late, high tackle from Lică Movilă, punched the Romanian so hard that he broke his jaw in two places. Fortunately for Souness none of the officials saw what he did, because if they had have done he would not have taken any further part in the European Cup that season.

Liverpool went on to win the game 1-0, taking the lead midway through the first half. The move started when Johnston raced down the left wing with the ball but was sent flying by yet another lunging tackle. Kennedy delivered the resulting free kick into a crowded penalty area and the pint-sized Sammy Lee connected with it to score a rare headed goal.

At the end of the match a number of the Bucharest players made it clear to Souness that he could expect to be on the receiving end of some severe retaliation when the two teams met again. If Souness had hoped that their rage had cooled by the time he reached Romania, then he was to be disappointed; even the security officials at the airport greeted him with threatening gestures. When he took to the pitch he was harangued by the waiting crowd and, predictably, he was on the receiving end of a number of vicious tackles but, to his credit, he followed Fagan's advice not to go looking for trouble and kept his composure, arguably being the best player on the pitch.

As Liverpool only had a slender lead from the first leg, Fagan impressed on his players that Bucharest mustn't be allowed to score an early goal. He could not have hoped for a better start, however, as Rush scored an invaluable away goal after only 11 minutes of play. The Romanians cleared away a Lee corner but, in doing so, left Rush unmarked on the edge of the penalty area. Souness fed the ball back to Rush, who ran towards goal and chipped the ball over the outrushing keeper. That left Bucharest needing to score three goals without reply if they were to win the tie and, while they did manage to equalise from a free kick shortly before half-time, the Liverpool defence wasn't to be breached again. With six minutes of the game remaining Fagan's men secured their place in the European Cup Final when Rush pounced on a mistake by his defensive marker to score again.

Before Liverpool could think of becoming European champions once more, they had to focus their attention on retaining the league title. They won only one of the three matches played between the two games against Dinamo Bucharest and were in danger of ceding ground to their title rivals, Manchester United. Liverpool's form in the league continued to stutter but United were unable to capitalise, winning only one of their remaining eight games.

Fagan's side duly took advantage of United's loss of nerve, avenging their away defeat at Coventry by thrashing them 5-0 at Anfield, with Rush scoring four times. That put Liverpool on the verge of another league triumph and they travelled to Notts County a few days later knowing that a win would give them their fifth league title in six years. Fagan's men, in keeping with their lacklustre end to the season, could only manage a 0-0 draw but, with Manchester United failing to win again, the solitary point proved to be sufficient. Liverpool had just crept over the line and, while they could and should have done better, in the end they simply didn't need to.

· ·

Both Joe Fagan and Jim McLean came on to the pitch before the start of extra time, exhorting one last push from their shattered players. There was little they could say in respect of game plans as such words would have little effect now; the match would be decided by those who kept their nerve, by those who kept their head while all about were losing theirs. Dalglish's spirit was certainly willing but his 33-year-old legs had little left to give, so Fagan replaced him with Michael Robinson, hoping that the Irishman's prodigious work-rate would stretch the tired Dundee United defence. McLean, meanwhile, decided to keep faith with the 11 players that had started the game. They hadn't let him down yet.

Liverpool started extra time as the stronger of the two sides. Their sheer determination to win the game slowly got the better of their opponents, whose exertions to find an equaliser had clearly taken a lot out of them. Craig Johnston, in particular, was a barely containable bundle of energy on the right wing. Maurice Malpas had managed to keep him in check for most of the game, but the part-timer's limbs were weary now and the Australian was starting to take advantage. Joe Fagan had no particular desire to change his side, given how well they were playing, but a substitution was forced on him when Lawrenson was caught late in a tackle by Kirkwood. The foul was neither intentional nor malicious, but it did for Lawrenson all the same, with the Irish international being replaced by yet another Scot, the young Steve Nicol.

The first clear-cut chance in extra time fell to Robinson, who only had the goalkeeper to beat after receiving a fine pass from Whelan. McAlpine spread himself low and wide, while simultaneously trying to force Robinson to shoot from as acute an angle as possible. The ploy worked as the Irishman dragged his shot narrowly wide of the post, causing Fagan and the other Liverpool coaches to leap from the bench in expectation before burying their heads in their hands. Liverpool's dominance continued into the second period of extra time, with their best move coming with only five minutes of the match remaining. Souness released the ball to Johnston on the right wing, who skipped past a tired challenge from Malpas before cutting inside and running at the heart of the Dundee United defence. Johnston ran into the right-hand side of the penalty area, drawing Hegarty towards him and thus leaving Rush unmarked ten yards from goal. Fagan instinctively demanded that Johnston pass the ball to Rush, even though he knew there was no chance of the Australian hearing him, and then roared with disappointment as Johnston opted to shoot instead, sending the ball high over the bar. That was the last real opportunity for either side to score, and so it would all come down to penalties.

. . . .

If Dundee United wanted to join Liverpool in the European Cup Final they would have to beat the Italian champions AS Roma. It was the greatest test that McLean's side had ever faced and, unlike all their other European Cup ties that season, the first leg was played at Tannadice. Unsurprisingly, the match was a sell-out, with the city's inhabitants flocking to see a star-studded Roma side that included Italian World Cup winners Bruno Conti and Francesco Graziani, as well as the great Brazilian midfielder Cerezo. His compatriot, the sublimely talented Roberto Falcão, unfortunately had to miss the game through injury.

The first half ended goalless but both sides had decent chances to score, with Roma coming closest when a header from Graziani bounced off the bar. The second half, however, was a different story as the United players shed their inhibitions and took the game to the Italians. The first goal came only three minutes into the second period when a shot from Bannon ricocheted off a Roma defender and, in the ensuing melee, Sturrock managed to push the ball to Dodds who fired the ball past the goalkeeper from close range. United then poured forward in search of a second goal and, just over ten minutes later, they got it; a swerving shot by Stark from 20 yards that fooled the goalkeeper before crashing into the back of the net. The Italians remained on the back foot for the remainder of the game, with Tancredi having to make a fine save from an incredible header by Hegarty to keep the deficit down to two goals.

Not only did McLean's side have a two-goal lead over Roma but, crucially, they had also prevented the Italians from scoring an away goal. That meant that if United could get a goal in the return fixture Roma would have to score four times to win the tie.

The European Cup Final was due to be held at Roma's home ground, the Olympic Stadium, and there was now a real risk that they were not going to be part of it. Fear can make people do unpleasant things and the Italians were desperately afraid that they were going to miss out on a party in their own house. The Italians began their dirty tricks straight after the defeat in Dundee, excusing their poor performance by accusing the United players of taking drugs. It was a dreadful slur but Roma knew what they were doing. They were a much bigger club than United so they started to flex their muscles, embarking on a campaign of intimidation designed to cow McLean's side before the return fixture had even kicked off.

Things got no better when the United players went to Italy, with armed guards being placed on their floor in the hotel and abuse being yelled at them as they made their way to the ground in their coach. Christians being transported to their doom in the Colosseum were probably made to feel more welcome. When the visitors came out on to the pitch Jim McLean was greeted with banners denigrating him while the players had to dodge oranges hurled at them by the Roma fans. The Dundee United players had never experienced anything like it before, and in front of a hostile crowd of nearly 70,000 spectators they wilted in the fierce afternoon sun.

United's best chance of getting the result they needed came early in the game after the referee had ruled out a Bruno Conti strike for offside. Bannon charged down the left wing, beat his marker and delivered a cross into the penalty area which landed at the feet of Ralph Milne. Despite being unmarked a couple of yards to the right of the penalty spot, he hit his shot over the bar.

A goal at that point in the game could have crushed the Italians, leaving them with an almost impossible task. Having dodged that bullet, however, Roma never looked back. With Falcão back in their side the Italians took the game to the Scots, scoring midway through the first half from a header by Roberto Pruzzo. The Italian striker then scored again shortly before half-time, shooting the ball past McAlpine despite being heavily marked by the United defence. The tie was all-square at the interval and, with another 45 minutes still to play, the advantage clearly lay with the home side.

Pruzzo was given an excellent opportunity to score his hat-trick 13 minutes into the second half when he was put through one-on-one with the United keeper. McAlpine could only thwart the Italian striker by pulling him to the ground, with the subsequent penalty easily being converted by the Roma captain, Di Bartolmei. The hosts had got the three goals they needed and proceeded to hold on to their lead for the remainder of the game without too much difficulty. Sadly, even though they had won the tie, the Italians were unable to be gracious in victory. Several Roma players and officials charged towards McLean at the end of the match, shouting abuse and taunting him, clearly intent on starting a fight. McLean was protected from the frenzied pack by his coaching staff, but still had to dodge missiles hurled from the crowd as he made his way back to the dressing room.

It was a dreadfully sad way for United's European Cup dreams to end, but there was to be one further sting in the tail for McLean and his men. Months later allegations surfaced that Roma had attempted to bribe the French referee, Michel Vautrot, via a middleman ahead of the second leg. There has never been any evidence that Vautrot received the monies intended for him, or that he was even aware of any attempt being made to influence him. Indeed, it is impossible for a dispassionate viewer of the game to see any proof that a conspiracy took place.

Conti had a goal disallowed for offside which could easily have been given, there was nothing suspect about Roma's two first-half goals and the penalty awarded to the Italians in the second half was indisputable. It would be wrong, therefore, to assert that Dundee United were denied a place in the European Cup Final by a dodgy referee; they were simply beaten by a better side on the day.

The 1984 European Cup Final promised to be a fascinating encounter. Roma had won all of their European Cup ties at the Olympic Stadium without conceding a single goal, while Liverpool had won all of their away ties. In a contest between the unstoppable force and the immoveable object, something was going to have to give. It hardly seemed fair that the Italians had home advantage for such an important match but there was little that Liverpool could do to change the situation and, to their credit, they didn't seek to.

In the hostile environment of the Olympic Stadium it was vital that the visitors showed that they would not be cowed. As Fagan's men walked back to the dressing room, after having had their pre-match walkabout on the pitch, they launched into an impromptu version of a Chris Rea song, continuing to belt it out as they marched past Roma's dressing room. The Roma manager revealed later that he had been giving his team-talk at the time and confirmed that the singing had unnerved his players. Later, as Liverpool lined up in the tunnel waiting to go out on to the pitch, they started singing the song again and, while their behaviour may have baffled the Italians, it clearly did their confidence no harm at all.

Liverpool had seized the initiative and they started the game well, calming the crowd by keeping possession of the ball and frustrating their hosts. It only took 14 minutes for them to take the lead, albeit with a rather fortuitous, scrappy goal. Johnston crossed the ball from the right wing and Whelan got his head to it just ahead of goalkeeper Tancredi, who really should have caught it. Tancredi tumbled to the ground and the ball fell to a defender but, almost comically, he thumped it against the prostrate goalkeeper's head and the ball rebounded straight into the path of Phil Neal, who gleefully poked it into the net.

Liverpool continued to play well for the remainder of the first half with Souness dominating midfield, outshining Brazilian duo Falcão and Cerezo. Yet, with just a few minutes of the half remaining, Roma showed that they weren't about to lie down and meekly accept defeat. Bruno Conti received the ball on the left wing and after his first attempt at crossing the ball was blocked by Lawrenson, he picked up the rebound and lofted the ball into the penalty area. The Italian centre-forward Roberto Pruzzo got in front of Hansen and then skilfully directed a looping, backwards header over Grobbelaar's outstretched arms.

The first half ended with the scores level and, with two goals scored already and all to play for, the second period looked to be an enticing prospect. However, recent European Cup finals had proved to be dull games, with the previous six all ending in 1-0 scorelines, and there were to be no further goals from open play in this match.

Roma started the second half the stronger of the two sides but they were unable to find a way past the Liverpool defence and, as the game wore on, both sides became increasingly cautious, fearful of making a mistake that would hand the game to the opposition. Liverpool's game was based on keeping possession of the ball and they were so successful at this that they reduced Cerezo to tears; he later complained that his efforts at trying to win the ball back from Liverpool had left him feeling like a bull tormented by matadors. Indeed, he did so much chasing and harrying that he went down with cramp and had to be substituted as a result. The game limped into extra time and eventually ended in deadlock and so, for the first time in the history of the competition, the winners of a European Cup Final would have to be decided by a penalty shoot-out.

Fagan picked the five players who would take Liverpool's penalties and then left it to Graeme Souness to decide the order in which they would take them. First up was the young Scot, Steve Nicol, who had come on as a substitute for Craig Johnston and courageously volunteered to take one of the penalties. He was a versatile player and would go on to have a fine career for Liverpool, but unfortunately his talents didn't extend that night to converting a spot-kick. He blasted the ball over the bar and when Roma captain Di Bartolomei scored his side's first penalty the situation started to look a little bleak for Liverpool.

The ever-reliable Phil Neal helped to calm his side's nerves a little when he scored the next penalty and then Bruno Conti handed the visitors a lifeline by hitting his penalty over the bar. With the contest evenly poised Souness scored his penalty, but that strike was then evened out by Righetti whose shot beat Grobbelaar. Rush scored the next penalty to put Liverpool back into the lead and then came one of the moments which defined the Zimbabwean keeper's career.

Liverpool's two previous attempts at winning the European Cup had ended at the hands of CSKA Sofia and Widzew Łódź and mistakes by Grobbelaar had been crucial in both of those defeats. He needed to make amends and the shoot-out against

Roma gave him the perfect opportunity. Prior to the shoot-out Fagan had urged Grobbelaar to try and distract the Roma players before they took their penalties. So, when Francesco Graziani stepped up to take his kick, Grobbelaar wobbled his legs as if they were made of spaghetti. The trick clearly worked, with the Italian's shot clipping the top of the crossbar before flying into the night sky. That meant that if Alan Kennedy could score his side's remaining penalty Liverpool would be champions of Europe once again.

It was an unenviable task but the full-back stepped up to become the hero of the hour, just as he had been against Real Madrid three years earlier. Kennedy ran up to the ball and gave the impression that he was going to hit it towards the right-hand side of the net. Then, at the last moment, he deceived Tancredi by side-footing the ball into the other corner. Roma were crestfallen; they had hoped to win the game's greatest club competition on their home ground but had been undone by the inherent cruelty of a penalty shoot-out. It was, however, a magnificent triumph for Fagan who in his first year as Liverpool manager had led the club to an unprecedented treble of trophies, silencing all those that had earlier questioned his age and experience.

Roma's defeat to Liverpool cast a long shadow over the Italian club. The fans turned on their talismanic star, Roberto Falcão, castigating him for a poor performance in the final and his unwillingness to take one of the penalties in the shoot-out. He only made a handful of further appearances for the club before returning to Brazil, while Di Bartolomei never played for Roma again. On the tenth anniversary of the defeat, weighed down by personal problems, Di Bartolomei committed suicide by shooting himself through the heart.

Darker days also lay ahead for the victors. Liverpool reached the European Cup Final again a year later, but their rioting fans caused the deaths of 39 innocent spectators in the crumbling Heysel Stadium. English clubs were banned from competing in European competitions as a consequence and it would be 21 long years before Liverpool would once again grace a European Cup Final.

Joe Fagan had announced his retirement shortly before the ill-fated match against Juventus and the ensuing disaster inevitably overshadowed his departure from the club. He was replaced by Kenny Dalglish and Liverpool continued to dominate English football for the remainder of the decade, winning a league and FA Cup double in 1985/86, another title in 1987/88 and a further FA Cup in 1988/89. The last of those triumphs occurred in the shadow of the terrible tragedy at Hillsborough, when 96 Liverpool fans perished in a death-trap of a stadium in Sheffield. It was an awful blow for the club and, despite winning another league title the following season, their long reign at the top of English football was almost at an end. Formidable rivals in the shape of George Graham's Arsenal and Alex Ferguson's Manchester United were on the rise and, at the time of writing, Liverpool's long wait for another league title continues.

While Fagan's tenure as Liverpool manager lasted for only one further year after the 1983/84 European Cup, Jim McLean held on to the reins at Dundee United for another nine seasons. His team continued to be one of the top sides in Scotland but failed to win any trophies during this period. Instead there was a succession of near-misses, with McLean's side losing a League Cup Final in 1984 and Scottish Cup finals in 1985, 1987, 1988 and 1991. The most galling disappointment, however, was their defeat in the 1987 UEFA Cup Final. Their route to the final included two memorable victories over Terry Venables's Barcelona (Gary Lineker, Mark Hughes, et al) as well as another triumph over Borussia Mönchengladbach.

The two-legged final against IFK Gothenburg should have been McLean's crowning glory, with a narrow 1-0 defeat in

Sweden in the first leg giving the United faithful hope that they could win the trophy back at Tannadice. It wasn't to be, however, as Gothenburg managed to get a 1-1 draw and, with it, an aggregate victory.

Even though Dundee United finally managed to win the Scottish Cup after McLean retired, his time in charge was undoubtedly the club's finest hour. McLean built a succession of fine teams, all largely based on homegrown talent, and United fans rarely went through a season without seeing their team competing in Europe. One of the clearest indications of the quality of players produced by McLean came at the 1986 World Cup finals in Mexico, when more players in Scotland's 22-man squad came from Dundee United than from any other club. Indeed, more United players went on that trip than Celtic and Rangers players combined. Over the years McLean suffered more than his fair share of defeats in semi-finals and finals, but at least he took his club that far, giving Dundee United fans memories that will never fade.

• •

Joe Fagan didn't want penalties. Jim McLean didn't want penalties. In truth, nobody out on the pitch wanted penalties, especially the poor souls who would have to take them. The first player to make the long walk from the centre circle to the penalty area was the Dundee United left-winger, Eamonn Bannon. He placed the ball on the spot, patiently awaited the referee's permission to take the kick and then picked his spot, placing the ball low to Grobbelaar's right-hand side. The Scots had got their noses in front and next up was the young Liverpool player, Steve Nicol. He looked confident as he strode up to take the kick, but his contact was too firm and the ball flew high above the crossbar. 'Early days,' said Joe Fagan firmly to those congregated around him, though he was evidently trying to reassure himself as much as he was them.

Paul Sturrock converted United's next penalty to give his side a 2-0 lead, leaving Liverpool's Phil Neal with the unenviable task of having to score if his side were to have any real chance of winning. The right-back had converted many crucial penalties before, including one in a European Cup Final, and he made no mistake with this one, smashing it high into the corner of the net. Davie Dodds was up next and Dundee United fans had their hearts in their mouths as he strode up to take it. If this went in they would almost be able to smell victory. But Dodds, scorer of so many goals in so many vital games, scuffed his kick, allowing Grobbelaar to make a relatively simple save. Nevertheless, United would stay in front if Souness didn't score with his penalty. This was the moment for the captain to demonstrate why he was the captain and he didn't disappoint, cracking the ball high into the left-hand corner of McAlpine's net.

With the scores level after three penalties apiece those watching back home could barely believe their eyes as McAlpine picked the ball out of the back of the net and then placed it on the penalty spot, clearly intent on taking the next kick himself. Grobbelaar stood on the goal-line and grinned eagerly at his opposite number, before wobbling his legs as if they were made of spaghetti. McAlpine smiled back and then repeated what the Liverpool goalkeeper had done, the two men engaged in a ridiculous schoolyard jape during the most important moment of their careers. It was a moment that those watching would never forget; a glorious jumble of gamesmanship, humour and bravado. McAlpine scored, but few would ever remember that.

Liverpool were behind again but their next penalty taker was Ian Rush, scorer of almost 50 goals that season. The Welshman made no mistake with his kick, sliding the ball into the same side of the net that Neal and Souness had smashed theirs. Dundee United's final penalty of the regulation five was due to be taken by their most enigmatic player, Ralph Milne. His away goal against Roma had secured his side's place in the final and his last-minute strike had kept them in it. If he could score now, then Dundee United would surely have one hand on the trophy.

Milne studiously ignored Grobbelaar's antics on the goal line and then strode up purposefully towards the ball. His strike was firm and true and it easily evaded Grobbelaar's dive, but it was ever so slightly off target, clipping the underside of the bar before bouncing back out. The inconsolable young man walked away, desperately alone, barely noticing Alan Kennedy, who he had tormented throughout the game, striding in the opposite direction.

If the Liverpool left-back scored it would all be over, so the Dundee United fans prepared themselves for the worst. The more morose among them reflected that their side only ever seemed to win trophies when they were in Dundee, and on their neighbour's ground to be precise. And so it turned out; Kennedy deceiving McAlpine by shaping to shoot to his left and then placing the ball to his right. Liverpool may have deserved their triumph, but that didn't ease the pain of the Dundee United players who had reached yet another final only to be beaten again. The cameras focused on the cavorting Liverpool players and only those in the ground could see Grobbelaar comforting McAlpine; two kindred spirits hugging in an embrace of mutual respect. An English side may have won, but the night really belonged to Scotland's golden generation. It was therefore fitting that the honour of lifting the huge silver trophy fell to Souness, who jubilantly lifted it aloft before brandishing it at the Liverpool supporters. The lions were rampant once more.

5
None Shall Sleep

World Cup Final, Olympic Stadium, Rome, 8 July 1990

Argentina v England

Argentina

Sergio Goycochea

Oscar Ruggeri

Juan Simón

José Serrizuela

Néstor Lorenzo

Roberto Sensini

Pedro Troglio

Jorge Burruchaga

José Basualdo

Diego Maradona (captain)

Gustavo Dezotti

England

Peter Shilton

Stuart Pearce

Mark Wright

Terry Butcher (captain)

Des Walker

Paul Parker

David Platt

Paul Gascoigne

Chris Waddle

Peter Beardsley

Gary Lineker

Referee: Edgardo Codesal (Mexico)

Bobby Robson shook hands briefly with Carlos Bilardo as their sides lined up for the national anthems, his eyes settling on the man whose team had beaten his in such contentious circumstances four years earlier. He looked for something in his face, some small element of contrition perhaps, but there was nothing to see there but grim determination. Both men were taking charge of their teams for the last time after eight years in the job; one of them due to be feted for evermore and the other destined to live forever in the world of ifs, buts and maybes. If it was a fair world then the triumph would surely be Robson's, but he had learnt the hard way what a desperately iniquitous place the world could be.

The World Cup Final was the tenth fixture between England and Argentina and few of their preceding games had been dull. Indeed, the history of their clashes as so dogged by controversy that there wasn't even agreement between them over how many games they had actually played against the other. Robson was well aware of the bad blood that had developed over the years between his countrymen and the Argentineans; a volatile brew that drew its fire from both sport and politics. He wished that it wasn't so; that the game could be played in a friendly, respectful and honourable manner, but he feared that the weight of history was simply too great for that to happen. If he was to become the second English manager to win the World Cup then his players would have to tear the Argentinean's grip on the trophy away finger by finger, and that would be no easy matter.

As the Argentinean national anthem was played Robson began to feel a twinge of sympathy for his opponents. It was being jeered relentlessly by the largely Italian crowd, with their venom directed at the side's captain, the reviled Diego Maradona. No one should have to suffer that treatment, thought Robson to himself, hoping against hope that the English fans were not indulging in this orgy of hate, but knowing in his heart that they were. His eyes moved across to the section of the stadium where they were housed, or secured more like, with massed ranks of Italian police keeping them apart from all of the other spectators. They were being treated as if they were savages but, sadly, they had brought it on themselves with their thuggish behaviour over the years; the horror of Heysel still fresh in Italian minds. It's time to show who we really are, vowed Robson to himself; time to rise above the past and be worthy kings once more.

· ·

English football was in poor shape at the beginning of the 20th century's final decade. If you wanted to watch a game then you would have no alternative other than to visit a decrepit stadium, often disfigured by vile racist chanting that would routinely go unpunished. Football hooliganism had dogged the game for many years and, despite much effort by the authorities to eradicate it, remained a stubborn thorn in its side.

The nation had wearily grown used to seeing shaven-headed yobs rampaging at football grounds at home and, even more embarrassingly, abroad. Their loutish behaviour muddied the game's reputation and was one of the principal causes of dwindling attendances, with many families wisely steering clear of the mini war-zones that blighted football grounds on a Saturday afternoon.

Aggregate attendances for league games had been declining since the 1950s, barring a blip after England won the World Cup in 1966, and reached their nadir in the 1985/86 season when they shrunk to a level half of that reached 30 years earlier.

It was hardly surprising that so few people went to watch football matches that year, given the dreadful events that had occurred at the end of the previous season. In May 1985, 56 spectators perished when fire engulfed a wooden stand at Bradford's Valley Parade ground and then, a couple of weeks later, 39 people died at the European Cup Final in the Heysel Stadium as they tried to escape rampaging Liverpool fans. UEFA, heartily sick of years of English hooliganism, duly banned all of their clubs from European competition, not just Liverpool.

During that period of exile the nation suffered a further tragedy when, in 1989, 96 Liverpool fans were crushed to death during an FA Cup semi-final at Hillsborough. The fences that had been erected to keep hooligans from encroaching on to the pitch now claimed the lives of innocent spectators, whose only crime was a desire to watch their team play football. Bradford, Heysel and Hillsborough were an unholy trinity of tragedies for English football; three massive nails knocked into its seemingly inevitable coffin.

The national game was clearly on its knees but, encouragingly, there was cause for a little cautious optimism. By the time of the 1990 World Cup aggregate league attendances had risen for four consecutive years, the first time since the Second World War that had happened. The Hillsborough disaster had also spurred the authorities into taking action to address its root causes, with Lord Justice Taylor's report into it recommending the introduction of all-seater stadia and the removal of the life-endangering security fences.

English clubs may have still been banned from European competition but the domestic game was healthy enough, with another fine Liverpool side gracing the league and a vibrant young Arsenal team rising up to challenge them. Nevertheless, the national game was still in desperate need of a fillip; some good news that it could rejuvenate itself with. Few held out much hope that the England side would be its source but, to everyone's great surprise, their 1990 World Cup adventure proved to be just that.

The man who led England to the World Cup finals was in his eighth and, as it transpired, last year in the job. Bobby

Robson was appointed as the manager of the national side in 1982, shortly after England's exit from the World Cup in Spain. The popular favourite for the post was the irascible Nottingham Forest manager Brian Clough but Robson, a far more diplomatic and accommodating figure, proved to be much more to the FA's liking.

His international managerial career didn't get off to the best of starts, however, with England failing to qualify for the 1984 European Championship finals after finishing second in their qualifying group behind Denmark; a 1-0 defeat at Wembley to the Danes effectively determining England's fate. That was Robson's first defeat in a qualifying game for a major championship but, impressively, it also turned out to be his last. While he was in charge of the national side England lost only one of 28 qualifying matches; a record that any manager would be proud of.

Robson had made his name as a manager with the unfashionable Suffolk club, Ipswich Town. He took over in 1969 and, after enduring a few difficult years, built a team that was capable of taking on much bigger sides. In his last ten years in charge of the club Ipswich only once finished outside the top six in the league, and that was in 1978 when they won the FA Cup with a surprise victory over Arsenal. Ipswich had their strongest spell in the two seasons before Robson became the England coach, with consecutive second-place finishes in the league and, most impressively, a UEFA Cup triumph.

Robson was a popular manager with his players, garnering their respect through his genuine, unquenchable zeal for the game. Like all great coaches he had a gift for making his players feel special, building them up to believe that they were capable of achieving great things which, more often than not, became a self-fulfilling prophecy.

Robson may have been a kind and likeable man, but that didn't protect him from suffering terrible abuse from the tabloid newspapers. They spent most of the 1980s vilifying him, especially after England had lost a game; their criticism of him harsh, unrelenting and, in hindsight, unwarranted. Robson went on to become the second-most successful manager in the history of the national side, staying loyal to his players when lesser men would have been tempted to lay some blame at their door when things occasionally went wrong.

Like Robson, Carlos Bilardo was appointed coach of the national side in the wake of the 1982 World Cup finals. Argentina had failed to defend the trophy they won at home four years earlier and with a change of personnel came a change of style. The previous incumbent, César Luis Menotti, a lank-haired socialist, advocated attacking football that entertained the crowds. Bilardo, by contrast, was an arch pragmatist whose instincts were frequently defensive, if not destructive. His sole objective was to win and every act had to serve that end, even if that meant berating his players when they kicked the ball out of play to help injured opponents obtain treatment.

The Argentinean squad bequeathed to Bilardo included the peerless, but all-too-human, Diego Maradona. His natural talent for football was evident at a young age, with the tyro demonstrating his ball-juggling skills on television before he was even a teenager. Capable of electric bursts of pace, Maradona could run with the ball as if it were attached to his feet and, despite only growing to a height of 5ft 5in, his strong build and exceptional balance gave him a low centre of gravity that made it extremely hard to knock him off the ball. Dribblers were supposed to belong to an earlier age but Maradona showed that, in the right feet, the art was far from dead.

When Argentina hosted the World Cup in 1978, Maradona was very nearly a part of it despite only being 17 years old. He was in Menotti's 25-man squad but was one of the three players discarded when the group had to be whittled down to 22. Menotti didn't feel that the young Maradona was mature enough to cope with the pressure of a World Cup that the hosts were expected to win and, with his best interests at heart, he decided to leave him out. Maradona had no choice other than to wait for four long years before fulfilling his dream to play at a World Cup finals but, when it finally came, it proved to be a frustrating and unsatisfying experience. A surprise 1-0 defeat in their opening game against Belgium resulted in Argentina finishing second in their group and being paired in the next round with Brazil and Italy. It was the toughest possible draw they could have got and when he came up against the very best defenders in the world, the relatively inexperienced 21-year-old Maradona came up short.

Maradona was still playing his club football in Argentina prior to the World Cup finals and he struggled when faced with an unfamiliar, watertight Italian defence. Argentina fell to a 2-1 defeat and worse was to come in the following game against Brazil. Maradona had managed to keep his composure against the Italians but was unable to contain his frustrations as Brazil comprehensively outplayed his side. Three minutes from the end of the game, with Argentina 3-0 down, he buried his foot deep into a Brazilian player's crotch and was duly sent off. The player who was supposed to set the 1982 World Cup on fire thus departed the competition in the most shameful of circumstances; dismissed for an act of childish petulance because the other boys wouldn't let him win.

Maradona moved to Barcelona after that debacle and completed the final stage of his footballing education, learning how to cope with the defensive methods that European sides employed as well as the faster pace of their game. When Bilardo was appointed as the coach of the national side his first move was to make Maradona the captain. The maverick midget had secretly longed for the post for years, amassing over 200 captain's armbands on his travels around the world in anticipation of the great day when he was appointed to lead the national team. Bilardo's decision thus proved to be a wise one, forming a bond between the two men that was to sustain them through two consecutive World Cup finals.

Bilardo built Argentina's 1986 World Cup squad around Maradona, doing all that he could to satisfy the diminutive genius's every whim. The authoritarian Bilardo devised a rigorous programme for his players, monitoring their diet, sleep and leisure activities closely but Maradona, in keeping with his elevated standing in the squad, was exempted from the tough regime, being allowed to do pretty much as he pleased. Bilardo's willingness to placate his captain clearly worked, with Maradona committing himself to the cause by regularly jetting backwards and forwards between Europe and South America so that he could play for the national side.

Bilardo unleashed his Maradona-led Argentina at the 1986 World Cup and his side opened the tournament with a victory, defeating South Korea 3-1 with all three goals being created by Maradona. A 1-1 draw with Italy followed, in which Maradona scored, and then a 2-0 victory over Bulgaria took Argentina into the second round where they met old rivals Uruguay. It was their first meeting in the World Cup since the 1930 final and this time it was the Argentineans that emerged victorious, winning 1-0. Bilardo's side had reached the quarter-finals and there they would play their other great historical enemy: England.

It is a given that the two nations most interested in the World Cup Final are those that are taking part in it, but this was particularly so for England's clash with Argentina. The game had the feel of a fierce local derby in which pride, honour and respect are at stake and, while the depth of feelings it invoked for the combatants were real enough, it left the rest of the world slightly cold. There were grievances here that had to be experienced to be truly understood and the other watching nations could only look on, puzzled by how two countries at opposite ends of the globe could possibly have become such implacable enemies.

The match that the rest of the world had wanted to see was Italy versus West Germany; the hosts against the best side in the tournament. They had both been defeated in the semi-finals and the watching neutrals didn't hold out much hope for the game that they were being served up with instead. Statisticians had calculated that the 1990 World Cup finals were on course to be the lowest scoring of the 14 held to date, and there was little prospect that the final would do much to alter that outcome. Both England's and Argentina's defences had been in impressive form, with Carlos Bilardo's side having conceded just three goals in six matches and Bobby Robson's side four. The final threatened to be a dour affair, but those that knew their football history knew better; England versus Argentina was many things, but it was never dull.

The match began, as expected, with a cavalcade of fouls. There was simply too much passion, too many unsettled scores, for the game to be anything but. Bobby Robson's side were on target to win the tournament's Fair Play award, but the composure and self-control that they had shown throughout the competition was now being sorely tested by the Argentineans. Ankles were clipped, shins kicked, hair pulled and nails dug into the softest, most vulnerable part of their anatomy. The English players were only human and they responded with their own particular brand of retribution; crunching tackles, jarring shoulder-barges and dead-eyed stares. There were 22 men on the pitch but all those watching, including the officials, knew in their hearts that number would be reduced before the game was over; the only question being by how many.

. . . .

The first encounter between England and Argentina took place at Wembley in 1951 and, in contrast to what was to come, it was a relatively civilised affair. The hosts won with a Jackie Milburn goal four minutes from time and few could have predicted the degree of enmity that the two nations would eventually have for each other.

The first signs of trouble came a couple of years later when England travelled to Argentina to play two games; a Buenos Aires League XI versus an FA League XI followed by a full international. The home side won the first game 3-1 but, to their frustration, the defeat was not recognised by the English who sniffily dismissed it as an unofficial friendly. The visitors made seven changes for the next match, bringing in all their big guns for the game that really did matter. Sadly, the argument as to which was the better of the two sides that year was never really settled; the game being abandoned after 22 minutes because of a waterlogged pitch with the two teams level at 0-0.

Relationships between England and Argentina were still pretty good up until this point, but that all changed in the 1960s as a succession of games altered each nation's perception of the other for the worse, and perhaps irrevocably. The third clash between the two nations (or the fourth if you're an Argentinean) came in the group stage of the 1962 World Cup finals in Chile. The English ran out clear 3-1 winners but many of their players were less than impressed with the behaviour of the Argentineans, protesting that the South Americans had kicked and punched them and stood on their heels. It was the first game between the two nations in which the dark side of Argentinean football had made an appearance but, sadly, it wasn't to be the last. If that encounter had left a bad taste in Englishmen's mouths, it would be as nothing compared to what was to come four years later.

England met Argentina in the quarter-finals of the 1966 World Cup and the outcome hinged on the dismissal of Antonio Rattín after 36 minutes. Argentina's 6ft 4in tall captain had been following the small German referee around for much of the game, constantly offering his opinions and protesting at his decisions. Rudolph Kreitlein eventually had enough of his authority being questioned and instructed Rattín to leave the pitch. Rattín refused to go and was soon joined on the pitch by his manager and an assortment of other Argentineans who all felt the need to get involved. They were duly followed by FIFA officials, and then the police, as the whole affair descended into a very sorry mess. Eight minutes of heated discussion and debate elapsed until Rattín finally accepted the inevitable and slowly walked off the pitch.

Without their captain the Argentinean ship was effectively holed beneath the water-line. They defended deeply for the remainder of the game, hoping that they could survive until the end of extra time and succeed in the coin-toss that would have determined the winners (penalty shoot-outs may be bad, but they are at least an improvement on what preceded them). Hurst's headed goal 13 minutes from the end of normal time put an end to that ploy and the Argentineans, with only ten men on the pitch, were in no position to respond.

Many of the England players subsequently complained about how the Argentineans had conducted themselves, attributing to them a long litany of offences, including kicking, spitting, pinching and ear-pulling. Alf Ramsey was so incensed with the treatment meted out to his players that he famously refused to allow them to swap shirts with their opponents at the end of the game. Ramsey may not have been one of life's natural diplomats but he surpassed himself afterwards by describing the Argentinean players as 'animals', thus single-handedly doing more damage to Anglo-Argentine relations than any other event prior to the invasion of the Falkland Islands.

The events of 1966 effectively cast the die for all subsequent clashes between England and Argentina, with the game starting a succession of grievances that both nations have added to over the years. Two years after the World Cup Argentina's Estudiantes de la Plata took on Manchester United in the Intercontinental Cup and, rather than take the opportunity to prove Ramsey wrong by showing their fairer side, they carried on where Rattín's team had left off, kicking and spitting their way through the two-legged tie. At the heart of this cynical team was one Carlos Bilardo, who was to be the source of much more misery for the English before he was done. Two 'friendly' matches were then played between England and Argentina in the 1970s and both of them had their unsavoury moments; the English captain Emlyn Hughes and Oscar Glaria exchanging blows at the end of the first half in the 1974 contest at Wembley and Trevor Cherry having his two front teeth knocked out by Daniel Bertoni in Buenos Aires in 1977.

There was then a brief, but perceptible, thaw in relations between the two countries after Argentina's victory at the 1978 World Cup. Two members of the winning squad, Osvaldo Ardiles and Ricardo Villa, signed for Tottenham Hotspur shortly after that triumph, a transfer the like of which may be routine today but which shocked and surprised English football in the late 1970s. The two Argentineans soon became very popular, not only in north London but all over the country. When Spurs reached the FA Cup Final in 1981 Ardiles even became the theme of their obligatory novelty record, 'Ossie's Dream'. The song reached number five in the pop charts and Villa's magnificent winning goal in the replay against Manchester City is still regularly voted as the best FA Cup Final goal of all time.

A year earlier, England and Argentina had met in a friendly at Wembley and, for once, it really was friendly. Out of respect for his newly adopted country Ardiles opted not to play, but he ended up missing a wonderful game of football that flowed from end to end and, refreshingly, was not persistently punctuated by foul play and cynicism. The hosts ran out 3-1 winners but the star of the night was not an Englishman. The Wembley crowd was enraptured by the 19-year-old Diego Maradona, standing to applaud him after he had slalomed his way past four defenders before steering his shot narrowly wide of the post. He, and they, wouldn't make the same mistake six years later.

For a few short years, it appeared that the relationship between England and Argentina had turned a corner. Then, on 2 April 1982, the Argentineans invaded the Falkland Islands. Before it was over hundreds of young men lost their lives in a conflict which, though it restored a measure of pride and prestige to an economically depressed England, appeared to belong to an earlier, colonial age. A few unseemly scuffles on a football pitch were one thing, but this was war in all its devilish horror.

The hostilities drew to a close just as that summer's World Cup was kicking off in Spain; England having qualified for the tournament while the Argentineans were automatically given a place as holders of the trophy. The two nations were in opposite halves of the draw and so couldn't meet unless they both progressed to the final. To the relief of FIFA that nightmarish vision never came to pass, with both England and Argentina failing to progress beyond the second round. Unsurprisingly, no friendly matches were arranged between the two nations in the following few years and so it was only at a World Cup finals that they could possibly meet. Fate decreed that they would.

Argentina reached the quarter-finals of the 1986 World Cup with relative ease while the English, by contrast, made rather a meal of it. An opening defeat to Portugal was followed by a desperate 0-0 draw with Morocco in which England lost their two top midfielders; Bryan Robson through injury and Ray Wilkins through dismissal. That left Bobby Robson's side staring down the barrel of elimination from the tournament with their last opponents being Poland, who had finished in third place at two out of the last three World Cups. To everyone's great surprise England then suddenly came alive, scoring three goals in 25 first-half minutes to beat the Poles, and they then dismissed Paraguay in the second round by the same scoreline.

England's six goals were all scored by a striking partnership introduced for the crucial game against Poland and then, unsurprisingly, retained for the tie with Paraguay. It was spearheaded by Gary Lineker, lethal penalty area predator and future football pundit. He started his career with hometown club Leicester City and then moved in 1985 to Everton for what proved to be a pivotal season in his career. He was the top goalscorer in England, and won both the Football Writers' and Players' Player of the Year awards and then the Golden Boot for finishing as the leading scorer at the World Cup. After that Lineker's career, and arguably his life, was never the same again.

A move to Barcelona followed shortly after and he proceeded to become the third-highest England scorer of all time, with an impressive 48 in 80 internationals. Lineker was adept at timing runs into the penalty area and finding space in which he could get a shot at goal, perfecting the art to such a degree that there were few more dangerous six-yard-area goal poachers in the world at the time.

Lineker's striking partner was the diminutive Geordie Peter Beardsley. He was not an out-and-out front-man like Lineker but acted instead as the link between midfield and attack, arguably being more of a midfield player that joined the attack than a forward that tracked back into midfield. Their partnership worked because they both gave each other the space to do what they did best; Lineker prowling inside the penalty area while Beardsley played further out, taking defenders with him and thus making the penalty area less crowded for his striking partner. Those seeking proof of the effectiveness of their relationship need look no further than this fact: Lineker scored 25 of his 48 goals for England in the 29 games that he played alongside Beardsley.

Robson's side's other great strength was its defence, which had conceded only one goal in four World Cup matches prior to meeting Argentina. At its base was arguably England's finest ever goalkeeper, Peter Shilton. Robson's predecessor, Ron Greenwood, had been unable to decide who his first-choice goalkeeper should be so often selected Peter Shilton and Ray Clemence for alternate matches. One of Robson's first acts as England coach was to end this peculiar arrangement, making Shilton his number one.

Shilton was rarely out of the England side over the following eight years, eventually becoming the nation's most capped player with 125 appearances. One particularly impressive aspect of Shilton's career was its longevity. He set a national record by playing over 1,000 league matches and his England career stretched over two decades. He made his debut for the national side in 1970 (when the youngest member of England's 1990 World Cup squad was still only three years old) and made his final appearance at the age of 40. During that period Shilton played in 17 World Cup finals matches, a British record, and established a world record by keeping clean sheets in ten of them.

Playing in front of Shilton was the imposing centre-half Terry Butcher. He may have lacked pace and sophistication but had character in abundance. Some players, when faced with a hostile crowd away from home, can almost vanish on the pitch but Butcher positively revelled in such occasions, being inspired by them rather than overawed. Never one to shirk his responsibilities, the aptly named Butcher threw himself into 50-50 challenges without hesitation and, more often than not, came out of the collision with the ball at his feet. At 6ft 4in tall

Butcher used his stature to intimidate the opposition, snarling and fist-shaking his way through matches. He was often no easier on his team-mates, shouting and screaming at them before a game to get them motivated for the challenge ahead.

Butcher started his career at Ipswich Town under Robson's tutelage and was a key member of the side that won the UEFA Cup in 1981. He won the vast majority of his 77 caps under Robson, but it would be a mistake to attribute his lengthy international career to misplaced favouritism. Butcher played eight times for England before Robson took over as manager and was a key part of the England defence that conceded just one goal in five matches at the 1982 World Cup.

The 1986 World Cup quarter-final between England and Argentina was the first competitive clash between the two nations since the infamous match in 1966 when Rattín was dismissed and their first meeting since the Falklands War. Both sides made the right noises prior to kick-off, stressing that they were there just to play a game of football and refusing to answer any questions from journalists that veered into the realms of international politics. The truth, however, was that England were facing an Argentinean side burning to take revenge for the injustice and humiliation that they believed had been heaped on them by the English over the previous two decades.

The first half was fairly uneventful, with neither side making any clear-cut chances, but in a four-minute spell early in the second half the game suddenly burst into life, and not without a little controversy. England midfielder Steve Hodge attempted to clear the ball away from the edge of his own penalty area but instead sliced it back towards his own goal. Maradona immediately seized the opportunity, dashing for the ball at the same time as the England goalkeeper. Shilton was a little slow coming off his line, thus allowing Maradona to jump for the ball a fraction of a second ahead of him.

If the diminutive Argentinean had attempted to head the ball then Shilton would have punched it to safety with ease, but Maradona didn't do that. Instead he flicked his left wrist at the ball, sending it above Shilton's clenched fist and into the unguarded net. The referee, who clearly didn't see what had happened, awarded a goal and was immediately surrounded by incensed Englishmen who tried desperately to alert him to what Maradona had done. It was to no avail and the goal, which Maradona infamously later attributed to the 'Hand of God', stood.

No sooner were England trying to get one goal back than they were left needing a second, with one moment of shameless cheating being followed by one of sublime beauty. In an echo of his effort at Wembley six years earlier, Maradona ran with the ball from near the halfway line, evaded the challenges of four Englishman and then slid the ball past Shilton. 'You have to say that's magnificent,' said Barry Davies, commentating on the game for the BBC. And it was.

England duly fought back, Lineker scoring his sixth goal of the tournament and then almost netting again in the game's dying minutes, but it wasn't to be. The day belonged to Argentina, and to Maradona in particular, who in a few short minutes had shown the genius and devilry that was to define his career. As the dust settled it was England's turn to feel cheated, just as Rattín and his side had 20 years earlier. While Argentina attributed their victory to Maradona's majestic second goal, England blamed their defeat on his brazen handball. And so the story of England versus Argentina turned, with injustice following injustice and grievance following grievance. Of such tales are true epics made.

Argentina never looked back after beating England, going on to beat Belgium in the semi-finals and then West Germany in the final. Football is supposed to be a team game but, in 1986, Maradona made even the fiercest devotees of team sports doubt it. Never before or since has one individual dominated a World Cup finals as Maradona did in Mexico, single-handedly making an ordinary side into the champions of the world. It was a tribute to his talent that, even when among the best players in the world, he was able to stand head and shoulders above them all.

One curious postscript to Argentina's 1986 World Cup victory is the rather bizarre reaction of their irascible coach, Carlos Bilardo. One would have expected him to have been jubilant but, rather bizarrely, that was not the case. He prided himself on how well his teams defended set pieces, the fruits of hours of careful practice, but in an eight-minute spell the Germans scored twice from corner kicks to level the game. Bilardo was livid, and even the small matter of his side scoring a winning goal five minutes from time couldn't settle him down.

While his players gleefully celebrated their triumph, the inconsolable Bilardo retired to his hotel room to brood alone. It wasn't conventional behaviour, but then Bilardo was not a particularly conventional man. He had qualified as a doctor and practised as a gynaecologist but, despite being a man of science, was still quite superstitious, even refusing to allow his players to eat chicken as he believed it brought bad luck.

. . . .

One of the encounters that most people wanted to see was Terry Butcher being reunited with Diego Maradona; the English defender with the build of a lumberjack and the slippery, but oh-so-talented, Argentinean striker. The last time that the two men had been together was in a small room following England's defeat to Argentina in the quarter-finals of the 1986 World Cup. They had both been selected for a routine drugs test and, while they waited, unable to exchange words, had used sign language to discuss Maradona's controversial first goal. Butcher queried how it had been converted and his bête noire responded by clarifying that he had scored it with his head. A clear lie, but given that he was confronting a very angry man who was almost a foot taller, a perfectly understandable one.

Butcher undoubtedly wanted to mete out some retribution after what had happened four years earlier, but he resolutely resisted the temptation; focusing on the game in hand rather than on settling old scores. He wasn't the only veteran of that previous clash, with Shilton, Beardsley, Lineker and Waddle also re-acquainting themselves with the Argentineans that had ended their last assault on the World Cup. In a perfect world, they would have conquered their demons by beating the same XI that they had faced in Mexico, but Bilardo's side had moved on since then, with only Maradona, Burruchaga and Ruggeri surviving from that previous encounter.

The first half ended up fulfilling the fears of the neutrals as there were few clear-cut chances for either side, just a seemingly endless blur of recriminations and reprimands. The Mexican referee clearly had his work cut out as he tried in vain to create a flowing game of football from the most unpromising of materials. The laws of the game required him to halt play every time a foul was committed, but doing so only succeeded in killing off whatever little momentum the match developed. It was therefore with a heavy heart that he blew his whistle to bring the goalless first half to an end; a World Cup Final deserved to be so much better than this.

• •

Argentina automatically qualified for the 1990 World Cup as the defending champions, but England had to get there the hard way. They were drawn in a group alongside Poland, Sweden and Albania, with the winners being assured of a place in the finals while the runners-up only went through if they were one of the two best-placed teams in the three UEFA qualifying groups composed of four teams.

The Poles were initially considered to pose the greatest threat to England's prospects, but it turned out to be the Swedes who should have been most feared. They visited Wembley for England's first qualification match and came away with a creditable 0-0 draw. The press was unimpressed with the result and Robson came under even greater pressure a month later when his side could manage only a 1-1 draw in a friendly with Saudi Arabia, with one outraged tabloid responding with the venomous headline, 'In The Name of Allah, Go'. Robson stayed and guided England to successive victories over Albania (2-0 away from home and then 5-0 at Wembley), which took them to the top of the qualifying group. England's next game was at home to Poland and, given that they had already dropped a point to the Swedes at Wembley, a victory was imperative. Robson's men didn't let him down, cruising to a 3-0 victory.

England's penultimate qualifying game was away to Sweden and while a victory would have been welcome, what Robson's side needed to do most of all was avoid defeat. They managed to achieve that, with the 0-0 scoreline mirroring the result of their previous encounter at Wembley, but the occasion is best remembered for Butcher's display of heroics after clashing heads with a Swedish striker. He played on despite blood streaming from his wound, his white shirt ultimately ending up the same colour as those worn by his predecessors when they won the World Cup in 1966. That result meant that Robson and his men needed just a draw in their final fixture away to Poland in order to qualify for the finals. The Poles, who had three matches still to play, were still in with a chance of qualifying themselves, however, so were hardly lacking in motivation.

The game was played in Katowice, a grim city deep in the heart of Poland's mining heartland. The Poles often played important games there, knowing that the venue would discomfort the opposition, and they duly had the best of the night, dominating possession and putting the English defence under incredible pressure. Shilton put in a superb performance, belying his 40 years with some excellent saves. The pressure gradually began to recede as the Poles ran out of energy and ideas but then, in the final minute, Tarasiewicz hit a venomous strike from 25 yards that evaded Shilton's reach before cannoning back off the crossbar. If the ball had gone in the net there would barely have been time for England to restart the game, let alone find an equaliser. The result meant that Robson's side finished second in their group behind Sweden and qualified for the finals, but only by virtue of that single hard-won point.

Most of the credit for England's qualification had to be given to the side's defenders. Not only did they hold out away to Sweden and Poland, but they also did not concede a single goal in any of their other group matches. Alongside Shilton and Butcher in that watertight defence were two Nottingham Forest players, Des Walker and Stuart Pearce. Walker's chief attribute was his pace, which he used to great effect to stop strikers from getting into goalscoring positions. He was at his peak in 1990, consistently putting in strong performances for Forest and England and eventually attracting the attention of future England coach Sven-Göran Eriksson who took him to Sampdoria in 1992.

The side's left-back, Pearce grew up in the shadow of Wembley Stadium, though there was little in his early career to suggest that he would play 78 times for his country. After failing a trial with Queens Park Rangers, Pearce played non-league football with Wealdstone for several seasons while working as an electrician for Brent Council. His potential was eventually spotted by Coventry City and Pearce grabbed the opportunity, playing so well for them that Brian Clough signed him for Nottingham Forest. Scarcely believing his luck, Pearce continued to work as an electrician in his spare time, even advertising his services in the Forest matchday programme. Pearce's caution was unjustified as not only did he become an irreplaceable member of Clough's side but, within two years of joining Forest, he had also made his debut for the national side.

Pearce was an infamously aggressive defender who would have no compunction about clattering into an opposition player if he felt that he was having too much of an impact on the game. The Forest fans affectionately nicknamed their fiery, snarling hero 'Pyscho'; his no-nonsense style of playing, non-league roots and the fact that he had done a 'real job' before becoming a professional footballer all helping to make him a genuine working-class hero. Though Pearce was undoubtedly hard he was never reckless, being booked only five times during his England career and never being sent off. While he was not particularly quick or especially skilful, Pearce could hit the ball with devastating pace and scored many goals from free kicks and penalties as a result.

The Football Association organised a number of friendly matches to help Robson prepare his side for the finals, with their fixture against Czechoslovakia proving to be pivotal for their fortunes in Italy. Given the impact that he was to make at the 1990 World Cup, it seems curious now that Paul Gascoigne wasn't an automatic selection for Robson's squad. The England manager was well aware of Gascoigne's burgeoning natural talent, but wanted to be convinced that he could apply it at the highest level of the game before including him in his group for Italy. The young midfielder was a frustratingly inconsistent player, being just as capable of destroying himself as the opposition, as his later career demonstrated so effectively.

Robson introduced Gascoigne to international football slowly, carefully nurturing his talent. Gascoigne played seven times for England prior to the friendly against Czechoslovakia, but only came on as a late substitute in six of them. One of those substitute appearances came in England's home victory over Albania, when he scored one goal and set up another. Rather than viewing Gascoigne's performance as a triumph, Robson complained that there should have been two balls on the pitch: one for the young midfielder and one for the rest of his team. While England fans dreamt of Gascoigne waltzing through defences to score the winning goal in the World Cup Final, Robson had nightmares about the maverick Geordie giving the ball away in dangerous positions and handing the game to the opposition. Gascoigne was still very much an unproven quantity at international level and so Robson needed to be persuaded that he was mature enough to cope with the strains and stresses of a World Cup.

Gascoigne's last chance to make it into Robson's squad for the finals came in the friendly against Czechoslovakia, less than two months before the start of the tournament. He knew that his future lay in his own hands, or more accurately, at his feet, and he responded by showing just what he was capable of, both good and ill. Clearly tense and agitated, Gascoigne's performance was initially energetic but lacked direction and he had to be told to settle down by the referee after a couple of rash tackles that could easily have resulted in a booking. Once Gascoigne calmed down, however, he became the most impressive player on the pitch; setting up England's first three goals before scoring the fourth. England won 4-2 and a suitably convinced Robson knew that Gascoigne was a risk he could no longer afford not to take.

Gascoigne's future England career may have looked bright, but sadly the same could not be said for Robson. In the run-up to the World Cup, Football Association secretary Bert Millichip told the press that Robson would have to win the tournament if he was to keep his job. Dutch side PSV Eindhoven spied an opportunity to recruit an experienced international coach and acted quickly, approaching Robson about becoming their manager. Robson's contract only lasted until January 1991 and, naturally concerned about his future, he asked Millichip to give him an indication as to whether he would be offered a new one. Robson failed to receive any guarantees about his future employment so obtained permission to speak to the Dutch club about their vacancy. This inevitably leaked out to the press and the tabloids had a field day, accusing Robson, among other things, of betraying his country. The criticism was harsh and unfair, but Robson had come to learn over the years that the press rarely presented reports about the England manager in a reasonable and balanced way.

Meanwhile, the years between the 1986 and 1990 World Cups were rather forgettable for Argentina. A year after their triumph in Mexico the world champions hosted the Copa America, the South American equivalent of the European Championships. Argentina were expected to coast to victory, especially as they were playing at home but it didn't turn out that way. Maradona was tired after the end of a long season in Europe, was troubled by injury and, to top it all, he had also come down with the flu. A victory over Ecuador and a draw with Peru was sufficient for the hosts to qualify for the semi-finals, but they then lost that game to Uruguay 1-0, their neighbours gaining a measure of revenge for their defeat in the World Cup a year earlier. Bilardo's dispirited side then capped their misery by losing the third-place match to Colombia. One win, one draw and two defeats on home soil was hardly the form of champions.

If the summer of 1987 had been one for Argentina to forget then 1988 proved to be even worse. West Germany were hosting the European Championship finals that year and they organised a 'Four Nations Cup' as a warm-up event, inviting Argentina, the USSR and Sweden to take part. Bilardo's side met a strong Soviet side in the semi-finals, crashing to a 4-2 defeat, and then lost 1-0 to the Germans in the third-place match. There may not have been too much shame in losing to the Soviets and Germans, but the same could not be said of their next defeat. Argentina travelled to Australia to take part in a four-team tournament organised as part of the nation's bicentenary celebrations. Their first two matches both ended in draws; a disappointing 2-2 stalemate with Saudi Arabia, followed by a more acceptable 0-0 draw with Brazil. But then they suffered real humiliation. They were thrashed 4-1 by Australia who, though playing at home, could not have been described at the time as being anything more than a minor football nation.

Given the disappointments of the previous two years, Bilardo was in desperate need of a decent performance at the 1989 Copa America. The tournament started well enough for his side, with Argentina finishing top of their first-round group. The four nations that qualified for the final stage of the competition formed a group in which each side played each other, rather than playing semi-finals and then a final. Maradona, again complaining of tiredness and injury, desperately wanted to win a Copa America, but was unable to prevent his side from disappointing their fans once more. Argentina succumbed to consecutive 2-0 defeats to Brazil and Uruguay and could then only draw 0-0 with Paraguay. It was a blessing for Argentina that, as holders of the World Cup, they were automatically granted a place in the following year's tournament. If they had needed to qualify their poor form might have prevented them from getting to Italy at all.

The root cause of Argentina's decline was a gradual, but perceptible, diminution in the quality of Maradona's performances. His cocaine habit steadily reduced his effectiveness as a footballer and his other, wide-ranging, extra-curricular activities hardly helped. Argentina played five matches in 1990 prior to the World Cup finals but won only one. There were defeats to Mexico and Scotland and draws with Austria and Switzerland, none of whom had particularly strong teams. An away victory over Israel in their final game before the World Cup restored a little hope, but Argentina's fans must have feared that their stay in Italy would be a short one. Bilardo opted to stay loyal to those that had served him well in Mexico, retaining seven of the side that beat West Germany in his squad. He was much more ruthless with the remainder of the 1986 squad, however, discarding 15 of them and replacing them with a new generation of talent.

One of the players that Bilardo brought in after 1986 was the flaxen-haired striker with the looks of a rock star: Claudio Caniggia. He played in the forward line alongside Maradona and the two men soon struck up a good partnership on the pitch, as well as becoming strong companions off it. Indeed, Maradona was so impressed with Caniggia that he told Bilardo that he wouldn't play in the finals unless his friend was selected. Caniggia was one of the fastest footballers ever to play the game, making quite an impression when he ran at full pace against opposition defences with his long, golden locks flowing in the wind.

In keeping with recent tradition Argentina, as winners of the previous World Cup, played the opening game of the 1990 tournament. Their opponents from Cameroon were a relatively unknown quantity, but they were not expected to cause the reigning champions too many problems. In a decision that was bound to irritate his captain, Bilardo opted not to include Caniggia in the starting line-up for the game against Cameroon. It was a curious decision, especially given that an injured toe prevented Maradona from being fully fit.

The match was played in the newly renovated San Siro stadium in front of a Milanese crowd that were clearly on the side of the underdogs. They cheered the Africans to the rafters, while whistling the Argentineans, and especially Maradona, for all they were worth. Not much was expected of the unknown Africans, especially given that they were being coached by a Siberian who didn't even speak the same language as his players. Naturally wary of the champions, Cameroon started the match by defending in large numbers and the Argentineans duly had the best of the opening minutes. As the first half wore on, however, the Africans came to realise that they were playing a team that they had no need to be frightened of. Bilardo's uninventive and uninspired side soon started to give ground and it was the Africans that came closest to scoring in the first half, with Lorenzo having to clear the ball off his goal line to prevent an own goal.

Belatedly recognising his error, Bilardo brought on Caniggia for the start of the second half in place of a defender. The change in personnel also allowed Maradona to play a little deeper and avoid the worst of the Africans' tackling. Cameroon had two brothers playing in their side but, within a six-minute spell, their fortunes diverged widely. First, Kana Biyick was sent off for tripping Caniggia, though it did appear accidental, and then Omam Biyick leapt athletically above the Argentinean defence to head the ball into the net from a free kick. It was hardly a classic goal, with the ball squirming under the body of the goalkeeper who really should have done a lot better.

Admirably, the Africans kept coming forward, looking to increase their lead rather than to just hold on to it. Then, two minutes from the end of the game, Caniggia raced up the pitch with the ball in a desperate search for the equaliser. He managed to hurdle two hefty challenges, but was unable to avoid the third, with the giant Massing colliding with him so heavily that the African lost a boot in the process. It certainly wasn't an advert for the beautiful game and Massing was rightly dismissed by the referee, leaving Cameroon with just nine men on the pitch. The Africans may have had virtually the entire world on their side, but few of those watching could defend their attempts to stop Caniggia, their tackles being as clumsy as they were reckless.

Cameroon's nine men managed to hold on for a famous triumph, though their subsequent progress to the quarter-finals did allow their surprise victory to be seen in its proper context. Maradona, who was clearly not in the imperious form that he had been in Mexico, duly blamed the defeat on others: the referee for not protecting him from the Africans' harsh tackling and Bilardo for not picking Caniggia from the start. The Argentinean coach admitted that it was the worst defeat of his career and later tried to lift his players' spirits in his own unique way, telling them that if they were going to get knocked out playing like that then he hoped the plane crashed on their journey home.

• •

The start of the second half witnessed a renewed effort by England, their forward plays digging deeper and deeper into the Argentinean defence. The driving force behind the attacks was Gascoigne; a brash, ebullient presence whose passes probed and prodded the soft belly of the Argentinean rearguard. The best player in the world was supposed to be the tubby maestro in the dark blue shirt, but it was England's own podgy genius who was showing him how the game should be played. The second period was only a few minutes old when Gascoigne charged at the heart of the Argentinean defence with the ball at his feet, evading lunges from Lorenzo and Serrizuela before thumping a shot at goal which Goycochea did well to push on to the crossbar.

The other England player most troubling Bilardo's side was Gary Lineker. They may have known all about him after their last clash in Mexico, but stopping him was another matter altogether. Monzón, who had replaced Ruggeri at half-time, was having difficulty tracking Lineker's runs, having to rely more than once on Juan Simón to nick the ball off the English striker as he readied himself to strike at goal. Lineker was inevitably on the end of a number of rough challenges, some of which were designed just to deprive him of the ball while others definitely had more sinister intent. To his credit the Englishman retained his composure, refusing to retaliate when every sinew in his body must have screamed for revenge.

Peter Beardsley was also suffering, being constantly kicked and jostled from behind. Ten minutes into the second half he received the ball a few yards outside the penalty area, shielding it as best he could from Serrizuela who climbed all over his back. Beardsley turned swiftly to face the goal and immediately felt his legs collapse beneath him, hearing the referee's whistle as his face thudded on to the turf. The position of the free kick was tailor-made for Stuart Pearce, who strode up confidently and took the ball out of Lorenzo's hands, staring at him remorselessly as he did so. Goycochea lined the defensive wall up well enough, but there was little he could do to stem the pace of Pearce's shot; a rifle blast that shaved the heads of the Argentinean defenders as it rocketed into the roof of the net. As England's supporters celebrated wildly the Italian police looked on nervously, not knowing which would be worse; Englishmen raging in defeat or Englishmen drunk on victory.

• •

There were good grounds for being both optimistic and pessimistic about England's chances of success at the World Cup. On the one hand, Robson's side had qualified for the finals without losing a game or even conceding a goal; having lost only once in 19 outings prior to going to Italy. On the other hand, however, their qualification had been a mightily close thing: if the shot from Tarasiewicz in the game against Poland had been an inch or two lower then they wouldn't have been going at all. Consequently, few believed that England had much chance of returning home with the trophy and that doubt hardened when the draw for the first round was made. Rather bafflingly, England were one of the six top seeds but they still had the misfortune to be paired with the Netherlands, who were the reigning European champions, Jack Charlton's upcoming Republic of Ireland side and Egypt.

The draw seemed almost to have been designed to bring back bad memories for Robson's team. England had qualified for the 1988 European Championships in West Germany with ease and went there as one of the favourites to win the trophy. Their first-round group, which included the Netherlands, the Republic of Ireland and the USSR, looked tough but manageable. A victory in the opening game against the Irish was expected but, despite playing well, they somehow lost 1-0. Next up were the great Dutch side of Gullit, Rijkaard and Van Basten and England matched them for an hour, before eventually falling to a 3-1 defeat. Those two defeats eliminated England from the tournament and a meek 3-1 loss to the USSR in their final game piled further misery on their travelling fans. England would not only have to face the Irish and the Dutch again in Italy, but the sequence of matches would also be the same. It was almost as if Bobby Robson had failed his GCSE in international football management and was being forced to take a re-sit.

Robson pinned a lot of his hopes on the team's two wingers, Chris Waddle and John Barnes. Like Stuart Pearce, Waddle had started his career in non-league football after failing several trials with professional clubs. He spent a couple of seasons playing for Tow Law Town in County Durham while working full-time in a sausage seasoning factory, before finally getting his chance with Newcastle United. Waddle soon made his way into the first team and went on to play alongside Peter Beardsley and Kevin Keegan in the side that won promotion back to the First Division in 1984. His career took off after that, with a move to Tottenham Hotspur and his

England debut both coming in the following year. Waddle's excellent technique, creativity and adeptness at running past defenders with the ball attracted the attentions of foreign clubs and in 1989 he moved to France to play for Olympique de Marseille.

Robson's first choice on the left was Jamaican-born Barnes, an exciting player who could dribble his way through crowded back-lines, make defence-splitting passes and score memorable goals. He started his career with Watford, helping them to gain promotion to the First Division for the first time in their history in 1982, and then joined Liverpool in 1987 for what proved to be his finest years as a footballer. Barnes won a league title in 1988, the FA Cup in 1989 and was at his peak in 1990, having been the most impressive cog in the Liverpool machine that steamrollered their way to another championship. He scored 28 goals for his club that season and was also voted Footballer of the Year by the press. Barnes was undoubtedly a fine player but he often struggled to replicate his wondrous club form for his country, the reasons for which were endlessly discussed at the time but, frustratingly, seemed to elude full explanation.

England's opening game was against the Republic of Ireland and, with almost 80 per cent of the players that started the game plying their trade for English clubs, both sides knew just what to expect. England succeeded in drawing first blood with Lineker scoring after just nine minutes. He managed to get on to the end of a superb through-ball from Waddle, evading the Irish keeper who tried to bring him down with an outstretched leg and then keeping his feet long enough to be able to poke the ball across the line.

The English ought to have killed the Irish off after that early goal but instead they held back, allowing themselves to be dragged into an unseemly scrap with a team that specialised in harrying opponents and disrupting their rhythm. The Irish, led by English World Cup winner Jack Charlton, could hardly be described as exponents of the beautiful game; their football functional, pragmatic and heavily reliant on long balls being thumped up to the strikers. Barnes had two Irish players tracking his every move and, as the game wore on, he became pretty much imperceptible. Waddle was playing well, however, and after an hour of play he went on a mazy run that took him past a couple of defenders and into the Irish penalty area. Kevin Moran brought him crashing to the floor but, inexplicably, the German referee failed to award a penalty that could have sealed England's victory.

In an attempt to stiffen the midfield and protect the slender lead, Robson took off Peter Beardsley and replaced him with Liverpool's central-midfield enforcer Steve McMahon. He had only been on the field for a few minutes when he lost the ball on the edge of England's penalty area and Kevin Sheedy pounced on his mistake, dispatching a hard shot past Shilton into the corner of the net. England came back at the Irish and tried to restore their lead, with Terry Butcher having their best chance shortly before the end of the game when he had a free header at goal following a free kick. If he had directed the ball back across the Irish keeper then he probably would have scored but, instead, he tried to head inside the near post and succeeded only in steering his effort embarrassingly wide of the net.

The game duly ended in a 1-1 draw and, while no one could fault the effort put in by both sides, it had been a poor match to watch. The spectacle had not been helped by the weather which the English and Irish appeared to have brought with them, the strong winds and driving rain being more typical of a league game in February than a World Cup match played in the Sardinian summer. An unimpressed Italian newspaper led with the headline 'No football, please, we're British' while *The Sun*, disappointed with England's second successive failure to beat the Irish in a major tournament, demanded that the

English team be brought home. It was an inauspicious start for Robson's side and their next match was against the Dutch, the reigning European champions. It was a game that England fans feared they would have to watch from behind their fingers.

England may not have had the winning start that they wanted but they were still in a much better position than Argentina, whose opening defeat to Cameroon meant that they would be eliminated if they lost their next game to the USSR. In a nod to his medical training, Bilardo took a scalpel to the side that had been humiliated against Cameroon, dropping five of the players that had started that game and giving Caniggia, who had now proved his worth, his first start of the tournament. The game was only nine minutes old when Bilardo suffered another setback; his goalkeeper, Nery Pumpido, breaking his leg in a clash with one of his own team-mates. Pumpido had a dreadful tournament, conceding a poor goal against Cameroon and then being stretchered off the pitch in agony in his next game, a victim of friendly fire.

Replacing Pumpido in goal was Sergio Goycochea, who was to have quite an impact on the tournament before it was over. Three minutes later the Soviets were denied a clear penalty when Maradona, in a sad echo of events four years earlier, handled a goalbound header as he stood at the near post defending a corner. The referee, standing only a few feet away from Maradona and with no players between them must surely have seen it, but somehow didn't. It was the first piece of good fortune that the Argentineans had experienced in the tournament and from that moment on things started to look up for them. If a penalty had been awarded against them, and the Soviets had scored, then perhaps Argentina would have disappeared without trace, but on such moments can entire campaigns turn.

Within 15 minutes Argentina were in front; Troglio scoring with a fine header from a cross by Olarticoechea, though the goal was due in no small measure to the Soviet defence's shambolic marking. The USSR were then reduced to ten men two minutes into the second half when Caniggia claimed his third victim of the competition; Bessonov sent off for tugging the golden boy's shirt and pushing him to the floor when he was clear through on goal. Once again, Caniggia's pace had caused a defender to commit a rash challenge and be dismissed as a result. Then, 12 minutes from the end, Burruchaga latched on to a dreadfully misplaced back pass and made certain of the victory. The Soviets were out, but the Argentineans were still alive and kicking, just.

Three days later England took on the Netherlands and Robson shocked the watching world by making key changes to his team. He had been a fierce defender of the 4-4-2 formation in his eight years as England manager, regularly dismissing demands from the press that he field a five-man defence as many continental nations commonly did at the time. Robson had long argued that it made sense to stick with a system that the players understood but, on the verge of one of his most important games as England manager, he dramatically changed tack and selected a team that included five defenders. It has never been clear whether this was his own initiative, or a result of senior players asking him to change the formation. Perhaps, in the end, it was a bit of both. Robson had seen his four-man defence torn to shreds by Gullit and Van Basten in the European Championships two years earlier and was acutely aware that something would have to change if England were to avoid a repeat of that debacle.

Robson had to remodel his team to accommodate the change of strategy, bringing in Paul Parker as a wing-back and Mark Wright as the side's sweeper. A forward had to be sacrificed to accommodate the extra defender and it was Beardsley who stepped aside, with Barnes coming infield to play alongside Lineker. The replacement of a striker with a defender would, at first glance, appear to be a defensive move but, counter-intuitively, it actually made England more adventurous. With three central defenders to guard the goal Pearce and Parker had greater freedom to attack on the wings, while Gascoigne had greater licence to surge forward without having to worry about leaving the defence unprotected.

Against all expectations, England had the best of the game against the Dutch. Des Walker shackled Van Basten while Rijkaard was kept so busy trying to keep Barnes and Lineker in check that he struggled to break out of defence. Gascoigne, meanwhile, was simply brilliant. Even Parker, who had never played as a wing-back before, responded with a performance so adept that no one watching the game would have guessed at his inexperience in the role.

England played well in the first half but it was in the second period that they had their best chances to score. They twice got the ball into the Dutch net but both goals were rightly disallowed, the first for a handball by Lineker and the second because no Dutchman got a touch on Pearce's indirect free kick.

Lineker had a good chance to score in between those two incidents, but sliced his shot wide of the net following a delightful exchange of passes with Barnes. Then Steve Bull, who had been brought on for Waddle, was presented with a glorious opportunity to score. Lineker lofted a fine ball into Bull's path as he accelerated into the penalty area but, with only the Dutch keeper in front of him, he directed his header well wide of the goal. There was still time for Gascoigne to evade two Dutch defenders with a beautiful piece of skill on the byline, before sending an inviting cross into the six-yard area that narrowly escaped Lineker's reach. England deserved to win but they just couldn't get the goal that their performance merited; the match duly ending in a 0-0 draw. Robson's side might not have won a game at the World Cup yet but there were, at long last, good grounds for some cautious optimism.

• •

England's goal brought the Argentineans out fighting, Bilardo screaming at his players from the sidelines and Maradona urging his team forward. They soon pushed the English back towards their own goal and threatened to overwhelm them, firing searing shots at Shilton. Des Walker had contained Maradona magnificently in the first half, diligently tracking his every move and never allowing him to turn with the ball at his feet. Indeed, he was so successful that the Argentinean captain had voluntarily moved back down the pitch in order to escape his attentions. This should have been a positive development for Robson's side but it actually worked out to Argentina's advantage, with Maradona finding more space in which to work his magic.

Argentina's first decent chance to level the scores came midway through the second period, when Maradona collected the ball deep within his own half and swayed swiftly between two desperate Englishmen who feared that he was going to repeat his glorious solo effort from four years earlier. Seeing Walker bearing down on him, Maradona quickly flicked the ball into the path of Troglio while continuing his forward run. Troglio headed up the left wing with the ball, attracting the attentions of Paul Parker who carefully shepherded him away towards the touchline. A rapid back-heel dispatched the ball to Sensini and he curled a pass into the path of Maradona who, 20 yards from goal, caught the ball full on the volley. His shot rose and then dipped sharply through the night air, forcing a magnificent save from Shilton who tipped it over the bar with his fingertips.

That scare re-ignited Robson's side, sending them forward in search of a second goal that would surely see the Argentineans off. Waddle was having a fine game on the right wing, combining well with Parker and taking full advantage of the absence of full-backs in Bilardo's 3-5-2 formation. His best move of the match came after his fellow Geordie, Gascoigne, hit a delightful cross-field pass straight to his feet. Waddle advanced at the rapidly retreating Monzón, constraining the speed of his run as he waited for Parker to pass him on the overlap. Sensing his team-mate's arrival behind him, Waddle nonchalantly knocked the ball into the space behind Monzón, knowing that Parker would get there first. The England right-back did just that, immediately cutting the ball back to Waddle whose shot from the edge of the penalty area cannoned back off the post before being cleared to safety by a much-relieved Serrizuela.

· ·

Argentina's final group game was against Romania, with their playmaker, Gheorghe Hagi, 'the Maradona of the Carpathians', taking the opportunity to show the real one how the game should be played. Romania dominated possession of the ball and created the best chances, but it was the Argentineans who scored the game's opening goal. They won a corner and Maradona took it, floating a ball into the six-yard area for Monzón to head past the goalkeeper. It was a great moment for the tall defender, but fate would have darker things in store for him before the competition was over.

The Romanians stormed forward in search of the equaliser that their play deserved, missing one glorious opportunity before Balint scored with a header that Goycochea had little chance of saving. Romania only needed a draw to ensure their qualification for the second round and, having got back on level terms, they were content to keep possession of the ball and let the match peter out. Bilardo's side had been outplayed for the second time in three games but, in the end, it didn't matter; they had still made it through.

England's group, meanwhile, was delicately poised prior to the final set of games, with all four teams having earned the same number of points and scored and conceded the same number of goals. The Egyptians had surprisingly held the Dutch to a 1-1 draw in their opening game and then secured another point in a sterile 0-0 draw with the Republic of Ireland. That meant if the teams still couldn't be separated after they had completed their third matches, FIFA would have to determine the qualifiers by drawing lots. That prospect didn't appeal much to Robson so he set out to win the game against the Africans by reverting to his usual 4-4-2 formation, clearly not fearing the Egyptians anywhere near as much as he had the Dutch.

England's clash with Egypt turned out to be another poor game, just as their tie against the Irish had been, with Barnes and Waddle contributing little on the wings. The Egyptians were initially content to play for a draw, passing the ball around their defence without much intention of doing anything more adventurous.

England toiled away and finally got the breakthrough after 58 minutes; Gascoigne lifting an inch-perfect free kick into the penalty area and Wright climbing athletically above the defence to head the ball past the keeper for the only international goal of his career.

That goal meant that the Egyptians had no choice other than to come out of defence and, in doing so, showed that they should have done so much earlier. They put England on to the back foot, forcing Shilton to make a fine save, but Robson's men managed to hold on for the victory, though their performance had hardly been impressive. The Egyptian goalkeeper, meanwhile, was so upset by his team's elimination that he needed medical attention after going into hysterics. The group's encounter between the Irish and Dutch ended in a 1-1 draw which meant that England finished as group winners; a rather unlikely-looking conclusion after the two draws in their opening two matches.

The format of the 1990 World Cup was kind to Argentina; the arithmetic of reducing 24 teams to 16 allowing the four best-placed third-placed teams in each group to progress to the second round. Argentina had done just enough to squeak into one of those places, but their punishment for failing to live up to expectations and win the group was a mouth-watering clash with Brazil. Their South American rivals were strong favourites to win, having beaten Argentina in the Copa America a year earlier as well as finishing top of their group after getting the better of Sweden, Costa Rica and Scotland.

The tie was played in Turin and the predominantly Italian crowd heartily jeered Maradona, just as the Milanese had done in Argentina's match against Cameroon. Brazil took the game to the reigning champions and almost scored within the first minute; Goycochea saving a shot from Careca with his legs after the striker had beaten Simón and Monzón. Brazil continued to pour forward, winning a succession of corners, but they just couldn't get the goal that would surely have presaged more. Dunga did manage to beat the goalkeeper with a header, but could only watch in frustration as it bounced back off the post. Maradona and Caniggia, meanwhile, were forlorn figures; waiting in vain at the other end of the pitch for passes that never came.

Brazil continued to dominate in the second half. Careca almost scored with a cross that caught Goycochea too far off his line, the back-pedalling goalkeeper just getting his fingers on to the ball and pushing it on to the post. The ball was cleared but it fell to Alemão, whose shot from 25 yards out was diverted on to the same post by Goycochea that had been hit moments earlier.

Argentina may have been on the ropes but they only needed one lucky punch and, nine minutes from the end, that was exactly what they got. Maradona received the ball inside the centre circle, with his back to the Brazilian goal, then turned, skipped past a couple of Brazilians and escaped into the space in front of him. Four defenders immediately sensed the danger and hurried to block his run. In doing so, however, they left Caniggia unmarked on the left-hand side of the penalty area. Ricardo Gomes tried to halt the attack by shoving Maradona to the floor, but the Argentinean captain managed to get the ball away to Caniggia as he fell. The pass was inch-perfect and the blond-haired striker collected the ball, took it around the goalkeeper and blasted it into an empty net. The Brazilians' fear of Maradona had been so great that they had momentarily forgotten how to defend, and one moment was all it took for Maradona and Caniggia to make them regret it.

Argentina almost doubled their lead two minutes later as Brazil desperately chased an equaliser. Basualdo ran with the ball from the halfway line, breaching the Brazilian defence just as Maradona had done, but was then tripped from behind by Ricardo Gomes as he neared the edge of the penalty area. The Brazilian was duly sent off and Maradona almost scored from the resulting free kick, with only a fine save from the goalkeeper keeping the ball out of the net.

There was still time for one last chance for Brazil but Müller, who only had the goalkeeper to beat, somehow managed to hit his shot wide of the post. The Argentineans celebrated wildly at the end of the game while the bemused Brazilians trooped dejectedly off the pitch, with many of their fans in tears at the injustice they had witnessed. Brazil had won their first-round group at a canter and had deserved better than to have been paired with the reigning world champions in the second round. They had then outplayed Argentina, only to see all of their fine work undone by a few moments of genius. Quite simply, Brazil had been mugged.

England's reward for finishing top of their group was a second-round tie against Belgium in Bologna, though the squad nearly didn't make it there. On their aeroplane flight to the northern Italian city a well-meaning pilot invited Paul Gascoigne into the cockpit, but soon came to regret the decision when the errant Geordie grabbed the controls and sent the plane into a steep dive.

The Belgians were a decent side, having finished fourth at the previous World Cup finals in Mexico, and so Robson opted to bring back the five-man defence that had served him so well against the Netherlands.

The match turned out to be a thrilling, closely fought contest, with the Belgians troubling Robson's back-line far more than the Dutch had managed to. They pierced the English rearguard early on in the game, forcing Shilton to make a good save from a shot by Versavel and then coming close to taking the lead when a strike from Jan Ceulemans hit the post. Barnes partnered Lineker up front again and, in a moment which could have made so much difference to his World Cup campaign, had a goal incorrectly disallowed for offside. Waddle, given a freer role than he would have had if England had used a 4-4-2 formation, played well, running at the Belgian defenders from all angles and causing them a variety of problems as a result.

The best player on the pitch was the Belgian midfielder Enzo Scifo, who eclipsed even Gascoigne. He was unlucky not to score in the second half when his well-struck shot from 25 yards beat Shilton but, fortunately for England, not the post. Robson tried to gain an advantage midway through the second half by making a double substitution, replacing Steve McMahon with the Aston Villa midfielder David Platt and bringing on Steve Bull in place of Barnes, who was struggling with a groin injury. However, neither of the teams could break the deadlock within 90 minutes of play so half an hour of extra time was needed. It was a trial for the tired players, with Des Walker limping and many more simply shuffling round the pitch, mere shadows of the players they had been earlier in the game.

The match was virtually over, with a penalty shoot-out beckoning, when Gascoigne finally came to England's rescue. He received the ball midway in the England half and, with what little energy he had left in his legs, raced up the pitch and won a free kick halfway inside the Belgian half after being bundled over. Gascoigne picked himself up and lofted a perfectly weighted pass towards Platt who was moving to the edge of the six-yard area. Platt swivelled round as the ball reached him and then volleyed an unstoppable shot past the helpless Belgian goalkeeper. Cue jubilation on the pitch, in the stands and in living rooms all across England. Even Bobby Robson danced a little jig on the touchline.

In the celebrations that followed few reflected on Gascoigne's booking for an unnecessary challenge on Scifo near the end of normal time. It went almost unnoticed at the time, but that caution was to have massive consequences for both the player and his team before the World Cup was over.

Platt's last-minute winner was a career-changing moment, just as Lineker's hat-trick at the previous World Cup had been. Platt was initially pleased just to be in the England squad, never expecting to get a game ahead of Bryan Robson and Steve McMahon, but left Italy with foreign clubs vying for his signature.

It was a remarkable turnaround in fortunes for a player discarded by Manchester United when he was a trainee, being advised by them to accept an offer from Crewe Alexandra if he wanted to stay in professional football. Platt served his apprenticeship in the lower leagues before moving back into the big-time with Aston Villa, whom he drove to second place in the league in the 1989/90 season.

Platt was initially a striker and only moved back into midfield as his career progressed, though his goalscoring instincts clearly never left him. He scored regularly for club and country, with his total of 27 for England in 62 appearances being an excellent record for a forward, let alone a midfield player.

Argentina moved on to Florence for their quarter-final against Yugoslavia, a talented side who had recovered from a 4-1 thrashing from West Germany in their opening game to win their following three matches against Colombia, the United Arab Emirates and Spain. Yugoslavia started the stronger and had some good chances to score but, like the Brazilians before them, they could not convert them. It was a tough game, with five Argentineans being booked and Šabanadžović being sent off for Yugoslavia after incurring his second booking within the first half an hour of the game; no mean feat in so short a period of time.

With the advantage of an extra man Argentina started to create more chances to score, with Ruggeri coming closest when he headed the ball against the bar during the second half. The match remained goalless at the end of 90 minutes so both sides had to continue to search for a winner in extra time. It was Argentina who nearly broke the deadlock when, just before the end of extra time, Burruchaga put the ball into the net. Contentiously, though, it was ruled out as the referee judged that the Argentinean had handled it prior to scoring. Two hours of football had failed to produce a goal so the match progressed to a penalty shoot-out. It was quite an achievement for the Yugoslavians to have got that far, having played with only ten men in fierce heat for a full 90 minutes. They may have been the moral victors, but a quarter-final of the World Cup is no place for ethics.

Penalties may be an unsatisfactory way of determining a game, but there is no denying their drama. Serrizuela scored Argentina's first and then the skilful Stojković hit his shot against the bar, giving the South Americans an early advantage. The next two penalties were scored and then Maradona, facing a cacophony of boos and jeers, stepped up to take his. To the evident delight of the crowd, and probably much of the watching world, his poorly taken kick was easily saved by the Yugoslavian goalkeeper.

Savićević scored next to level the shoot-out and the European side were given a great opportunity to take the lead when Troglio hit his shot against the post. Brnović's penalty, however, was struck even more weakly than Maradona's and Goycochea saved it without too much difficulty. Dezotti converted Argentina's next penalty to leave Hadžibegić with the responsibility of having to score if Yugoslavia were to stay in the competition. He took his penalty fairly well but Goycochea was equal to it, saving the ball to his left. Argentina had once more been the weaker of the two sides but, yet again, had made it through. It was almost as if they were fated to make the final.

· ·

Waddle's strike against the post galvanised the English, with Gascoigne even attempting to advance up the pitch by knocking the ball between Maradona's legs. The cheeky effort didn't quite come off but that didn't prevent it from being cheered to the rafters back home; beating Maradona was good but humiliating him, now that really was special. Such impertinence did not go down well with the Argentineans and Monzón soon took out his frustrations on Lineker's right leg, his tackle so vicious that the referee had little alternative other than to brandish a red card in his disbelieving face. Maradona led the protests, pleading to the official with his hands in prayer, but the Mexican was unmoved, gesturing simply to Monzón that his World Cup was over.

The World Cup Final had already been a pretty fraught affair, but Monzón's dismissal just ratcheted the emotions up even higher. The English were enraged by the ferocity of his tackle, which had left Lineker limping so heavily that it was questionable whether he would be able to continue, while the

Argentineans felt persecuted by the officials once more. First Rattín, now Monzón: would referees forever be on the side of the English? It was a time for cool heads and calm hearts but Bilardo was worried, fearing that the combination of being both a man and a goal down would prove too much for his players to cope with. His fears were realised a few minutes later when Waddle jinked past two players before being upended in the penalty area, the brave referee pointing immediately to the spot.

While the Argentinean players crowded around the beleaguered official, their tempers clearly at boiling point, there was a fierce debate going on over who was going to take the spot-kick. Lineker was England's nominated penalty taker, but he still hadn't recovered fully from Monzón's attempt to separate his limb from the rest of his body and concerns were clearly being expressed as to whether he was up to it. After all, this was no ordinary penalty. Both Pearce and Platt willingly offered their services, but Lineker made it known that the responsibility was his and would remain his.

Lineker placed the ball on the penalty spot and glanced quickly at Goycochea, who was standing confidently on his line, exuding belief. His kick was decent enough but the Argentinean goalkeeper guessed correctly, getting enough of his right palm on to the ball to force it on to the post. The ball bounced back out and Platt was first to it, managing to get his shot in before he was bundled over. Goycochea was equal to that strike as well, however, punching it out for a corner. Maradona puffed out his cheeks with relief and anyone looking carefully would have seen a defiant glint in his eye; this World Cup Final wasn't over yet.

• •

England's quarter-final opponents were Cameroon, conquerors of Argentina in the tournament's opening match. The Leeds United manager, Howard Wilkinson, had watched their matches for Bobby Robson and reported back that England pretty much had a bye into the semi-finals. Over-confidence would hardly help the English players, though, and their troubles started before the match had even begun. As they waited in the tunnel to go on to the pitch they heard the Africans coming, singing their tribal chants loudly and enthusiastically. Cameroon's players were noticeably fearsome and the less-well-built Englishmen clearly feared that it was going to be more like Rorke's Drift than a game of football. It soon became evident that the vast majority of the crowd in Naples were on the side of the African underdogs and, in a hot and humid atmosphere, England belatedly realised that they had a real fight on their hands.

Robson selected Platt ahead of McMahon and, while that made England more of an attacking force, it did leave them without a holding midfielder in front of the defence. Given that his team had three central defenders on the pitch, it was clearly a risk that Robson felt he could afford to take, but the wisdom of this approach was soon tested. Cameroon started the match the stronger of the two sides and Shilton had to make a good save from Oman Biyik to prevent them from taking the lead. England struggled to keep possession and Gascoigne became noticeably agitated, repeatedly complaining to the referee rather than concentrating on his football. It was therefore against the run of play when Platt scored after 25 minutes, heading the ball down through the goalkeeper's legs following an excellent cross from Pearce. England held on to their lead until half-time but it flattered them. Cameroon had been the better side, and both teams knew it.

Cameroon made a change at the interval, bringing on their 38-year-old striker Roger Milla. It was an inspired substitution, with Milla being instrumental as the Africans turned the game on its head in a devastating four-minute spell. Their first goal came after a tired-looking Gascoigne brought Milla down in the penalty area with a clumsy and needless challenge. The penalty was converted by Kunde, though there was a suspicion that Shilton should have got closer to it than he did. Cameroon then brought on Ekeke and within a couple of minutes of being on the pitch he put his side in front, chipping the ball over the outrushing Shilton after exchanging passes with Milla. The Cameroon players celebrated joyously, piling on top of each other by the corner flag, with their goalkeeper running all the way up the pitch to jump on to the mass of writhing bodies.

Cameroon's lead was no less than they deserved, and some of the more rumbustious England players released their rage and disappointment with some rugged challenges. Pearce was booked and then Oman Biyik almost added a third goal with an impudent back-heel that would have made England's task almost impossible.

Robson's dishevelled side were on the ropes so they reverted to type; dispensing with the new-fangled 5-3-2 formation and returning to the traditional 4-4-2. England slowly started to force their way back into the game and it was Gascoigne, well aware that he had to redeem himself for giving away a penalty, who was at the heart of the revival. He threaded a fine pass through to Platt, but he dragged his shot wide of the post when he really should have scored. Then, seven minutes from the end of normal time, England were handed a lifeline. Lineker tried to get on to the end of a pass from Wright but was upended and the referee, correctly, pointed to the penalty spot. Lineker picked himself up and, with nerves of steel, sent the Cameroon goalkeeper the wrong way with his spot-kick.

England were playing extra time for the second game in succession and this time they only had ten fit men. Wright had cut his eye badly in a clash with Milla but had no alternative other than to stay on the pitch as Robson had used all of his substitutes. Unable to head the ball, Wright was sent to play out of position on the right-side of midfield, Parker replaced him in the centre of defence and Trevor Steven was moved to right-back. England were, quite literally, all over the place.

Robson's side continued to ride their luck in extra time, with Shilton saving yet again from Oman Biyik, a header this time, and Steven hooking the ball away from an empty net before a Cameroon player could get on to the end of it.

Just before the end of the first period of extra time the erratic Gascoigne finally found redemption. He ran forward from deep in the England half and played a delightful pass through the heart of the Cameroon defence for Lineker to latch on to. Lineker got to the ball, but then had his legs taken from beneath him by the goalkeeper before one of the African defenders clattered into his back. Both challenges deserved a penalty and the referee had no hesitation in pointing to the spot. England's opening penalty was the first that they had been awarded in over four years but, like the proverbial bus, another one came round nearly as quickly. Lineker placed his first penalty to the left-hand side of the goal and Nkono dived that way for the second but the Tottenham Hotspur man, who had only practised taking penalties one way, slammed it straight into the centre of the net instead.

England held on for the victory, with Parker finally getting a grip of Milla and preventing him from influencing the game, but it was a mightily close-run thing. After the game, even Robson admitted that he didn't quite know how they had managed to win it. Ultimately, it was English nous that was decisive; their brave, never-say-die attitude contributing as much to their triumph as Cameroon's defensive lapses had resulted in their defeat. West Germany awaited England in the semi-finals and Robson knew that, if his side played that poorly again, they could be on the wrong end of a real hammering.

In the other semi-final, Argentina faced World Cup hosts Italy. The venue was the southern city of Naples so Maradona, knowing that his side had their backs against the wall, opted to indulge in an outrageous display of gamesmanship. The Argentinean captain had joined Napoli in 1984, following an unsuccessful spell with Barcelona, and the locals had taken to him immediately, with over 70,000 fans crowding into the stadium just to greet him when he signed for the club. Napoli were the proverbial sleeping giants, never having won a championship during their entire history, despite being one of the nation's best-supported sides. Napoli finished eighth in the table in Maradona's first season, third the year after that and then, in 1987, won a league and cup double. The celebrations in the city were joyous and lasted for days, with grateful Napoli fans painting huge murals of Maradona on the sides of buildings and naming their newborn sons after him. A UEFA Cup triumph followed in 1989 and, in the year of the World Cup, a second league title.

For his fans in the deep Italian south, Maradona could do no wrong. Those who supported clubs in the north of Italy, however, viewed him very differently. To them he was a strutting, posturing irritant that denied their sides titles and explains why, when Argentina played in Milan and Turin, he was subjected to such harsh cat-calling.

Maradona was not alone in being loathed by the residents of rich northern cities, with Napoli fans also being regularly insulted by those who begrudged paying taxes to help support the less-well-off south. Maradona had a keen understanding of the ongoing hostility between north and south and was well aware of his popularity among the people of Naples. He therefore sought to divide and conquer, provocatively encouraging the city's residents to support him and, by extension, Argentina. Maradona's attempt to recruit the Naples crowd on to his side predictably enraged the north but it had some impact on the Napoli fans, with support for the Italian side being more muted than it had been in Rome where they had played all of their previous games.

Maradona's attempt to undermine the Italians was borne out of genuine fear. Italy may have had a kind draw in the tournament but they had still negotiated it with ease. The hosts had beaten Austria, the USA, Czechoslovakia, Uruguay and the Republic of Ireland on their way to the semi-finals without conceding a goal. However, three of their victories were only secured by a single goal and there was an increasing suspicion that the Italians just weren't prolific enough to win the competition. While Bilardo kept faith with the same side that had started against Yugoslavia the Italian coach inexplicably left the talented Roberto Baggio, who had scored one the best goals of the tournament in the match against Czechoslovakia, on the bench.

The semi-final was only 17 minutes old when the Italians drew first blood; Toto Schillaci gleefully volleying the ball into the net after Goycochea had parried a shot from Gianluca Vialli. The Italians held on to their lead for the remainder of the first half but started the second period in a much more hesitant fashion, seemingly unsure whether to try and increase their lead or hold on to what they had got. Bilardo's side seized on the Italians' indecision and played some of their best football of the tournament, getting their just rewards halfway through the second period when Caniggia headed in a cross from Olarticoechea. He was greatly assisted by the Italian goalkeeper who went to intercept the ball when he really should have stayed on his line. It may have been the first goal that he had conceded in the tournament but, with his side just over 20 minutes away from a World Cup final, it was still an inexcusably poor error of judgement.

The enigmatic Roberto Baggio was belatedly brought on as a substitute a few minutes later but even he was unable to turn the game back in his side's favour, his best effort coming from a free kick that Goycochea saved well. Argentina remained the stronger of the two sides, even after being reduced to ten men when Giusti was dismissed for pushing Baggio over. There were no further goals after extra time so, for the second consecutive game, Argentina had to surrender their fate to a penalty shoot-out.

The Italians initially subjected the Argentineans to a tougher duel than Yugoslavia had, scoring their first three penalties. The Argentineans simply responded in kind and waited, threateningly, for their opportunity. It came when Roberto Donadoni struck Italy's fourth kick far too near to Goycochea, who saved easily. Perhaps inevitably, given the controversy that he had added to the occasion with his pre-match comments, it was Maradona who was given the chance of putting his side into the lead. He got it right this time, atoning for his miss against Yugoslavia by sending the goalkeeper the wrong way with a well-taken penalty. Serena had to score to keep his nation in the competition but his blast at goal couldn't beat Goycochea who dived to his left to save it. The Argentinean, who had only gone to Italy as the team's reserve goalkeeper, had become the hero of the hour, remaining unbeaten by five out of the ten penalties taken against him in the two shoot-outs. Somehow Argentina, who had performed so poorly throughout most of the tournament, were in the World Cup Final; a scarcely believable, and desperately unfair, outcome.

· ·

There may have been just ten minutes of the match left to be played but that felt like an eternity to the watching England fans; each second having to be dragged reluctantly from the future. Goycochea's penalty save had given Argentina hope and, even though they only had ten men, they succeeded in pushing England deeper and deeper into their own half. Bobby Robson was almost beside himself on the touchline, gesturing frantically to his players to break out of defence and swarm up to the other end of the pitch. That was easier said than done, however, as a siege mentality had evidently settled on the English players, who instinctively defended the battlements for all they were worth.

England's ultra-defensive approach was an open invitation to the Argentineans and to Maradona in particular. He stood at the heart of midfield and directed assaults on the English goal, almost as if he were a footballing equivalent of Napoleon Bonaparte. Wave after wave of blue-shirted attacks crashed on to the rocks of Butcher, Walker and Wright, but there was a growing suspicion that they couldn't hold out forever.

What Argentina needed most of all was a moment of magic from their captain and they duly got it. Maradona picked the ball up 30 yards from the English goal and slipped it into the path of Troglio, who advanced past Platt's tired tackle and drew Walker out of defence towards him. The Argentinean midfielder promptly switched the ball across the pitch to Burrachaga and he deftly shielded it from Wright before flicking it up in the air into the path of the onrushing Maradona. The ball hovered invitingly at knee height and Maradona cracked it for all he was worth, his shot shaving Butcher's horror-stricken face as it made its way into the top corner of the net.

Argentina's late equaliser changed the complexion of the match in an instant; the ten men looking as if they were 12 and England appearing a pale shadow of the side they had been just a few minutes earlier. Of greatest concern to Robson was the young Gascoigne. He was clearly rattled by Maradona's goal and struggled to maintain his composure as a consequence. The ball was fed to him a number of times as England tried to get back into the match but his passes were as wild as they were inaccurate. Frustration soon got the better of him and he released it with a lunging tackle that scythed through Basualdo's legs. The Argentinean crashed to the floor and his team-mates immediately surrounded the referee, demanding that he punish Gascoigne as he had punished

Monzón. For one heart-stopping moment it looked as if the referee was going to do just that, but to the utter disgust of Bilardo's players he opted to brandish only a yellow card. Cue tears of relief from Gascoigne.

• •

England fans were thrilled to see their team in their first World Cup semi-final for almost a quarter of a century, but few realistically expected them to progress any further. The Germans had started the tournament strongly, brushing the talented Yugoslavians aside 4-1 and then thrashing the United Arab Emirates 5-1, the only surprise being that they conceded a goal. In the second round they knocked out the Dutch 2-1 and then secured their place in the semi-finals with a 1-0 victory over Czechoslovakia. If that wasn't scary enough, Robson's side also had to contend with the fact that England hadn't managed to beat the Germans in a competitive match since the 1966 World Cup Final.

The side selected by Robson was, with one exception, the same that had started against Cameroon, with Beardsley being brought in to partner Lineker. The England manager also decided to persevere with his new 5-3-2 formation, opting to use Butcher as a sweeper so that Walker and Wright could mark the two quick German strikers, Klinsmann and Völler. The England side that started against West Germany had never played together before and would never play together again, meaning that the show was, quite literally, for one night only. And what a show it was; the best game of the tournament by a mile.

The Germans may have been the favourites but it was England who started the stronger. They won two corners within the opening minutes, the second of which came after Gascoigne rifled a shot at goal which was only just tipped around the post by the goalkeeper. It wasn't only England's attack that looked good as the defence was also holding up well, with Butcher performing the unfamiliar sweeper role competently, the bandaged Wright marshalling Klinsmann effectively and Walker reducing the dangerous Völler to a peripheral figure. The Germans meanwhile looked tense, clearly a little flustered at being bested by a team that they were expected to beat without too much difficulty.

The favourites slowly came back into the match, but England were still clearly the better side prior to the interval. Their most audacious attempt on goal came when Waddle tried to score from the edge of the centre circle after spotting the German number one off his line. The ball was arcing its way into the net before the keeper, back-pedalling, diverted it on to the bar at the last possible moment. In a sense it was academic, as the referee had already awarded the Germans a free kick for a foul committed by Platt in the build-up to Waddle's strike, but it was, nevertheless, a clear demonstration of England's self-belief and control of the game.

England's only disappointment from the first half was their failure to convert their superiority into goals. Many worried that the Germans would make them pay for that and, on 59 minutes, the favourites scored the game's first goal. Pearce gave away a free kick close to the edge of the penalty area and the ball was played short to the German left-back, Brehme, who struck it at goal. Parker tried to get in the way of the shot, as he had been instructed to, but the ball ricocheted upwards off his leg and ballooned over Shilton who had come off his line to stop Brehme's shot. It was a freakish goal to concede in any game but, in a finely balanced World Cup semi-final, it was cruelty almost beyond belief. The abiding image of that moment was Shilton sitting down in his goal, disappointment and disbelief written all over his face.

Undeterred, Robson's side chased an equaliser, with the lively Gascoigne being the most dominant player on the pitch. With 20 minutes remaining, and in desperate need of a goal,

Robson once again reverted to 4-4-2, replacing Butcher with midfielder Trevor Steven. There were only ten minutes of normal time remaining when Lineker (who else?) got the goal that England so desperately needed. Parker, grateful for an opportunity to atone for his luckless role in the game's opening goal, lofted the ball into the penalty area but the German defence failed to clear it. It then fell to Lineker, who touched it past his marker with his thigh before smashing it low past the keeper. For the second game in succession he had kept England's World Cup dreams alive in the game's dying minutes.

Rather than going in for the kill, England played out the remainder of normal time. In retrospect that may have been a mistake as it gave the Germans time to settle themselves, and they duly went on to be the stronger of the two teams in extra time. Klinsmann started to look more threatening in front of goal, forcing Shilton to make a good save from a header before shooting just past the post. Then came the iconic moment for which Paul Gascoigne shall forever be remembered. Eight minutes into extra time he received the ball in England's half of the pitch and evaded two Germans before the ball started to get away from him. Gascoigne lunged for it, but succeeded only in upending the opposing right-back, Thomas Berthold, who had got to the ball a moment earlier. It was an unnecessary foul, though certainly not malicious, but, crucially, Gascoigne had committed it in front of the German bench.

While Berthold rolled on the floor, a little dramatically it has to be said, the German coaches jumped to their feet and protested vehemently. They knew what they were doing and the Brazilian referee responded as they hoped he would, booking Gascoigne and, in doing so, ruling him out of the final should England reach it. If the foul had been committed anywhere else on the pitch Gascoigne probably would have got away with it, but instead he was left to rue his fate, his face puckering and tears rolling down his flushed cheeks.

Gascoigne's World Cup may have been almost over but England's was still very much alive. To get to the final they needed Gascoigne to be at his most incisive, but his spirit was shattered by the booking and he slowly drifted out of the game.

Still, England did have chances to score. A venomous shot from Waddle beat the German keeper but smashed into the post, with Platt missing the rebound by no more than the length of his boot. Platt then managed to get the ball in the net early in the second period of extra time but the referee wrongly ruled it out for offside. England continued to push for a winner but it was the Germans who came closer, with a shot from Buchwald cannoning off the same post that Waddle's strike had hit.

Extra time ended without any goals being scored and the inevitable penalty shoot-out awaited the exhausted players. It was England's first shoot-out in a major tournament and it should be remembered that, at the time, no one foresaw just what a wretched record they would come to have. Indeed, England fans would often scoff at how poorly other nations performed in such shoot-outs. After all, how difficult could it be to score from 12 yards? Sadly, England, and their supporters, were about to find out.

The shoot-out started well for England with Lineker, Beardsley and Platt all converting but, ominously, the Germans were just as efficient. Stuart Pearce stepped up to take England's fourth penalty and few worried that he would fail to score. He was a regular penalty taker for Nottingham Forest and one of the best kickers of a dead ball in the English game. But, to the horror of all England supporters, Pearce, for once, failed. He smashed the ball at the centre of the goal but the German keeper, diving to his right, managed to keep it out with his legs. The Germans then heaped the pressure on to England by scoring their penalty.

An exhausted-looking Waddle walked up to the penalty spot next, needing to score to keep his nation in the World Cup. The weight of expectation was far too great and the Marseilles winger collapsed underneath it, sending his penalty over the bar. It was all over now.

The 1990 World Cup Final would therefore be a repeat of the previous final of four years earlier, with the Germans having the opportunity to avenge their defeat in Mexico. One consequence of Bilardo's side's cynical, scrappy approach to the game was that four of their players would miss out through suspension. Giusti was absent after his sending-off against Italy while Batista, Olarticoechea and Caniggia had all collected enough bookings to warrant their exclusion. The absence of Caniggia was particularly frustrating, given that his most recent booking was for the self-inflicted crime of handling the ball as it went over his head. Caniggia was one of the few Argentinean players who looked capable of scoring and his fruitful partnership with Maradona was one of the reasons why his side had managed to go so far in the competition.

The 1990 World Cup had been a bad-tempered affair, with more players being sent off than in any other previous tournament, and its final was a fitting epitaph. It was a game bereft of imagination, sportsmanship and grace and remains, by common consent, the worst World Cup Final there has been. It even started inauspiciously, with the Argentinean national anthem barely being audible above the sound of Italians jeering the widely detested Maradona. Bilardo's approach was so defensive that it appeared Argentina's game plan was to win the World Cup by triumphing in a third consecutive penalty shoot-out. If that was their strategy, then it was poorly conceived; had they never seen the Germans take penalties?

The impressive Buchwald managed to keep Maradona quiet in the first half, but although they dominated possession the Germans struggled to make any clear chances. They shifted up a gear after the interval and a succession of goalscoring opportunities soon came their way. Berthold and Völler missed when it seemed easier to score, Augenthaler was denied a clear penalty when he was tripped by Goycochea, even though the referee was only feet away, and Brehme went close with a shot from 25 yards that Goycochea did well to turn around the post.

Then, on 64 minutes, came the game's most infamous moment. Pedro Monzón committed a dreadful challenge on Klinsmann and was duly dismissed, the first player to be sent off in a World Cup Final. The watching world was finally put out of its misery 20 minutes later when the Germans were awarded a penalty for a foul on Völler by Sensini. Brehme duly converted the spot-kick, with Goycochea being unable to save his side this time.

The Argentineans, knowing in their hearts that the game was over, then lost what little was left of their composure. Dezotti was sent off two minutes from time for trying to throttle Kohler and then Maradona was booked for his overly fierce protestations at the referee's decision. His team-mates shamelessly shoved and jostled the referee as he tried to restore order, confirming people's worst suspicions about the true nature of this Argentinean side.

Maradona left the pitch in floods of tears at the end of the game, but few were shed for him. Everyone had wanted to see the world's greatest footballer doing only what he could do but he was a pale shadow of the presence that he had been in Mexico; more prima donna than Maradona. As well has having two players sent off, Argentina also set another unwanted record in becoming the first team to fail to score in a World Cup Final. Of the nine men still on the pitch at the end of the game, the only one who had been in Argentina's World Cup-winning side four years earlier was Diego Maradona. It was truly the end of an era.

Bilardo resigned as national coach after the World Cup and within a year Maradona had been banned from the game for 15 months following a positive drugs test for cocaine. In his absence, however, Argentina went from strength to strength, winning the Copa America in 1991 and again in 1993. They were expected to qualify for the 1994 World Cup with ease and won three out of their first four qualifying games. That put them in a strong position to win their group, which was important as only the side that finished top was guaranteed a place at the World Cup. However, they could only manage a 0-0 draw at home to Paraguay in their next game so had to win their final match at home against group leaders, Colombia. Few expected them to falter and none predicted the outcome: a disastrous 5-0 defeat that so humiliated the nation that one Argentine magazine printed an entirely black front page in response.

Argentina's new manager, Alfo Basile, had initially been deprived of Maradona's services because of his drugs ban but soon found out that his team could do perfectly well without him. The shocking defeat to Colombia resulted in a mass popular call for Maradona's return, however, and he was duly welcomed back into the fold, helping Argentina to win a two-legged play-off against Australia for the last remaining place at the World Cup.

A national hero, Maradona was duly made captain of Argentina's squad for the 1994 World Cup in the USA and initially all went well. He led the team to a 4-0 victory in their opening tie against Greece, scoring a fine goal in the process, though there was something in his celebration, when he stared dementedly down a television camera lens, which made you wonder just what was in his system.

A 2-1 victory over a strong Nigerian team followed in which Maradona had a hand in both goals (though not literally this time) and it seemed to many observers that Argentina were good enough to reach their fourth World Cup Final in five attempts. However, after the match Maradona was led off the pitch by a nurse for a dope test and was never seen in the World Cup again; a cocktail of drugs being found in his urine sample which inevitably resulted in his expulsion from the competition. His side never recovered from the shock, losing 2-0 to Bulgaria in their final group game and then 3-2 to Romania in the second round, though at least it was the best match of the tournament.

After England's heroics at the 1990 World Cup there were high expectations that the nation could go one better in the USA. Even though some of the old warriors were no longer around there were enough talented young players coming through to enable a nation to dream of glory once more. In retrospect, however, the 1990 World Cup was the end of an era for the national side, rather than a brave new beginning. Bobby Robson left to manage in the Netherlands, where he would be much more appreciated than he ever was as England manager, while Gascoigne's burgeoning natural talent remained largely unfulfilled. He seemed to have the world at his feet after the 1990 World Cup, but injury, ill fortune and self-destructive behaviour conspired to rob him of the chance to seize the game's greatest prizes.

Robson was replaced by Graham Taylor, a well-meaning soul who created strong domestic teams but looked out of his depth as an international manager. His England side qualified for the 1992 European Championship finals in Sweden without too much difficulty but crashed out of the tournament at the group stage without winning a game.

Taylor was pilloried as a result, famously being depicted as a turnip, while his under-use of some of England's most creative players was widely mocked. Chris Waddle only played one more full game for his country after the 1990 World Cup and Peter Beardsley also featured little. Things then went from bad to worse as England failed to even qualify for the 1994 World Cup finals in the USA, a fate that would have been almost unthinkable a few years earlier when they almost conquered the world.

The legacy of the 1990 World Cup for English football was not success on the football pitch, however, but the revival of the national game. Robson's players were largely oblivious of how World Cup fever had gripped the nation while they were away, but when their plane landed at Luton airport they soon found out. They were greeted with scenes not witnessed since the days of Beatlemania, with 70,000 England fans welcoming their heroes at the airport and another 150,000 cheering them through the streets of Luton as they toured in an open-top bus. Goodness knows what would have happened if they had actually won the World Cup.

On the same day that the players arrived back home UEFA decided to re-admit English club sides to European competition; Manchester United marking the nation's return by winning the 1991 European Cup Winners' Cup with a victory over Barcelona. Before the decade was out Alex Ferguson's side confirmed the nation's re-emergence as a major football power, winning the 1999 Champions League Final with a thrilling triumph over Bayern Munich.

The Premier League opened its doors in the summer of 1992 and its willingness to allow wall-to-wall coverage of its matches helped to create the commercial behemoth which, for better or worse, continues to dominate the national game to this day. Slowly, but surely, English football emerged from the dark days of Heysel, Hillsborough and hooliganism and England's 1990 World Cup adventure played a key part in its rehabilitation. If only they had won it. If only.

• •

Bobby Robson's reaction to Argentina's late equaliser was to return to the formation he knew best: 4-4-2. He sacrificed his old warrior, Terry Butcher, and brought Steve McMahon on in his place, instructing him to become Maradona's shadow. The change of personnel worked as planned, with the Argentinean captain struggling to have any meaningful influence on the game. With their most important player neutered, Bilardo's side slowly began to retreat, opting to hold out for extra time and the penalty shoot-out that had served them so well in previous rounds. Meanwhile, Gascoigne's fortunate reprieve injected new life into his tired limbs; the shock of almost being dismissed jolting him back into form.

Gary Lineker had already saved his nation twice during the tournament; his two penalties disposing of Cameroon and his two goals in two minutes defeating the Germans. Now, in the dying moments of the game, his moment came again. He won a free kick on the right-hand side of the pitch, ten yards outside of the penalty area, and Gascoigne immediately grabbed hold of the ball, placing it carefully on the steamy turf. The young Geordie was particularly indebted to Lineker as the Spurs striker's late double ensured that he ended the match without incurring a caution that would have ruled him out of the final. Gascoigne's lofted kick flew towards the six-yard area and Platt got his head to it, flicking it backwards in an arc above Goycochea's outstretched fist. The ball struck the base of the post and rebounded straight out to Lineker who reacted instantly, thumping it into the roof of the net.

There was still time for the Argentineans to kick off but it has never been clear when the match actually ended. The ball soon made its way to the corner flag in England's half of the pitch and Parker tried to waste a little time by keeping it out of the opposition's reach. He was dealing manfully with the combined attentions of a number of Argentineans until Sensini came rushing in, knocking him clean off the pitch. All three officials immediately ran to the scene as they knew what was about to happen, though they were unable to prevent the inevitable brawl that ensued. In the midst of the melee the referee spotted Dezotti trying to choke Wright and duly thrust a red card in his face though, in reality, half a dozen other offences had been committed that deserved such a response.

When the two sets of warring players had finally been separated, the Mexican referee made it known there was no time left to play football, which hardly improved the mood of the Argentineans. They eventually calmed down enough to collect their losers' medals but never accepted the defeat with grace, let alone congratulate the victors. Not that anyone in England really cared. The nation's first World Cup triumph for almost a quarter of a century was greeted with utter delirium back home, with impromptu street parties being held throughout the nation, many of which lasted the whole night long. When the dawn came up it felt like the national game had entered a new era; reborn, revived, resurrected. Truly, things would never be the same again.

6
The History Boys

UEFA Champions League Final, San Siro Stadium, Milan, 23 May 2001

Bayern Munich v Leeds United

Bayern Munich

Oliver Kahn

Thomas Linke

Patrik Andersson

Samuel Kuffour

Bixente Lizarazu

Willy Sagnol

Stefan Effenberg (captain)

Owen Hargreaves

Hasan Salihamidžić

Mehmet Scholl

Giovane Élber

Leeds United

Nigel Martyn

Ian Harte

Dominic Matteo

Rio Ferdinand (captain)

Danny Mills

Harry Kewell

Olivier Dacourt

David Batty

Lee Bowyer

Alan Smith

Mark Viduka

Referee: Dick Jol (Netherlands)

Football players come and go, as do managers; the one constant at any club being its supporters. Cyril Ormsby had followed Leeds United since he was a boy, watching their glory years under Don Revie and keeping the faith in the dark years after his departure. He rested as he climbed the steep steps towards his allotted seat, catching his breath while he admired the magnificent stadium laid out in front of him. This was only the second time that he had travelled abroad to watch his beloved Leeds, the other trip having taken place a quarter of a century earlier when he visited Paris to watch them play in the 1975 European Cup Final. It should have been the crowning glory for Revie's great side but they fell at the final hurdle, losing to the club that they would be taking on tonight: Bayern Munich.

Cyril had bored his children and grandchildren for years with stories of that final and how Leeds had been robbed of their rightful triumph. Revie's side had dominated English football in the late 1960s and early 1970s, intimidating opponents with a unique mixture of undeniable skill and downright menace. Their European Cup Final against Franz Beckenbauer's all-conquering Bayern Munich was a much anticipated 'clash of the titans' but Leeds, not for the first time and certainly not for the last, were undone by poor refereeing, players losing their nerve and downright bad luck. Leeds had the best of the game against the Germans, being unlucky not to be awarded two penalties in the first half.

Both offences were committed by the not-so-saintly Beckenbauer; the first for a handball and the second when he bundled Allan Clarke over. The referee's dismissal of both appeals was bad enough, but he would commit a graver offence before the game was over.

The incident burned most strongly into Cyril's memory of the final came midway through the second half, with the game still goalless. Johnny Giles lifted a free kick into the penalty area and Lorimer got hold of the ball, thumping it past the helpless goalkeeper. Then, while Leeds were celebrating and the Bayern players were walking up the pitch for the kick-off, the ever-alert Beckenbauer appealed for the goal to be disallowed for offside. The French referee, Michel Kitabdjian, duly consulted his linesman and decided to award a free kick to the Germans instead; a desperately bad decision as the offending player, Billy Bremner, certainly hadn't been interfering with play.

The Leeds side built by Revie had a much-remarked-upon habit of 'choking' just as they were on the verge of winning a trophy, having finished as runners-up in the league five times in eight seasons, as well as having lost three FA Cup finals and a UEFA Cup Final. The Leeds fans, infuriated by the referee's decision and sensing yet another disappointment, could take no more. They started to riot, ripping up seats and throwing them on to the pitch.

With mayhem erupting in the stands Leeds fell apart on the pitch, conceding two goals in a ten-minute spell. The defeat was never accepted by the Leeds fans and even now, a quarter of a century later, they could still be heard chanting during games, 'We are the champions, champions of Europe!' That is why the Champions League Final of 2001 mattered so much to Cyril and his fellow Leeds fans: it was an opportunity to banish memories of what could, and probably should, have been; to right the wrongs that had been done to them a generation earlier. If revenge is a dish best served cold, then Leeds's act of retribution would be positively arctic.

. . . .

If it wasn't for the quick thinking of an airline pilot, Leeds United's adventures in the 2000/01 Champions League may never have come to pass. Three years earlier, following an away game at West Ham, the Leeds squad piled into a specially chartered Emerald Airways plane at Stansted airport for the short trip back up to Yorkshire. It was a journey they would usually have made by coach but, in an attempt to ease the stresses created by a busy fixture list, the club opted to travel by plane instead. It almost proved to be a disastrous decision. Within a few seconds of leaving the ground the plane's starboard engine exploded, violently shaking the aircraft. Flames engulfed the stricken engine and trailed into the night sky while the cabin was a riot of noise, with alarms shrieking and passengers screaming in fear.

Normal procedure required the pilot to circle the airfield before making an emergency landing, but he wisely judged that there wasn't enough time to do that before the entire plane caught fire. Instead he took the plane straight back down to the ground and, a few heart-stopping seconds later, it hit the runway with such force that the nose wheel collapsed. The plane then slid on for some distance before finally coming to rest in the grass at the end of the runway. The Leeds party escaped quickly from the burning plane, running away to safety. If that plane had not landed in one piece then the club would have lost almost their entire squad, a large proportion of which would play in Leeds's great Champions League run three years later. They would also have lost the man who was soon to become the side's manager; the charming Irishman David O'Leary.

He had joined Leeds in the autumn of his playing career, following a long and successful spell at Arsenal as an elegant centre-half. He had been recruited by Howard Wilkinson to help bolster the Leeds defence, but injuries resulted in him playing only a handful of games for the club and he was eventually forced to retire. O'Leary had played under George Graham at Arsenal for a number of years and when the Scotsman succeeded Wilkinson as Leeds manager, he accepted an offer to become his assistant. It was an excellent opportunity for O'Leary as Graham was one of the most successful managers in the game at the time and great things were expected of him at Leeds.

Graham had won numerous trophies with Arsenal, with his side's success being based largely on the paucity of its defence. He applied the same methods in Yorkshire and, while his team certainly didn't concede many goals, they also didn't score many either. In his first season in charge Leeds conceded fewer goals in the Premier League than champions Manchester United but managed to score only 28: the lowest in the league. This hardly made Leeds exciting to watch; when a local newspaper fitted a heart monitor to a fan at one particularly dull home game they found that he was more animated by the anticipation of a meat pie than by the football he was being served with. Graham's methods eventually started to bear fruit, however, and in his second season at the club Leeds finished in fifth place in the league, earning a place in the UEFA Cup as a reward.

The 1998/99 league season started reasonably for Leeds, but not so well for Tottenham Hotspur who were soon on the lookout for a new manager. Their covetous eyes landed on George Graham and he jumped at the opportunity to return to London. He invited O'Leary to go with him to Spurs but the Irishman, who had moved his home to Yorkshire a few years earlier, declined the offer. O'Leary was put in temporary charge of the side and the club's chairman was so impressed by their performance away to AS Roma in the UEFA Cup that he decided to offer him the manager's job. Terms were soon agreed and it didn't take long for O'Leary to put his imprint on the team, dropping some of the senior players and replacing them with talented youngsters from the club's academy. O'Leary had tried on many occasions to persuade Graham to give them a chance in the first team, but the Scotsman could never be convinced that they were ready to make the step up. With Graham no longer around O'Leary was able to act on his instincts and give the young players the chance he felt they deserved.

O'Leary had the good fortune to become manager of Leeds as an unusually large crop of talented youngsters were graduating from the club's academy. The first inklings of this bounty came when Leeds won the FA Youth Cup in 1997 with a number of players who would go on to have successful careers in the game. Keeping goal was Paul Robinson, who was handed his debut in O'Leary's first match in charge after he had been given the job on a permanent basis. It took a few seasons for Robinson to make the goalkeeper's position his own but he eventually went on to have a long and distinguished career for Leeds, Tottenham and Blackburn Rovers. The ultimate vindication of his abilities came in 2003 when Sven-Göran Eriksson gave him his England debut, with Robinson playing in all of England's games in their run to the quarter-finals of the 2006 World Cup.

Playing in front of Robinson in that successful youth side was centre-half Jonathan Woodgate. Having played in that position himself, O'Leary was a good judge of centre-halves and he soon became enamoured of Woodgate's potential. The youngster had all the facets needed to be a top-class defender, being quick, strong in the air and comfortable with the ball at his feet. O'Leary gave Woodgate his debut while he was still the caretaker manager and the youngster did so well that he retained his place in the side for the remainder of the campaign. His performances also so impressed England manager Kevin Keegan that he gave the 19-year-old his first cap at the end of the season.

The most exciting player in that FA Youth Cup side was an Australian attacking midfielder, Harry Kewell. His talents had come to the attention of Leeds when he toured England as a member of an Australian youth side, with the club subsequently offering him a place in their academy. By the time of the FA Youth Cup victory he had already made his first-team and international debuts, having started for Leeds while Howard Wilkinson was still in charge as well as becoming the youngest-ever player to be selected for his native Australia. He established himself in the Leeds first team in Graham's second year in charge, and then appeared in every league game in the season when O'Leary took over.

The fourth notable graduate from that side was Leeds-born striker Alan Smith. He made a dramatic entrance into first-team football after being brought on as a substitute during a league match at home to Liverpool in one of O'Leary's first few games as manager. Leeds were a goal behind when he came on, with just over ten minutes of the match remaining, but the youngster scored with his first touch of the ball and then helped his side secure a thrilling 3-1 victory. That blistering start to his career raised expectations sky-high, but Smith had the character to rise to the challenge rather than being daunted by it. He soon gained a reputation for being a brave, hard-working target man who was prepared to stand up to tough challenges and fight his corner. Occasionally Smith's play was overly aggressive, with dismissals being the inevitable outcome, but his desire to succeed and undeniable passion for the club resulted in the Leeds fans adopting him as a true local hero.

Inevitably, not all of the members of that youth team went on to play professional football at the highest level. One of the casualties was a substitute goalkeeper called Nicky Byrne, though his subsequent career as a singer with the phenomenally successful band Westlife wasn't a bad consolation prize.

The combination of a novice manager and a team which included a number of teenagers made Leeds relatively unique in the Premier League, with O'Leary often calling his players 'babies' and highlighting his own relative lack of experience. The image he presented to the outside world, of Leeds being a wide-eyed group of innocents embarking on a grand adventure, was rather contrived but it did help to dampen the expectations placed on O'Leary and his young players and was clearly a shrewd move.

The younger contingent may have grabbed the headlines but the side couldn't have succeeded without the solid stock of experienced professionals that O'Leary had inherited from his predecessors. Even though a couple of years had elapsed since Howard Wilkinson was in charge a good number of his players were still at the club. The team's first-choice goalkeeper was Cornishman Nigel Martyn, who Wilkinson had recruited from Crystal Palace shortly before he was sacked. Martyn wasn't a flamboyant entertainer, but was well respected within the game for his consistent, dependable displays. Indeed, he was so reliable that it took a number of seasons for his talented understudy, Paul Robinson, to dislodge him from the team. Martyn played 23 times for England over a ten-year period, but was never able to make the goalkeeping position his own, with first Chris Woods and then David Seaman often being selected ahead of him.

The Leeds side also included two Irishmen from Drogheda, Gary Kelly and his nephew Ian Harte, who played at right-back and left-back respectively. Kelly joined the club as a striker but failed to make the desired impact and was about to be sent back home when Wilkinson decided to try him out as a full-back. Not only was Kelly's professional career saved as a result, but he also became part of Jack Charlton's Republic of Ireland squad at the 1994 World Cup finals in the USA later that season. Kelly spent his entire playing career with Leeds, rarely being displaced in the team, and was eventually capped 52 times for his country. Harte topped that by playing 64 times for Ireland and scoring 12 goals, an impressive haul for a defender who developed a reputation for being an effective taker of free kicks and penalties.

One of Wilkinson's final acts was to sign Lee Bowyer from Charlton Athletic for £2.5m, a record British fee for a teenager at the time. Bowyer was a naturally fit, aggressive midfield player who could be relied on to fight hard for the team, week in, week out. There were no doubts over his talent but his career was dogged by his inability to stay out of trouble, both on and off the pitch. Shortly after joining Leeds he was convicted of affray and fined £4,500 for throwing chairs around a McDonald's restaurant following a quarrel over his order. Then later in his career, when he was playing for Newcastle United, he managed to get sent off in a home game against Aston Villa for brawling on the pitch with his own team-mate, Kieron Dyer. An FA ban followed and, unsurprisingly, he was placed on the transfer list as a consequence. Bowyer was capped only once for England and the abiding impression he left is of a player that never quite fulfilled his potential.

O'Leary may have been part of the George Graham management team that delivered a succession of 0-0 draws, but he soon made it clear that there would be a change of emphasis now that he was in charge. The Irishman had been impressed with Kevin Keegan's swashbuckling Newcastle United side of the mid-1990s and had noted how the nation had taken them to their hearts. He wanted to emulate that team by playing fast, attacking football and, in doing so, create a side that top-class players would want to join at the expense of more glamorous rivals such as Arsenal, Chelsea and Liverpool.

O'Leary's stirring approach soon had the desired effect, with his team finishing the season in fourth place, a clear ten points ahead of fifth-placed West Ham United. It was the club's highest league placing since they had won the title under Wilkinson seven years earlier and a ringing endorsement of the O'Leary regime. Not only had the Irishman secured the club a place in the UEFA Cup for the following season, but Leeds had also finished one place higher than they had under George Graham in the previous season.

· ·

David O'Leary stood at the side of the pitch, looking nervously at his young players as the grandiose opening ceremony dragged to its conclusion. His heart told him that they could rise to the occasion and emerge triumphant, but his head was less sure. Bayern Munich were football aristocrats, with a playing squad whose cumulative value was well beyond what Leeds could afford. Six of the Bayern side had played in a Champions League Final before and one of the other five had taken part in a World Cup Final. They knew all about these big occasions and how to approach them, in contrast to his inexperienced charges who could only muster a couple of FA Cup Final appearances between them.

There was no doubt about it: Leeds were the clear underdogs. Indeed, some commentators dismissed the final as a mismatch; a contest between masters and pupils, veterans and novices, thoroughbreds and dark horses. O'Leary didn't care what the pundits thought. He'd seen enough of his young side to know that they had character in abundance. They'd been to the San Siro before and returned home undefeated and he knew in his heart that they could do it again. In fact, returning to a place that they had fond memories of would do them no harm at all. Little things like that mattered on a night like this.

O'Leary was immensely proud of what his young players had achieved, but part of him could hardly believe it. It barely seemed a few heartbeats ago that the club had won the FA Youth Cup, with four of that side having made it all the way to the Champions League Final; Kewell and Smith on the pitch, Robinson and Woodgate on the bench. There'd been many times when he'd wondered just how far this young team could go and now he was about to find out. The prize for the victors was football immortality, the promise of a free meal every night for the remainder of their lives. Dreams floated through the Italian night air, waiting to be seized by those that wanted them the most. O'Leary couldn't believe that anyone in the stadium wanted them any more than he did.

• •

A few months before David O'Leary became manager of Leeds, Bayern Munich also appointed a new head coach: Ottmar Hitzfeld. The club had suffered a relatively lean spell in the 1990s, failing to dominate German football to the extent that they had previously and their players were making more headlines in the gossip sections of the newspapers than they were in the sports pages. Bayern desperately needed a coach who could restore a sense of discipline and focus to the club so they turned to 'der General', who had a reputation for being able to handle star players who were a little too ready to believe their own hype.

Hitzfeld began his managerial career in Switzerland, where he had spent the majority of his playing career as a prolific striker. A successful spell with the Grasshopper club in Zurich attracted the attentions of Borussia Dortmund, who had failed to win a league title for almost 30 years despite being one of the best-supported clubs in Germany. Hitzfeld took over in 1991 and led the club to a second-place finish in the Bundesliga in his first season in charge, only missing out on the title by virtue of an inferior goal difference.

That success gave Dortmund entry to the following season's UEFA Cup, in which they knocked out Celtic and AS Roma on their way to the two-legged final. They were then outclassed by Italian giants Juventus, losing 6-1 on aggregate, but were awarded a very valuable consolation prize. The rules in place for allocating television income meant that the club received the vast sum of 25 million DM, which Hitzfeld used to make some significant improvements to his playing squad. Within two seasons Dortmund had finally won the Bundesliga and they didn't stop there. They fought their way to the final of the 1997 European Champions League, knocking out Alex Ferguson's Manchester United on the way and then, with delicious irony, defeated Juventus 3-1 to lift the trophy.

Dortmund's triumph was a magnificent achievement for Hitzfeld, but he paid a high personal price. The years of toil visibly aged him and his health deteriorated to such an extent that he had to take a year out of football management to recuperate. While he was away Bayern Munich struggled to deliver the level of success that their fans had become accustomed to, finishing as runners-up in the Bundesliga and being knocked out of the quarter-finals of the Champions League by the Dortmund side that Hitzfeld had built. The Bavarian club duly dispensed with the services of their Italian coach, Giovanni Trapattoni, and turned to Hitzfeld to restore their fortunes.

The club that Hitzfeld joined may have been Germany's equivalent of Manchester United, but they hadn't always held such an eminent position. Bayern Munich were founded in 1900 and it took them almost 70 years to win their second national championship. Their first triumph came in 1932, but success proved to be short-lived following the Nazi takeover of the country. The club's Jewish president was forced out and then held in a concentration camp before escaping to Switzerland, with Bayern's fortunes under the Nazi regime suffering predictably as a consequence. The damage done to the club in that period took many years to repair and when the Germans belatedly introduced a nationwide league in 1963 (the Bundesliga) Bayern weren't even a founder member.

Bayern won promotion to the Bundesliga in 1965 and it wasn't long before they embarked on the most glorious period in their history. With a team based around the peerless spine of Sepp Maier in goal, Franz Beckenbauer in defence and Gerd

Müller in attack the Bavarian club won four league titles and three consecutive European Cups in a glorious seven-year spell between 1969 and 1976. That trio were also at the heart of the West German side that won the 1972 European Championship and the 1974 World Cup, the latter triumph fittingly being won at the Olympic Stadium where Bayern played their home games.

When that great side broke up Bayern's fortunes inevitably took a dip but the arrival of a new decade brought with it a new period of domination, with Bayern winning six of the ten Bundesliga titles competed for in the 1980s. While there was no denying their supremacy at domestic level the new-look Bayern side were unable to repeat the success that Beckenbauer's group had achieved in the European Cup. They twice reached the final but suffered defeat both times, losing to Aston Villa in 1982 and then to Porto in 1987.

The 1990s began splendidly for Bayern, with the Bavarians winning another Bundesliga title, but any hopes that this presaged a further decade of dominance proved to be misplaced. They won only two of the following eight championships; a decent record for most clubs but little short of a disaster for a dynasty that had come to expect so much more. That period saw a great deal of change, both for the German nation and for its football teams. The end of the Cold War brought about the reunification of Germany in 1990 and, in the years that followed, vast sums of money started to flow into the domestic game.

Germany had the most successful economy in Europe and a combination of the sale of television rights, sponsorship and private investment pumped previously unseen levels of funding into the Bundesliga. This new-found wealth allowed German clubs to start hiring some of the world's best players and, just as importantly, enabled them to prevent foreign clubs from poaching their top indigenous talent. As the quality of players at German clubs improved so did their success in the Champions League which, inevitably, resulted in even greater levels of revenue. Borussia Dortmund's victory in 1997 was the first by a German team for 14 years, and in the following season's tournament three of the quarter-finalists came from Germany.

Bayern may have under-achieved in the years preceding Hitzfeld's arrival, but it should not be assumed that he inherited a playing squad that was in great need of an overhaul. Hitzfeld actually had some of the best players in Germany, if not the entire continent, at his disposal. Keeping goal was the Bavarian behemoth Oliver Kahn, who won virtually every honour in the club game, with only success at international level eluding him. Arguably, the pinnacle of his career came at the 2002 World Cup when he took an ordinary German side almost single-handedly to the final with a succession of impressive performances. His triumph was duly recognised when he became the first goalkeeper in the tournament's history to win the Golden Ball, the trophy awarded to the competition's best player.

One of Kahn's defining qualities was his unquenchable determination to win, which is a fine trait for any sportsman, but his desire not to lose was almost obsessive. On one occasion Kahn took part in a penalty shoot-out competition for charity in which children lined up to try and score against him in order to raise money for an orphanage. He duly saved every penalty, so great was his desire not to be beaten.

In front of Kahn in the centre of the Bayern defence was the powerful Sami Kuffour, who had left his native Ghana as a teenager to find fame and fortune in European football. Then, on the left of the defence, was the diminutive French international, Bixente Lizarazu. An ethnic Basque, he started his career with Bordeaux before arriving at Bayern following a short spell at Athletic Bilbao. A natural athlete, Lizarazu's energetic approach to the game served him well and he became a key part of the France side that won the 1998 World Cup and Euro 2000.

Ahead of him in midfield was the side's playmaker, Mehmet Scholl. A technically proficient footballer, Scholl was adept at dribbling through defences and taking free kicks, but his career was so bedevilled by injuries that he was fated to be one of the most talented German footballers never to appear at a World Cup finals.

Playing in front of Scholl was Brazilian striker Giovane Élber. He came to Europe at the tender age of 18 and spent virtually his whole playing career on the continent. Blessed with electric pace and an eye for goal, Élber regularly finished as Bayern's leading goalscorer in the six seasons that he spent with the club. Élber's main rival for the team's centre-forward role was the lofty Carsten Jancker. At 6ft 4in tall, Jancker should have been a dominant figure in the air but, surprisingly, that wasn't really where his talents lay. He was at his best with his back to the goal, getting hold of passes played forward and laying the ball off to his team-mates. Before eventually finding his way to Germany's biggest club, Jancker had to suffer the ignominy of failing a trial with Luton Town though, as we shall see, that didn't prove to be his greatest disappointment in the game.

Hitzfeld wisely retained these talented players and complemented them by bringing in some signings of his own, with his most prized acquisition being that of the irascible but prodigiously gifted central midfielder Stefan Effenberg. He started his career with Borussia Mönchengladbach in the late 1980s where his abilities caught the eye of Bayern who first signed him in 1990. The first half of Effenberg's career promised far more, however, than it actually delivered. His arrival at Bayern coincided with an alarming dip in their fortunes, with the club finishing only five points above the relegation zone in his second season there. Effenberg then moved on to the Italian side Fiorentina who were duly relegated from Serie A.

Despite his rather conspicuous lack of success Effenberg was still selected as part of the German squad for the 1994 World Cup in the USA. In their final group game the Germans were labouring against an unconvincing South Korea side, having raced into a 3-0 lead but then conceded twice. The alarmed German coach, Berti Vogts, decided to hold on to what he had got by substituting Effenberg with a more defensively minded player. As he walked off the pitch the travelling German fans cheered his substitution, which resulted in a clearly incensed Effenberg responding by 'giving them the finger'. Vogts was so enraged by Effenberg's behaviour that he sent him straight home from the tournament.

Effenberg's career was clearly in need of rehabilitation so he decided to reboot it by returning to his first club, Borussia Mönchengladbach. The following season he won his first honour in the game when his side won the DFB-Pokal, the German equivalent of the FA Cup. Effenberg then stayed at Gladbach for a few more seasons before Hitzfeld gave him a second chance at Bayern. What Hitzfeld most valued in Effenberg was what had got him into trouble so many times during his career: his tempestuous, driven character. A natural leader, Effenberg was capable of inspiring those around him and giving them confidence in their own abilities. He was never one to hide when the going got tough and Hitzfeld knew that this was the type of player he needed in his side if he was to take Bayern back to the summit of European football.

Hitzfeld then recruited two players that had started their careers in East Germany but, following the fall of the Berlin Wall, were now free to play wherever they wished. Jens Jeremies, a defensive midfield player renowned for his tigerish tackling, made his way west from Dynamo Dresden, while Thomas Linke, a central defender, had played previously in the East German First Division for Rot-Weiß Erfurt. Hitzfeld's final acquisition was an attacking midfield player, Hasan Salihamidžić. Like Jeremies and Linke, his career was greatly affected by the turbulence created by the end of the Cold War. Salihamidžić was born in Bosnia which proclaimed independence in 1992 following the disintegration of the communist Yugoslavian state. When conflict broke out between the newly created nation and Serbia Salihamidžić's father desperately sought a way to get his talented 15-year-old son out of the war-torn country, salvation coming in the shape of the German side SV Hamburg who offered him a youth contract. Salihamidžić gradually worked his way into their first team, playing so well that Hitzfeld eventually acquired him for Germany's biggest club. The Bosnian spent most of his career at Bayern but remained a strong patriot of the land of his birth, proudly scoring Bosnia-Herzegovina's first ever goal in an international match.

Hitzfeld's revitalised Bayern side got off to a flying start in the 1998/99 Bundesliga, winning eight of their first nine matches. By the halfway stage of the season they were six points clear at the top of the table and a consecutive run of eight victories between December and March put them into an almost unassailable position. There were only two sides that caused Bayern difficulties in the Bundesliga that season; Hitzfeld's old club Borussia Dortmund, who held them to a pair of 2-2 draws, and Hertha Berlin, who beat them 1-0 at home and drew 1-1 in Munich. Nevertheless, Bayern still ended the season as runaway winners of the Bundesliga, finishing 15 points ahead of second-placed Bayer Leverkusen.

Bayern's triumph in the Bundesliga was impressive enough, but there was an even greater prize awaiting them before the season was over. Hitzfeld had led the club to their first Champions League Final in a dozen years, disposing of such forces as Barcelona and Dynamo Kiev on the way. If

Bayern were to end their 23-year wait to recapture the trophy, however, they would have to beat another club with a proud history in the competition: Manchester United. Frustratingly for both managers their sides would be below strength for the final, with Giovane Élber and Bixente Lizarazu out injured for Bayern and Roy Keane and Paul Scholes suspended for United.

The last Champions League Final of the millennium was an eagerly awaited affair and few who witnessed its dramatic finale are likely to forget it, though Bayern Munich fans probably wish they could. One team's dreams were destined to end in bitter disappointment, and for most of the night it seemed likely to be Alex Ferguson (not yet a knight of the realm) and his men who would be returning home empty-handed.

Bayern went in front after only six minutes of play and then spent the remainder of the game trying to keep their lead rather than extend it; United dominating possession but unable to create any clear-cut scoring opportunities. The Germans occasionally broke out of defence on the counter attack and, with only a few minutes of the match remaining, Jancker was presented with a glorious opportunity to put the result beyond doubt. The ball came to him from a corner when he was standing on the edge of the six-yard area, unmarked with his back to the goal. Jancker had time to trap the ball, turn and shoot it past the keeper but, instead, he tried to score from a spectacular overhead kick. He struck the ball well enough but his shot cannoned back off the bar, leaving the way open for Manchester United to make a glorious comeback.

Bayern's failure to kill off United ultimately proved to be their undoing, though that seemed an unlikely outcome when the fourth official held up the illuminated board to communicate to the watching millions that there were only three minutes of added time left to be played. Indeed, the game was so close to ending that Bayern-coloured ribbons were being tied to the trophy and the UEFA president was walking down to the pitch to present the medals. The UEFA functionaries really should have known better, however, because this was 'Fergie Time'.

United won a corner and, though Bayern initially cleared it, Teddy Sheringham managed to latch on to a wayward Ryan Giggs shot and steer the ball into the net. Extra time loomed but Ferguson, sensing that the Germans were reeling on the ropes, drove his side forward in search of the winner. Their ambition was rewarded just a minute later when Sheringham got his head to a Beckham corner, sending the ball towards the goal for Ole Gunnar Solskjaer to poke it past the disbelieving Kahn.

The Bayern players were so distraught that even the shiny-domed referee, Pierluigi Collina, struggled to persuade them to continue with what little was left of the game. No side has ever come closer to lifting the European Cup before having the prize wrenched from their grasp and losing in such devastating circumstances left many of the Bayern players in tears. One of the night's most arresting images was the sight of Sami Kuffour, Bayern's impeccable Ghanaian defender, beating his fists on the pitch in frustration after the final whistle had been blown.

Bayern's last-minute misery in the Champions League Final wasn't to be the end of their disappointments that season. A few weeks later they met Werder Bremen in the final of the DFB-Pokal. They had beaten the north German side twice in the Bundesliga that season but, as so often happens in football, league form was to count for little.

Bremen went in front after only four minutes and then Jancker drew Bayern level by scoring an equaliser on the stroke of half-time. There were no further goals in the second half, or in extra time, so the winners had to be decided by a penalty shoot-out. Kahn saved the second of Bremen's penalties while Bayern scored their first four penalties, thus leaving Effenberg with the opportunity to win the trophy with his side's fifth kick. However, he sent his shot, Waddle-like, soaring over the bar to give Bremen a lifeline. The shoot-out went into sudden death and it was Bremen's goalkeeper, Frank Rost, who became the hero of the evening, scoring against Kahn before saving from Bayern's ageing Lothar Matthäus. Like Alex Ferguson's United, Hitzfeld's side had gone into the last few weeks of the 1998/99 season with a treble in sight but, in the end, had to settle for just one trophy. Football can be such a cruel game.

. . . .

Those commentators who predicted an easy victory for Bayern Munich soon felt confident they would be vindicated, with the German side dominating the early exchanges. It was their first Champions League Final since the heartbreaking defeat to Manchester United two years earlier and it was clear that they meant to banish the bad memories of that night by putting David O'Leary's young side to the sword.

Their control of the game seemed almost effortless, with Effenberg commanding the centre of the pitch and Scholl's intelligent passing and penetrating runs regularly piercing the Leeds back-line. Hitzfeld's formation enabled Élber, Salihamidžić and Scholl to run at the heart of the Leeds defence, outnumbering the two centre-halves and creating a host of openings as a result. The first chance of the game fell to Salihamidžić , whose shot from just inside the penalty area grazed the outside of Martyn's right post, though the Bosnian's rather blasé reaction suggested that another opportunity would come along soon enough.

The possession statistics evidenced Bayern's dominance, but they didn't convey anything that those watching the game hadn't already deduced for themselves. The German side were encamped in the Leeds half of the pitch and O'Leary gestured animatedly from the touchline for his side to break out and attack, but that was far easier said than done.

If Bayern weren't terrorising the centre of the Leeds defence, their two attacking wing-halves were causing havoc on the flanks. Lizarazu, in particular, was a constant thorn in Leeds's side, his advanced position tying down their right-sided players and preventing them from moving forwards. Indeed, it was a magnificent cross from the French player that created Bayern's next opportunity; Élber heading the ball over the bar when it seemed easier to score.

Hitzfeld was visibly disappointed by Élber's failure to convert that chance, but he didn't have to wait too long for the Brazilian to right that wrong. Effenberg made a robust, but fair, challenge on Bowyer as he snuffed out another attempt by Leeds to break out of their half of the pitch. He passed the ball cross-field to Scholl, who easily skipped past a sliding tackle from Harte and then clipped the ball into the penalty area. Élber was first to it, skimming his shot across the turf past Martyn's forlorn dive. The first goal had come after only 20 minutes of play and, if the game continued in this vein, it looked as if the Germans could be home and dry by half-time.

· ·

In preparation for his first full season as manager David O'Leary spent the summer of 1999 undertaking some significant surgery to his playing squad. His first foray into the transfer market had taken place a few months earlier, when he astutely brought local hero David Batty back to the club where he had started his career. The Leeds-born Batty had been a key plank of Howard Wilkinson's side that won the Second Division title and the championship within a three-year spell in the early 1990s, his tenacious, uncompromising style of play enamouring him to the club's fans.

Batty had never had a strong relationship with the schoolmasterly Wilkinson, however, and it became increasingly tense as Leeds's attempt to defend their crown failed miserably. To the surprise and dismay of Leeds fans he was sold to

Blackburn Rovers in 1993 where, within a couple of years, he was part of another title-winning side.

Batty subsequently moved on to Newcastle United and it was from there that O'Leary brought him back to Leeds. Re-signing a fan favourite was not just a sentimental gesture, but a clear declaration of O'Leary's ambition to return Leeds to the top of the English game. He needed an experienced player to give balance to his team of 'babies' and Batty, who was still a regular member of the England side, fitted the bill perfectly.

Despite not being particularly tall or well-built, there was no mistaking Batty's courage or desire to get 'stuck into' a game. He was often used as a deep-lying midfield player, playing just in front of the centre-halves with a brief to stymie opposition attacks and protect the defence. Not blessed with electric pace, Batty compensated by running tirelessly during games, achieving with endeavour what others accomplished by stealth.

In order to bring in new talent O'Leary had to release six of the club's players, with three of them being put out to pasture at neighbouring Bradford City. The most significant departure was that of the club's leading goalscorer for the previous two seasons, Jimmy Floyd Hasselbaink. He had made a big reputation for himself at Leeds and tried to use it as a lever to extract a huge increase in his salary. The amount that he asked for, however, was so far in excess of what other players were being paid that the club had no choice other than to refuse his demands. Hasselbaink duly handed in a transfer request and was eventually sold to Atlético Madrid for £12m, making Leeds a healthy £10m profit on what it had cost them to buy him in the first place. With the funds generated from these transfers O'Leary signed Eirik Bakke, a Norwegian midfield player, for £1.75m and then brought in Danny Mills to provide competition for Gary Kelly at right-back. The high point of Mills's career came at the 2002 World Cup finals when he was an ever-present in the England side following an injury to Gary Neville.

O'Leary's revamped side started the new season in an indifferent fashion, winning two and losing two of their first five games. The match that kick-started their new campaign into life was a much-enjoyed away win over George Graham's Tottenham Hotspur, with five further consecutive victories lifting them to the top of the table. They stayed there until early in the new millennium, when events off the pitch started to derail their season.

The fixture list had left Leeds without any games to play for a fortnight in mid-January and O'Leary thought about taking the squad abroad for a few days in the sunshine. He finally decided against it, opting to give his players time at home with their families instead. It was a seemingly mundane decision but it was to have massive consequences for the club's fortunes, not just that season but, arguably, for years afterwards.

O'Leary instructed his players to stay at home and rest, an edict that might have suited some of the older players, but it left some of the youngsters with more time on their hands than they knew how to fill. A group of them, including Lee Bowyer and Jonathan Woodgate, disobeyed O'Leary's orders and went on a heavy drinking session in Leeds city centre, with their ill-advised bender eventually turning into a scenario of nightmarish proportions.

A few days later police officers arrived at the Leeds training ground to interview Bowyer and Woodgate about an attack which had resulted in a student, Sarfraz Najeib, having his leg broken and his face fractured and bitten. The police carried out their investigation and, a couple of months later, Bowyer and Woodgate, among others, were charged with grievous bodily harm and affray. The trial date was eventually fixed to start in January 2001, over a year after the incident had taken place and, in the meantime, all the affected players could do was to wait for their day in court. Leeds decided to stand by Bowyer and Woodgate, picking them for first team matches on the basis that they were innocent until proven guilty. The FA, meanwhile, took a harder line, declaring that neither Bowyer nor Woodgate would play for England while the charges were hanging over them.

There was an inevitable furore over the incident and it had a predictably negative impact on the remainder of Leeds's season. Victories became less commonplace and Manchester United soon took their place at the top of the table. Leeds's form then picked up a little but a run of four consecutive defeats between late March and mid-April, including a chastening 4-0 hammering at home to Arsenal, saw them slip down into fourth place. There were only three places in the Champions League for English clubs at the time and it was soon clear where two of them were going, with Manchester United on course for another title and a run of eight consecutive victories cementing Arsenal into the runners-up spot.

That left Leeds and Liverpool to fight it out for third place in the table. O'Leary's side duly got it, but that was due more to a collapse in Liverpool's form than it was to their own performances. The Merseyside team were second prior to their five final fixtures but failed to win any of them, not even scoring a single goal. O'Leary's side could only draw their last two matches but that was enough to secure entry to the lucrative Champions League. Ironically, the pivotal moment came on the final day of the season when Liverpool were beaten by Bradford City, with David Wetherall, who had been sold to the Yorkshire club by O'Leary the previous summer, scoring the game's only goal.

While Leeds were qualifying for their first campaign in the Champions League, Bayern Munich were trying to banish the haunting memory of their last-minute defeat to Manchester United in the previous season's final. Hitzfeld showed his faith in his players by making far fewer acquisitions than he had the previous summer. He brought in Patrik Andersson, a central defender who had been part of the Swedish side that finished third at the 1994 World Cup, and a second Brazilian striker, Paulo Sérgio, who had played for Bayer Leverkusen for a number of seasons before moving to Roma in Serie A.

Unlike the previous season Bayern got off to an uncertain start in the Bundesliga, drawing their opening game at home to SV Hamburg and then losing away to Bayer Leverkusen, who would prove to be their chief rivals for the title. Eight wins from their next ten games pushed them back up the table, though that good run ended with a defeat to local rivals TSV 1860 Munich, who beat them twice in the Bundesliga that season. Bayern's steady progress in the league was matched by their performances in the Champions League and DFB-Pokal meaning that, by the start of May, they were still in with a chance of winning the treble of trophies that they had come so close to securing a year earlier.

Bayern's opponents in the semi-finals of the Champions League were Real Madrid, who they had already beaten twice during the second group stage of the competition by an aggregate of eight goals to three. Buoyed by those two victories, Bayern's prospect of reaching a second consecutive Champions League Final did not look unrealistic, but the Spanish giants had clearly paced themselves better. Bayern lost the first leg at the Bernabéu Stadium 2-0 and, though an early goal by Jancker back in Munich gave them hope, an equaliser by Nicolas Anelka before half-time effectively ended their involvement in the competition. The away goals rule meant that Bayern had to score three times without reply to reach the final and that was simply too much of an ask, with Élber's second-half goal being all they could manage.

In between the two legs of their Champions League semi-final, Bayern played in the final of the DFB-Pokal. Once again their opponents were Werder Bremen but there was to be no repeat victory for the underdogs; Hitzfeld's men exacting revenge for the previous season's disappointment with a 3-0 win. It looked at the time as if that would be their only triumph of the season, with Bayern trailing Bayer Leverkusen by three points in the Bundesliga.

Bayer only needed a draw from their final game of their season in order to win their first league title and they were widely expected to get it, especially given that their opponents were Unterhaching. They were one of the Bundesliga's smallest clubs and their ground, located in the suburbs of Munich, held just 15,000 spectators. Surprisingly, Bayer crashed to a 2-0 defeat while Bayern put three goals past Werder Bremen (again) to become league champions for a second consecutive season, albeit only on goal difference. Hitzfeld's side had been denied two trophies at the death a year earlier, but now experienced just what it was like to win one in such a fashion. Perhaps football wasn't such a cruel game after all.

. . . .

The longer the first half went on the more frustrated the Leeds players became. Bayern Munich were pulling them all over the pitch, maintaining their own rhythm while preventing the English side from developing any of their own. It was, perhaps, therefore inevitable that their tempers would become frayed and their patience exhausted. The first Leeds player to be cautioned by the referee was David Batty, his scything challenge on Effenberg temporarily halting another Bayern attack but only at the expense of a yellow card. Batty accepted his punishment without murmur, simply casting a fierce glance at the prone German as he calmly walked away.

The next Leeds player to have his name taken was Danny Mills, for whom Lizarazu's latest forward run was plainly one too many to have to contain by legal means. The most venomous tackle, however, was made by Alan Smith, whose two-footed dive at Kuffour's feet brought incensed Bayern fans to their feet. David O'Leary's heart was in his mouth as the referee marched towards Smith, his hand already reaching to his back pocket. To his great relief, and that of all watching Leeds fans, the card he flourished was yellow, but it could just as easily have been red.

Bayern continued to dominate the game and, five minutes before half-time, they had a glorious opportunity to double their lead. It started with Scholl whose jinking run took him past both Batty and Harte and into the penalty area. As the third Leeds player closed in on him he lofted the ball into Salihamidžić's path, the Bosnian gaining a vital half a yard on Mills whose desperate lunge connected only with his ankle. The contact was sufficient to bring Salihamidžić crashing to the floor and the referee pointed immediately to the penalty spot. There was little protest from the Leeds players as the offence was blatant but they were incensed by Bayern's attempts to get Mills sent off, with a number of the German side vigorously pointing out to the Dutch official that this was Mills's second bookable offence and that he should be leaving the pitch as a consequence. The referee waved their complaints away but soon had to intervene as the Leeds players started to push and jostle their opponents, their anger threatening to boil over into fisticuffs.

The furore took some time to die down and it plainly didn't help the nominated Bayern penalty taker, Mehmet Scholl. He stayed apart from the fray, nervously juggling the ball between his hands as he waited for the penalty area to clear so that he could take his spot-kick. Eventually he was able to place the ball on the ground and then struck it cleanly enough, but it was fired at the centre of the goal and Martyn wisely delayed his dive until the last moment, clearing the shot away with his legs.

There were no further chances for either side before half-time and neither of the two managers looked particularly pleased as they walked to the dressing rooms. O'Leary knew that his team were fortunate to still be in the game, while Hitzfeld was more than a little anxious that his side's dominance had only translated itself into a one-goal lead. Way above them in the stands Cyril Ormsby puffed out his cheeks and reached into his bag for his flask. As he sipped on his half-time tea he smiled gently at the worried young Leeds fan sat beside him, murmuring softly, 'Football's a funny game, son. If a German's missed a penalty, maybe it will be our night.'

. . . .

Leeds had done well to qualify for the Champions League, but O'Leary knew that if they were to make any real progress in the competition they would have to invest heavily in the playing squad. Finding the funds to do so was normally the stumbling block for such ambitions, but the Irishman soon found that his aspirations were matched by that of the club's chairman, Peter Ridsdale. In the summer of 2000 Leeds borrowed over £17m to spend on new players, which may be a relatively small sum for a modern-day Premier League club but, back then, it represented a massive investment.

The first to arrive at the club was French midfielder Olivier Dacourt, an aggressive ball-winner with a decent passing range, though his disciplinary record did leave a little to be desired. O'Leary needed another competitive central midfielder as David Batty was struggling with injuries and Dacourt, purchased for a club-record fee of £7.2m, was the ideal replacement. Next in was Australian striker Mark Viduka, who was signed from Celtic for £6m. A big, brawny forward, Viduka was surprisingly nimble for a man of his size and, as his record in Scotland showed, more than capable of finding the net on a regular basis. Finally, £4.25m was paid to Liverpool to acquire the services of Dominic Matteo, a versatile player who was equally at home in the centre of defence, at left-back or even on the left side of midfield.

Leeds entered the Champions League in the third qualifying round and, despite being seeded, still managed to end up being paired with TSV 1860 Munich, who had finished fourth in the previous season's Bundesliga. It was a tough draw, made harder by the fact that Batty, Kewell and Woodgate were out with injury and Matteo hadn't yet joined the club. That left O'Leary with no option other than to put three substitutes on to the bench who had never even played for the first team before. It was hardly the start that Leeds had wanted, with the eagerly awaited financial bonanza from getting into the group stage of the Champions League hanging delicately in the balance.

The first leg of the tie was played at Elland Road and it was memorable, not for Leeds's 2-1 victory, or for the quality of football, but for the dire performance of the Cypriot referee. It was not a particularly rough game but the referee still saw fit to dismiss three players, including Bakke and Dacourt for Leeds. Leeds's goals came from a Smith header in the first half and a dubious penalty 20 minutes from time, converted by Harte. One of O'Leary's main objectives for the game was to prevent the Germans from scoring an away goal, and he almost secured it, but deep into stoppage time Munich got a goal back. That left the Germans as favourites to progress to the next round as they only needed a 1-0 win back in Munich to dump Leeds out on the away goals rule.

O'Leary may have struggled to pick a team for the first leg, but his options for the return fixture in Munich were even more restricted. Leeds were facing one of their most important games for years but he didn't have any experienced central midfielders available, with Batty out injured and Bakke and Dacourt suspended following their dismissals in the home tie. The Irishman therefore had no option other than to make do and mend, playing Lucas Radebe, a centre-half, alongside Matthew Jones, a novice who wasn't even fully fit. If that wasn't bad enough, Gary Kelly also had to play out of position on the right side of midfield, while Bowyer was fielded in an unfamiliar role on the opposite flank.

Nevertheless, Leeds managed to emerge triumphant once again; Smith scoring the game's only goal after taking advantage of confusion in the Munich defence to win the ball and hit it low past the goalkeeper. It was an excellent result for O'Leary's young side and an even better one for the club's finances, with entry to the group stage of the competition guaranteeing millions of pounds of revenue.

Leeds were only third seeds in the draw for the first group stage so were expecting a difficult draw, but what they got was eye-wateringly tough. They were paired with AC Milan and Barcelona, two of the game's giants, and with only two sides qualifying from the four-team group it looked likely that their European campaign would be over before the leaves had fallen from the trees. Their first game was away to Barcelona, with O'Leary's already daunting task made much harder by the fact that Bakke, Batty, Kewell, Matteo, Woodgate and Viduka were all unavailable, the latter having gone to play for Australia at the Sydney Olympics. In front of a crowd of 85,000 spectators Barcelona duly took Leeds apart, with the Brazilian Rivaldo causing much of the damage. Retreating in the face of the Catalan onslaught, O'Leary's side defended too deeply and allowed their opponents far too much of the ball. They were 2-0 down within 20 minutes of the start and eventually succumbed to a 4-0 thrashing. Clearly, the Champions League was going to be every bit as demanding as Leeds had feared.

A week later Leeds played their next game in the competition; a home fixture against AC Milan. O'Leary was finally able to field a full-strength midfield and the impact that had on the team's performance was palpable. The midfield four of Bakke, Bowyer, Dacourt and Matteo didn't allow the Italians to have any time on the ball, constantly harrying them and denying them space in which to build attacks. The game was played in dreadful conditions, with the rain pelting down throughout, and the Italians struggled to create any clear-cut chances.

The match was on the verge of ending in a 0-0 draw when Bowyer struck a speculative shot from 20 yards out, the foul Yorkshire weather fortuitously coming to his aid. Milan's Brazilian keeper, Dida, managed to get to the ball without too much difficulty, but it was so wet and slippery that it squirmed out of his grasp and slipped into the net. It was a lucky win, perhaps, but it was a win nevertheless.

Leeds's victory over Milan wasn't the only reason for O'Leary to be joyful that night as, surprisingly, Barcelona lost 3-0 away to Besiktas. That left the group table finely balanced with all four teams level on three points after having won one and lost one game each. Leeds's next fixture was against the side from Istanbul and it would be a difficult one for the club, though not for any reasons that had anything to do with football. O'Leary's side had enjoyed an excellent run in the previous season's UEFA Cup, reaching the semi-finals after knocking out a number of prestigious sides, including AS Roma and Spartak Moscow. They were drawn against Turkish side Galatasaray in the last four but, in the evening before the first leg, events took a decidedly sinister turn.

Leeds fans were attacked in Istanbul's Taksim Square by a group of knife-wielding hooligans and two blameless onlookers, Christopher Loftus and Kevin Speight, were fatally wounded. They had not gone to Turkey with the intention of causing trouble but simply had the terrible misfortune to get caught up in a disturbance not of their making. The response of UEFA and Galatasaray was little short of disgraceful. Not only did the competition's administrators insist that the game went ahead regardless, but they also refused Leeds's request for a one-minute silence in honour of the two dead fans. Rather than show any remorse the Galatasaray fans in the stadium proceeded to shower the Leeds players with missiles, and then howled down an announcer who tried to read out a message of sympathy about what had occurred the previous evening.

Another trip to Istanbul was the last thing that Leeds would have wanted, but the draw dictated that they had to return. Besiktas approached the first match in Leeds in a respectful manner, bringing only a small number of supporters to Elland Road and then having their players give out flowers to spectators to commemorate the two murdered fans. Pleasingly, the game itself turned out to be one of Leeds's finest performances of the season.

Bowyer scored twice, his first coming after only seven minutes when he poked home a cross from Harte, and his second arrived a minute from time when he won the ball deep in his own half, played it forward, then raced up the pitch to get on the end of the move and slot it past the goalkeeper. In between those two strikes, Leeds scored four further goals. Viduka, back from the Olympics, scored Leeds's second after 12 minutes, flicking a header past the goalkeeper following a cross from Kelly. Ten minutes later Matteo scrambled home Leeds's third and, midway through the second half, Bakke rifled in a shot from just outside the penalty area to make it 4-0. A fifth was then added by Darren Huckerby in one of his rare Champions League appearances.

Barcelona unexpectedly lost at home to AC Milan that night which meant that Leeds topped the group table, equal on points with the Italians. Suddenly Champions League football didn't look so tough after all. Dreams of another goal-fest against Besiktas in the return fixture were not realised, however, with the Turkish side putting in a much more resilient performance at their own ground. The game ended 0-0 and, thankfully, there was no repeat of the dreadful violence that had occurred the previous time Leeds had visited Istanbul.

Paul Robinson made his first appearance in the competition, having been drafted in to replace the injured Nigel Martyn, and he performed admirably in daunting circumstances. O'Leary also had to make do without Alan Smith, who had already received enough yellow cards in the tournament to earn a one-game suspension. The group's other fixture between Milan and Barcelona ended in a draw too, meaning that a Leeds victory at home to Barcelona would confirm their qualification for the next round.

The visit of the Catalan giants to Elland Road was a major event for Leeds and the game got off to a wonderful start, with Bowyer scoring the first goal direct from a free kick after only five minutes, though the Barcelona goalkeeper should never have allowed the ball to sail over his head and drop into the far top corner of the net.

Barcelona came back strongly and Robinson had to make a number of excellent saves to keep Leeds in front. Rivaldo had destroyed the young Leeds side in their first encounter at the Nou Camp and it was the Brazilian who finally denied them a famous victory. Deep into stoppage time, with whistles echoing around Elland Road as Leeds fans frantically implored the referee to end the game, Phillip Cocu whipped in a desperate cross from the left-hand side. The ball was met by Gerard whose header struck the post but it bounced out conveniently to Rivaldo, who made no mistake from a few yards out. O'Leary's side had been moments away from qualifying for the next round, but the draw meant that they had to avoid defeat away to Milan if they were to realise that dream.

While Leeds and Barcelona were battling away in Yorkshire the Italians defeated Besiktas to claim the first of the group's two qualifying places. That left them with nothing to play for in their final game against Leeds but they didn't ease up. Milan attacked Leeds from the start and were awarded a penalty midway through the first half following a disputed handball by Gary Kelly. Robinson dived in the opposite direction to Shevchenko's spot-kick and was relieved to see the ball hit the opposite post and bounce away. It was, therefore, against the run of play when Leeds went in front; Matteo scoring with a header from a Bowyer corner after evading his marker. O'Leary's side hung on to their lead until midway through the second half when Serginho raced into the Leeds penalty area and slotted the ball past Robinson. The young goalkeeper had to make some good saves to keep the Italians from going in front, but Leeds resisted the pressure and duly got the draw they needed. Barcelona, meanwhile, hammered Besiktas 5-0 at the Nou Camp, but it was to no avail. They had been knocked out of the Champions League by the upstarts from Yorkshire, with that 4-0 thrashing in the first group game now having been well and truly avenged.

Unlike Leeds, Bayern Munich were one of the top seeds in the draw for the first group stage. That meant they received a relatively easy draw, with Paris St-Germain, Helsingborg and Rosenborg not expected to pose them too much of a challenge. Hitzfeld largely kept faith with his existing squad for the new campaign, making just one acquisition: French international right-back Willy Sagnol. He had started his career at Saint-Étienne before moving on to Monaco, where he established a strong reputation as an attacking wing-back. Bayern made a good start to the 2000/01 season, winning five of their opening six matches in the Bundesliga, and they carried that good vein of form into the first group stage of the Champions League. Helsingborg were beaten 3-1 away from home and then Rosenborg were defeated by the same scoreline in Munich.

All seemed to be going well for Bayern but then they embarked on their worst spell of the season. A Champions League defeat away to Paris St-Germain, with the French side scoring the game's only goal in the 90th minute, was followed a few days later by a home defeat to Hansa Rostock in the Bundesliga. Hitzfeld's side then won only two out of the next seven league matches, during which came the most embarrassing result of all: a DFB-Pokal defeat to FC Magdeburg. The East German club played in the fourth tier of German football and few expected anything other than a routine victory for Bayern. The minnows took the lead, however, and Hitzfeld's side only managed to secure an equaliser 11 minutes from the end of normal time. There were no further goals so the tie had to be settled by a penalty shoot-out; Jeremies and Élber both having their penalties saved to hand Magdeburg a famous victory.

Bayern nursed their wounds by beating Paris St-Germain in the Champions League, 2-0, with Salihamidžić scoring after three minutes and Sérgio one minute from the end of the game. That meant that Hitzfeld's team would qualify for the next round if they could win their penultimate group game at home to Helsingborg. The Swedish side initially looked to be out of their depth in the competition, having lost their first three matches and conceded 13 goals in the process. The Swedes restored a measure of pride with a home victory over Rosenborg and then travelled to Munich with only a slim chance of staying in the tournament. Bayern were frustrated by the Swedes, with the game ending in a 0-0 draw, but Hitzfeld's side still qualified for the second round, courtesy of Paris St-Germain's 7-2 victory over Rosenborg in the night's other fixture.

· ·

The second half started as the first period had ended, with the Germans clearly in the ascendency. Willy Sagnol was proving to be particularly effective, his rapid darts down the wing troubling the much more pedestrian Harte and his accurate crosses keeping Matteo occupied in the heart of the Leeds defence. He created a fine chance for Élber in the opening minutes but his shot was parried by Martyn and the ball cleared to safety by the ever-alert Mills.

It's often said that in a boxing contest it only takes one lucky punch for the underdog to get the upper hand and, ten minutes into the second half, the besieged Leeds side got exactly that. The move actually started with a Bayern attack; Sagnol advancing briskly down Leeds's left wing with the ball at his feet. He approached Harte, confident that he had the beating of the Irishman once more, but his belief was misplaced this time. Harte took the ball cleanly from his feet and, looking up, saw Kewell advancing into the space that Sagnol had left behind. Harte's pass to the Australian was not only accurate but also perfectly weighted. The ball landed right in Kewell's path and he soon had Kuffour backtracking as he bore down on Kahn's goal. He managed to skip past the Ghanaian's challenge but Andersson's clumsy tackle sent him flying, the referee immediately blowing his whistle for a foul.

The offence took place a few yards outside the penalty area, midway between its centre and left edge. Kahn took control of organising Bayern's defensive wall, placing his defenders as carefully as if he were arranging the side's annual team photograph. The Leeds players, meanwhile, did their best to hamper the German goalkeeper's efforts by trying to inveigle themselves into the wall.

The responsibility for taking the free kick fell to Harte, whose ability with a dead ball was uncontested among the Leeds players. He waited for Kahn to perfect his wall and then for the referee to signal that the kick could be taken, his concentration undisturbed by the long delay. His shot, when it eventually came, was unstoppable; thundering over the heads of the Bayern defenders and escaping Kahn's determined dive. Up in the stands Cyril waited for the young man next to him to finish jumping up and down before winking happily at him; a wordless gesture that conveyed a myriad of joyous emotions.

• •

The Champions League was in its most bloated form in 2000/01, with the 16 qualifiers from the first group stage being drawn into four further groups of four rather than playing knockout ties. Bayern's gentle introduction to the competition was definitely over as they were pitched against Arsenal (Thierry Henry, Patrick Vierra, Dennis Bergkamp, et al), Spartak Moscow (who had beaten Real Madrid at home in the previous round), and Lyon, who were about to embark on a run of seven consecutive French league titles. Leeds's reward for seeing off Barcelona was to face the holders of the Champions League trophy, Real Madrid. If that wasn't tough enough they also had to contend with the reigning Italian champions, Lazio, and Anderlecht, who had topped their first-round group ahead of Manchester United.

Bayern got off to a good start by beating Lyon 1-0 at home and then travelled to London to play Arsene Wenger's Arsenal. The English club started the stronger, with Henry and Kanu causing the Bayern defence problems and each of them creating a goal for the other. Henry scored after only three minutes and Kanu doubled Arsenal's lead nine minutes into the second half. Arsenal may have won the game if they had been able to hold on to their two-goal lead for longer but Bayern got a goal back almost immediately and then levelled the tie just ten minutes later. Arsenal conceded a free kick ten yards outside their penalty area and Mehmet Scholl scored with a delightful shot, despite slipping over on the pitch as he kicked the ball. It was a hard-won point against an excellent team and it moved Bayern to the top of the group.

Spartak Moscow were Bayern's next victims, being beaten 1-0 in Munich and then 3-0 at home. The Luzhniki Stadium had become a daunting place for teams to visit in that season's Champions League, with Arsenal, Bayer Leverkusen, Real Madrid and Sporting Lisbon all defeated there prior to Bayern's visit. The game was played on a badly cut-up pitch but Hitzfeld's side soon went in front; Mehmet Scholl settling his side down with a goal after 17 minutes. Scholl then scored again with an unstoppable penalty and Paulo Sérgio rounded off the victory with a headed goal three minutes before the end of the game.

Bayern needed just a draw away to Lyon to secure their qualification for the quarter-finals, but the French side inflicted on them their heaviest defeat in the Champions League for six years. Paulo Sérgio missed a good chance to score early in the game and from then on Lyon dominated the match, scoring twice in the first half and then again in the second half to win 3-0. That result meant that Hitzfeld's side had to avoid defeat at home to Arsenal in their final group game in order to reach the last eight. Bayern duly rose to the challenge, winning 1-0 after Élber headed in a cross from Salihamidžić.

Leeds's opening group game was at home to Real Madrid and O'Leary struggled once again to put out a team with a strong midfield, with Bakke, Batty and Dacourt all unavailable. The heart of the Real Madrid side included such luminaries as Luís Figo, Claude Makélélé and Steve McManaman and, unsurprisingly, they dominated Leeds's makeshift midfield. Leeds managed to hold out until midway through the second half but then two goals in three minutes decided the contest, Fernando Hierro scoring the first with a header and Raúl adding the second with a low shot that Robinson had no chance of saving.

Any disappointment that the Leeds fans felt was soon washed away when the club announced that it had agreed to pay West Ham United £18m for their highly-rated young central defender Rio Ferdinand. It was a world record fee at the time for a defensive player and the acquisition was a major coup for O'Leary. Ferdinand had it all: blistering pace, great technique, strength in the air and an unbelievable poise for a 22-year-old. If anyone had doubted the club's ambitions then this signing, above all others, confirmed that Leeds were aiming right for the top.

Ferdinand was signed too late, however, to be eligible for Leeds's next Champions League fixture, an away trip to Lazio. The Italian side were managed by Sven-Göran Eriksson and he had a number of world-class players at his disposal, including Hernán Crespo, Pavel Nedvěd and Juan Sebastián Verón. To their credit, O'Leary's young side refused to be overwhelmed by the occasion and they grew stronger as the game went on. Woodgate had an outstanding game at the heart of the defence, but it was Viduka and Smith who deservedly gained most of the plaudits. With ten minutes of the game remaining there was a beautiful interplay of passes between them; Smith knocking the ball to Viduka, who deceived the Lazio defence with an adroit back-heel back to Smith, who then slid the ball past the goalkeeper. The Italians were unable to find an equaliser and Leeds's three hard-won points moved them up to second place in the table behind Real Madrid.

The away victory over Lazio was followed by a break in Champions League fixtures until mid-February, giving O'Leary's side an opportunity to apply some much-needed focus to their faltering Premier League campaign. They won only three games out of 12 between mid-October and New Year's Day and duly ended the calendar year down in 12th place.

The last month of 2000, however, did see Harry Kewell and David Batty making a welcome return from injury. Batty's late substitute appearance in a home victory over Sunderland was his first game in over a year. He had suffered first with a heart condition after breaking some ribs and then, bizarrely, ruptured his Achilles tendon while pushing his children on a garden swing. The latter injury nearly ended his career and there were many who feared that the midfield dynamo would never be seen on a football pitch again. Batty worked hard to get fit and was rewarded with a rapturous reception from the Leeds fans when he finally returned to the fray.

The start of 2001 brought with it the long-awaited trial of Bowyer and Woodgate for an attack on a Leeds student. The trial was held at Hull Crown Court and, as the case dragged on, the two players responded in quite different ways. It was expected that both of them would struggle to keep their places in the team, with the pressure of the court proceedings and their inability to train having a significant effect. Rather than being swamped by his circumstances, however, Bowyer rose above them, playing some of the best football of his career. It was fortunate for him that many of Leeds's matches were played at a weekend, when the court wasn't sitting, but he still managed to make most of the midweek games, once even being flown by helicopter to Liverpool so that he could play against Everton. Woodgate, by contrast, visibly lost weight during the trial and didn't play again that season.

When Leeds returned to their Champions League campaign David O'Leary was in the novel position of having almost a full squad to select from. The next two ties were both against Anderlecht, with the first fixture at Elland Road turning out to be a fairly drab game. The Belgian side took the lead midway through the second half but a blistering free kick from Harte, ten yards from the right-hand corner of the penalty area, levelled the scores. Bowyer had raced to the game from his trial in Hull and had to endure some tough challenges from Anderlecht players who were attempting to goad him into retaliating. The young midfielder kept his composure and, four minutes from time, scored Leeds's winner. Alan Smith pounced on a mistake by the Belgian defence and steered the ball into the path of Bowyer, who slid the ball past the goalkeeper from the right-hand side of the penalty area.

That night Real Madrid defeated Lazio to pretty much end the Italian club's interest in the competition, with the Spanish side odds-on favourites to top the group. That meant that Leeds's return fixture against Anderlecht effectively became the decider for the second qualification place. With so much at stake it came as no particular surprise that the coach of the Belgian side, Aimé Anthuenis, tried to gain an advantage before a ball had even been kicked.

He dismissed Leeds as an average team, claimed that they had been fortunate to have won the first encounter and predicted that Anderlecht would win the second game easily. There was some substance behind the bravado, however, as the Belgians had a strong record at home, having defeated Manchester United, Dynamo Kiev, PSV Eindhoven, Porto and Lazio at the Constant Vanden Stock Stadium that season. Records are made to be broken, however, and Leeds proceeded to smash it in some style.

The match was only 13 minutes old when Leeds struck first; Smith scoring with a volley after Viduka had beaten the defender on the left-hand side of the penalty area and sent in a cross that Smith could hardly fail to convert. Leeds had lined up without Bowyer in the team, his trial precluding him from being in Brussels in time for the kick-off, but his replacement, Dominic Matteo, had an excellent game. Twenty minutes after the opening goal he sent over a looping cross that cleared the entire Anderlecht defence and Viduka read the flight of the ball perfectly, rising majestically to send a header past the stranded goalkeeper. Five minutes later Leeds were three up when Smith scored the best goal of the game; a deft chip over the advancing goalkeeper after a delightful sequence of passes had opened up the Anderlecht defence. The Belgians got a goal back 15 minutes from time but Leeds soon restored their three-goal lead, Harte scoring from a penalty given for a foul on Viduka.

While Leeds were hammering Anderlecht, Lazio and Real Madrid played out a draw in Rome. That meant that O'Leary's side qualified for the quarter-finals with two games to spare and were also in the enviable position of being able to visit the Bernabéu Stadium for what would be no more than a glorified friendly. Real Madrid won 3-2, but the Yorkshiremen came mighty close to getting a well-deserved draw against the reigning European champions. The difference between the two sides was a goal that should never have been given; Raúl punching the ball straight into the net from a Figo free kick. The Polish referee apologised to the Leeds players after the game, once he had seen a replay of the goal on television, but that, of course, didn't change the outcome. O'Leary rested Martyn, Batty and Dacourt for the meaningless home tie against Lazio but his weakened side still performed well, playing out an entertaining 3-3 draw.

• •

Football is ostensibly a game for the limbs but, more often than not, it can become a battle of wits; chess with muscles. Harte's equalising goal changed the nature of the match in an instant, transforming it from a succession of German onslaughts directed at a plucky English defence into a much more even contest. Hitzfeld's side still dominated possession of the ball but their play was visibly more cautious, the lingering memory of the last-minute defeat to Manchester United instinctively preventing them from committing too many men to the attack. The Germans were, in effect, stuck in no man's land; fearful of moving forward in numbers but unwilling to retreat into defence. Leeds, meanwhile, were content to let the Germans have the ball, waiting patiently for the opportunity to counter-attack; their young guns keeping their legs fresh for a blistering assault on the Bayern goal.

In an attempt to break the stalemate Hitzfeld decided to take off Scholl, who had never been quite as effective after his penalty miss, replacing him with the forceful striker, Carsten Jancker. His team-mates soon started to play the ball up to him, hoping that he could hold it up long enough for attacking moves to be built around him. Rio Ferdinand was wise to the danger, however, using his pace and aerial power to minimise the substitute's impact on the game. At the other end of the pitch there was a similar duel between Sami Kuffour and Mark Viduka, with the Ghanaian having to work hard to contain the burly Australian whenever Leeds had the opportunity to move forward.

The game's next chance fell to the English side, though it began once again with a Bayern attack. Another forward dash by Lizarazu tested the Leeds defence and Ferdinand did well to intercept his pass to Salihamidžić, sliding into its path and shepherding it to the feet of Dacourt. The Frenchman spotted Bowyer sprinting into the space previously guarded by Lizarazu and he quickly hoisted the ball into the gap. The young Englishman eagerly seized the pass and headed towards goal, his momentum only halted when Linke's last-ditch tackle pushed the ball out for a corner. Bowyer swiftly took the kick, sending the ball spiralling away from Kahn's grasp and towards the head of Dominic Matteo who had raced in from the edge of the penalty area.

The Leeds defender climbed above Andersson and his connection with the ball was sweet, though its outcome was less so, with his effort clipping the crossbar on its way out of play. The Bayern players were noticeably relieved; the ghosts of Sheringham and Solskjaer clearly visible in their panicked eyes.

• •

The quarter-finals of the 2000/01 Champions League were dominated by English and Spanish sides, with three teams from each nation reaching the last eight. The rules of the competition precluded Leeds from playing any of the other English clubs or Real Madrid (as they had been in the same second-round group). Instead, Leeds were drawn to play Deportivo La Coruña, the reigning Spanish champions, who had already knocked AC Milan and Juventus out of the competition.

The first leg was played at Elland Road and O'Leary's young team put in a bravura performance, playing fast, free-flowing football that forced Deportivo on to the back foot. Leeds's endeavours were rewarded midway through the first half when Ian Harte smashed a blistering free kick into the net from just outside the penalty area, abetted by Kewell who adroitly prevented the defensive wall from getting in the way.

Harte then played a key role in Leeds's second goal, sending over a cross from the left wing that Alan Smith headed past the goalkeeper. With momentum behind them Leeds piled forward and tried to extend their lead, their adventurousness paying off when, midway through the second half, Rio Ferdinand scored his first goal for the club. Harte was involved again, sending his corner to the near post where a Deportivo defender headed the ball over his own goalkeeper and into the path of Ferdinand, who then threaded the ball between the defenders standing on the goal line. A three-goal lead was an excellent advantage to take to Spain for the second leg, though their success at preventing Deportivo from scoring an away goal would eventually prove to be just as crucial.

In between the two games against Deportivo the trial of Lee Bowyer and Jonathan Woodgate came to an unexpected conclusion. While the jury were deliberating over the verdicts a Sunday newspaper published an article in which the victim's father claimed that the alleged assault was racially motivated. The prosecution had already stated in advance of the trial that there was no suggestion of there being such a motive for the attack so the judge felt he had no option other than to order a retrial. That meant that Bowyer was available to play away fixtures in the Champions League, his last such game having been Leeds's victory over Lazio in Rome four months earlier.

Leeds may have had a three-goal lead to take to Spain but Deportivo had already proved that season that they could overturn such a deficit. In the second group stage the Galician side went three goals behind to Paris St-Germain but then scored four times in the last 30 minutes to win the match. Therefore, the last thing O'Leary would have wanted was for his young charges to concede an early goal, but that's exactly what they did; Kewell conceding a penalty after only nine minutes. The spot-kick was converted and Leeds had to battle hard to prevent any further goals being scored before half-time.

The longer the match went on the more secure Leeds looked but, with 17 minutes remaining, the Spaniards scored again following a quickly taken free kick. Deportivo needed only one more goal to take the tie into extra time and they pushed hard for it, putting the Leeds defence under constant pressure for the remainder of the game. O'Leary's side held out, but only just; Deportivo hit the frame of the goal three times before the night was over.

Bayern's draw for the quarter-finals, meanwhile, was a mouth-watering encounter with Manchester United; the first meeting between the two clubs since their dramatic Champions League Final two years earlier. The first tie was played at a packed Old Trafford and this time it was the Germans' turn to get a late winner from a set piece. With just six minutes remaining Bayern won a free kick in the United half and Effenberg lofted the ball into the penalty area. Linke got to it first, flicking it into the path of Sérgio who ran in behind the United defence to tap it into the net. The joyous celebrations of the Bayern players left no one in any doubt as to just how much the victory meant to them; seven of them had been in the side that had lost to United at the Nou Camp and there were clearly some demons being exorcised that night.

Hitzfeld's side may have been making promising progress in the Champions League, but the same could not be said of their attempt to retain their Bundesliga crown. They had suffered uncharacteristic away defeats to minnows Unterhaching and

Hansa Rostock, while a further setback at home to Werder Bremen just prior to the first leg against Manchester United hardly helped their cause. After winning in Manchester they then proceeded to lose at home to FC Schalke 04, their chief rivals for the title. It was their second defeat to the team from Gelsenkirchen in the league that season and their bid for a third successive championship appeared to be heading for a disappointing end.

Manchester United travelled to Munich with great hopes of reversing the deficit from the first leg, though they would be without their talismanic midfielder David Beckham who had been suspended after being cautioned for a foul on Effenberg at Old Trafford, his third booking of the competition. The two players had clashed throughout the encounter in Manchester, their antagonistic relationship worsening after the German was booked for diving in an attempt to get the Englishman sent off. The suspension of Beckham forced Sir Alex Ferguson to re-organise the right-hand side of his midfield and Bayern took advantage after only five minutes, Élber converting a cross from the left wing that United had, uncharacteristically, left completely exposed.

Bayern kept coming forward and could have scored another couple of goals within the first quarter of the game, with Jancker's first effort hitting the bar and his second being well saved by the United goalkeeper. Mehmet Scholl then made two crucial interventions to put the tie beyond the English side, clearing an Andy Cole shot off the line and then, six minutes before half-time, getting on to the end of a move down the right of United's defence and shooting the ball low into the net. Ryan Giggs did get a goal back four minutes into the second half but Bayern, and Effenberg in particular, were playing too well to allow another great United comeback to take place. No further goals were scored and a much-needed, cathartic victory fell to the Germans.

After beating the side that had defeated them in the Champions League Final two years earlier Bayern were paired with the club that had knocked them out of the previous season's semi-final: Real Madrid. It was almost as if fate was handing them the opportunity to lay all their ghosts to rest in the space of a few weeks. The first leg of the semi-final took place in Madrid and the Germans started the stronger, with Effenberg and Scholl having early shots on goal. As the first half wore on, however, the hosts came back into the game, and their Portuguese galactico Figo was their main attacking threat. He brought a good save out of Kahn and the Bayern defence had to withstand further buffeting in the second half as the home side poured forward in an attempt to get their noses in front.

Madrid's English import, Steve McManaman, had a shot saved by Kahn and it was against the run of play when Bayern silenced the crowd with a shock goal. The ball was played forward to Élber who hit a bobbling shot from outside the penalty area, its last bounce deceiving the Spanish goalkeeper and escaping his efforts to keep it out of the net. Bayern managed to hold on to their slender lead for the remainder of the game, though they did suffer a setback 12 minutes from the end when Effenberg earned a caution that ruled him out of the second leg.

The absence of Effenberg for the return fixture was a problem for Hitzfeld. The German midfielder was the team's heartbeat, responsible for organising his colleagues on the pitch and driving them forward. His replacement, therefore, came as quite a surprise: a 20-year-old Canadian who had never previously started a game in the Champions League.

Owen Hargreaves grew up in Calgary and, like a number of his Bayern team-mates, his career was heavily influenced by the fall-out from the end of the Cold War. In a country dominated by ice hockey and not overly fond of football the young Hargreaves's talents could easily have been lost to the game, but he became the beneficiary of a great stroke of luck. Following the fall of the Berlin Wall Thomas Niendorf, who had previously worked in Dynamo Berlin's well-respected youth programme, relocated to Calgary. There he set up his own academy and one of his recruits was Hargreaves, who was thus able to access top-class coaching at a crucial phase of his development.

Niendorf helped Hargreaves to get a trial with Bayern Munich and they were sufficiently impressed to offer him a place in their youth scheme. Undaunted by the prospect of life in a country whose language he didn't speak, the 16-year-old Hargreaves eagerly grabbed the opportunity presented to him. All of the young players taken on by Bayern were naturally talented footballers, but Hargreaves's self-belief, determination and quiet, unflappable character gave him an edge over his contemporaries.

Just three years after arriving in Munich, Hargreaves impressed Hitzfeld enough to be promoted to the first team, making his Bundesliga debut as a substitute in August 2000. He then made 13 further league appearances that season as Hitzfeld gradually increased his exposure to senior football. Hargreaves's stellar rise continued apace when he won his first England cap a few months after his Champions League debut. He was eligible to play for the national side because his father was English, establishing an unusual record by becoming the first player to appear for England without ever having actually lived there.

Hitzfeld, wanting to protect his side's narrow lead from the first leg, instructed Hargreaves to play as a defensive midfielder, shielding the defence from the threat posed by Figo and McManaman. Hargreaves was an excellent ball-winner so the role suited him perfectly. Aside from the enforced introduction of Hargreaves, Hitzfeld fielded the same side that had beaten Madrid in the Bernabéu Stadium and they soon repaid his faith in them, doubling their aggregate lead after only eight minutes of play. Bayern won a corner and during a shambolic goalmouth scramble, which was almost unseemly in the rarefied heights of a Champions League semi-final, Élber headed the ball into the net.

Real Madrid came back at Bayern and got an equaliser just ten minutes later. That goal changed the entire outlook of the tie as one more goal for Madrid would give them victory, courtesy of the away goals rule. The reigning champions failed to take advantage of the opportunity offered to them, however, as it was Bayern that scored next. They won a free kick on 34 minutes and Scholl found Jeremies unmarked just outside the penalty area, his well-taken shot evading the dive of the Spanish goalkeeper.

That left the visitors needing to score two goals if they were to reach the final and the pattern of play throughout the second half was Madrid attacking while Bayern kept ten men behind the ball, only venturing out of their own half when the opportunity to counter-attack presented itself. There were further chances for both sides to score, but no more goals came, so Bayern reached their second Champions League Final in three years; most plaudits after the game going to the young Hargreaves whose masterly display in thwarting Madrid's attacks belied his lack of experience.

Back in the Bundesliga Bayern's fortunes had taken a turn for the better, with Hitzfeld's side responding to the disappointing defeat at home to Schalke by winning their next four matches.

In their penultimate games of the season Schalke succumbed to a last-minute defeat away to lowly Stuttgart while Bayern beat Kaiserlautern in injury time. Those two results tilted the odds in favour of the Bavarian side as they only needed a draw away to SV Hamburg to clinch the title. Schalke, meanwhile, had to beat already-relegated Unterhaching at home and pray for the best.

The scene was thus set for one of the most exciting ends to the season in the history of the Bundesliga. Schalke's game was replete with goals, with the side from Gelsenkirchen trading strikes with Unterhaching in a thrilling match. Schalke went two goals behind but then scored twice just before half-time to draw level. A third goal for Unterhaching put them back in front but Schalke were not to be denied, storming back with three goals in the last 17 minutes of the game to seal victory.

At the same time a much less eventful game was taking place in Hamburg. The match remained goalless until the 90th minute when the home side scored to put Schalke into pole position for the title. The club from Gelsenkirchen hadn't won a league championship for over 40 years and, on the conclusion of their game, their fans rushed on to the pitch, celebrating wildly with the ecstatic players who clearly believed that it was too late for Bayern to respond.

Haunted by the last-minute disaster in Barcelona, Bayern appeared to be destined for a repeat performance. What happened next was, for Schalke, almost cruel beyond words. Four minutes into injury time the Hamburg goalkeeper, a native of Gelsenkirchen and an ardent Schalke fan, inexplicably collected a back-pass when he could simply have booted the ball into the stands. Bayern were duly given an indirect free kick inside the penalty area and Effenberg, ever the leader, picked the ball up and directed proceedings as all 11 Hamburg players stationed themselves inside the six-yard area, clearly prepared to defend their goal for all they were worth.

Effenberg then rolled the ball to Patrik Andersson, who had never scored a goal for Bayern, somehow expecting him to breach the wall of bodies arrayed in front of him. Impressively, the Swede managed to do just that, his thunderbolt resulting

in jubilant celebrations among the Bayern players and much shedding of tears a few hundred miles away in Gelsenkirchen.
. . . .

As the game entered its final quarter of an hour it appeared increasingly likely that extra time would be needed to separate the two sides. A familiar pattern had established itself, with the Germans venturing forward tentatively while Leeds waited patiently for the opportunity to bolt upfield on the counter-attack. Both approaches to the game had their merits but neither looked likely to break the deadlock; Bayern's efforts repeatedly floundering on the rocks of Ferdinand and Matteo while Leeds's rapier thrusts were continually deflected by the central back three of Andersson, Kuffour and Linke. If there was going to be a goal then it appeared increasingly likely that it would be the result of a mistake, rather than through a glorious display of sublime skills.

And so it proved. The move started with Batty blocking Effenberg's forward run, forcing the Bayern captain to play the ball back to Linke as the Germans considered how best to restart their attack. The big East German received the ball easily enough but, slightly unnerved to see Viduka barrelling down on him, looked to play it sideways to the unmarked Lizarazu. Viduka's forceful run didn't succeed in its original purpose of winning the ball, but it startled Linke sufficiently that his pass wasn't as cleanly hit as it should have been. Lizarazu immediately saw the danger but was unable to do anything as Bowyer pounced on the stray ball, knocking it into space behind the Basque wing-back.

Suddenly the German back-line had to turn on its heels, chasing Bowyer as he bore down on Kahn's goal. Linke and Lizarazu both reached the young Leeds winger at the same time, clattering into him without regard to the consequences. Their vigorous challenges came too late, however, as Bowyer had already released the ball into the path of the rapidly advancing Viduka. The hefty Australian shaped to shoot, causing Andersson to throw himself down to block the expected strike but then, with the deftest of touches, Viduka halted the ball's motion instead.

In that split-second everything stood still, with even time itself seemingly suspended. All across the stadium Leeds fans instinctively started to lift out of their seats, their lungs filling in expectation of the roar to come. And then came the release; Viduka shooting the ball low past Kahn's outstretched palm. Goooooooooaaaaaal!!!

· ·

There were four Spanish entrants to the 2000/01 Champions League and David O'Leary's side ended up playing them all after being drawn against Valencia in the semi-finals. Valencia had conquered Arsenal in the previous round and were formidable opponents, having finished as runners-up in the previous season's Champions League. As with the quarter-finals the first leg was played at Elland Road, but this time O'Leary's side were unable to build up a lead to take into the away tie. Their best chances all came from headers; Alan Smith directing his effort wide of the goal, Matteo's attempt being well saved by the goalkeeper and Bowyer's hitting the crossbar. The silver lining on a frustrating evening was that Leeds had, at least, prevented the visitors from scoring a valuable away goal.

O'Leary's side were facing an uphill task to reach the final and things started to go wrong before they even reached Spain. UEFA's disciplinary commission reviewed the first leg and spotted Lee Bowyer stamping on Valencia's Juan Sánchez. Leeds vehemently defended their player, asserting that the contact was accidental rather than deliberate, but it was to no avail. The commission found him guilty of violent conduct and imposed a three-match ban, thus making arguably Leeds's most important player ineligible for the second leg.

Despite the great personal pressures brought about by the court case, Bowyer had probably had the best season of his entire career. He was Leeds's top scorer in the Champions League, with only Real Madrid's Raúl scoring more goals in the competition (and one of those should never have been given). If the FA had not prevented Bowyer from being selected for England because of the trial, there also seems little doubt that he would have made his international debut that season.

Losing Bowyer was a huge blow for Leeds and their bad luck didn't end there. Sixteen minutes into the game Sánchez (who else?) scored for Valencia when he steered the ball into the net with his upper arm. There were fierce protestations from the Leeds defenders but the referee was unmoved, awarding the goal to the home side.

Regardless of the fortunate nature of their goal, Valencia were still clearly the better of the two sides and Leeds, struggling to cope with a baking hot Spanish evening, were hard pushed to keep the score down to 1-0 at half-time. O'Leary urged his players on at the break, reminding them that they only needed to score once to reach the final on the away goals rule. The end of their brave European campaign, however, was only a few minutes away. Rather than getting the early equaliser that would have piled the pressure on their Spanish hosts, the young Leeds side collapsed in the first few minutes of the second half. Sánchez scored again, this time with a well-directed shot from 25 yards, and then Valencia's midfield playmaker Gaizka Mendieta put the game beyond Leeds's reach, shooting the ball low past Martyn from just outside the penalty area.

To cap Leeds's miserable evening Alan Smith was sent off just before the end of the game for a dreadful two-footed lunge on Rodríguez Vicente; the challenge a petulant release of pent-up frustration. Leeds badly missed Bowyer's drive and creativity and it's not too far-fetched to contend that his presence in the second leg could have resulted in a quite different outcome for Leeds.

The 2001 Champions League Final, therefore, was a contest between the defeated finalists from 1999 and 2000; an encounter that promised redemption for one side and unmitigated misery for the other. The final took place just four days after Bayern's dramatic Bundesliga triumph in Hamburg and Hitzfeld had almost a full squad to choose his team from, with only Jens Jeremies ruled out after being cautioned in the second leg against Real Madrid. In a curious way, that actually made Hitzfeld's team selection a little easier as it meant he could include Hargreaves in place of Jeremies, rather than having to relegate the hero of the semi-final to the bench. The rest of the team almost picked itself, with Kahn in goal, the French duo of Lizarazu and Sagnol playing as full-backs, Andersson, Kuffour and Linke forming the heart of the defence and Effenberg, Salihamidžić and Scholl providing midfield support for Élber, the sole striker.

Perhaps inevitably the contest proved to be a cautious affair, with both sides desperate not to succumb to defeat again. It was not one of the great European Cup finals and, if it is to be remembered at all, it will be for the fact that no other final has been so dominated by penalty kicks. The first was awarded after only two minutes when Andersson was penalised for handball. It was a harsh decision as the Swede was on the floor at the time and it appeared that the ball was kicked against him, rather than him using his arms to prevent the Spanish side from scoring. Mendieta converted to give his side an early lead and then a second spot-kick was awarded just five minutes later, the referee pointing to the spot after Effenberg was tripped over. The Valencia players tried hard to put Scholl off as he waited to take the penalty and their efforts clearly worked, with the German's tame kick being saved easily by the Spanish goalkeeper.

Bayern were still a goal behind at half-time so Hitzfeld made a key change to his side's formation, taking off the right wing-back Willy Sagnol and replacing him with a striker, Carsten Jancker. His ambition was rewarded five minutes into the second half when his side were awarded a second penalty after Carboni was adjudged to have handled the ball. It was another dubious decision as the unfortunate defender appeared to have been pushed on to the ball by a forceful challenge from Jancker, rather than have deliberately been trying to prevent a goalscoring opportunity. This time Effenberg stepped up to take the penalty, ignoring attempts by Valencia players to distract him, and he dispatched his spot-kick clinically.

There were no further goals, either in normal or extra time, so the winners had to be determined by a penalty shoot-out; a rather fitting outcome for a game dominated by spot-kicks.

The first kick was taken by Paulo Sérgio, who had come on in place of Scholl in extra time, and he blasted it over the bar. The Spanish side then scored their first two penalties but a miss from Zahovic, combined with successful strikes by Salihamidžić and Zickler, levelled the competition. No sooner had Bayern drawn level than they handed the initiative back to Valencia as Andersson, the hero of Hamburg a few days earlier, had his weak effort saved by Cañizares. The opportunity to put Valencia back into the lead then fell to the luckless Carboni, his spot-kick beating Kahn but hitting the underside of the crossbar and bouncing out to safety. Effenberg and Lizarazu then converted but Valencia responded in like terms to keep the scores level.

What turned out to be Bayern's last penalty fell to Thomas Linke, who sent Cañizares the wrong way with his spot-kick. The stage was thus set for Oliver Kahn to become the hero of the night and he duly rose to the occasion, saving Mauricio Pellegrino's kick to make Bayern Munich the champions of Europe for the first time in 25 years. Probably the most relieved man in the stadium was the young Owen Hargreaves; he was next in line to take a penalty.

Ottmar Hitzfeld thus achieved what only one other manager in the history of the game had managed to do at the time: lead two different clubs to victory in Europe's premier competition. There was almost nowhere for Hitzfeld to go other than down and, almost inevitably, that was what happened. Despite their Champions League triumph the signs of Bayern's decline were there for all to see. Hitzfeld's side may have won their third successive Bundesliga but it was by the narrowest of margins, with the total number of points won being ten short of that gathered in the previous season and 15 lower than when Hitzfeld won his first title with the club.

It wasn't that the other German clubs were catching up but, rather, that Bayern were slowing down. Their domestic dominance came to an end the following season when Hitzfeld's old club, Borussia Dortmund, finished top, with Bayern limping home in third place. They also lost their hold on the Champions League trophy after being defeated in the quarter-finals by Real Madrid, the pendulum swinging back towards the Spanish giants. A domestic league and cup double followed in 2003 for Hitzfeld's side but failure to retain the Bundesliga title the following season ultimately cost him his job. He deserved better but football is rarely a sentimental business; yesterday's achievements always counting for less than today's troubles.

There was, however, a happy ending for Hitzfeld. Bayern initially had some success after his departure but then started to struggle once again. Swallowing their pride, they duly asked 'Der General' to return. He soon worked his magic, leading Bayern to a league and cup double in 2008 before willingly handing over the reins to Jürgen Klinsmann when he became manager of the Swiss national side. There have been some great

German coaches over the years but, arguably, none greater than Hitzfeld.

Bayern Munich have gone from strength to strength in the new millennium but, sadly, the same cannot be said for Leeds United. Their performance in the first half of the 2000/01 Premier League season was pretty mediocre, though ten wins and three draws between late January and late April did lift them to third in the table. That meant that a place in the Champions League would be theirs again, if they could only hold on to it. The crucial match came a few days before the defeat to Valencia, Leeds losing narrowly away to Arsenal. That defeat dropped Leeds back down into fourth place and, despite thrashing Bradford City and Leicester City in their final two fixtures of the season, they eventually missed out on third by a solitary point.

Nevertheless, they started the following season with high hopes. Consecutive semi-final appearances in the UEFA Cup and Champions League gave them real belief that they could succeed in European competition once again, while their strong run in the second half of the previous season made them one of the favourites to top the Premier League. Initially all went according to plan with O'Leary's side winning five of their first seven league games, including a cathartic away victory at Arsenal. They maintained their good form up until Christmas and once again topped the table on New Year's Day.

The second trial involving Bowyer and Woodgate also took place that autumn and, almost two years after the assault had taken place, verdicts were finally reached. Bowyer was acquitted on all charges while Woodgate was found not guilty of grievous bodily harm, but guilty of affray. He was spared a prison sentence, receiving 100 hours of community service as his punishment instead, with the judge recognising the misery that Woodgate had suffered during the trial. The cloud that had hung over the club for the previous two years had lifted at last, leaving O'Leary and his players free to concentrate on football.

That should have been the moment when O'Leary's young side finally matured and realised their much-vaunted potential. Instead, it all went horribly wrong. The unlikely trigger was an away fixture against Cardiff City in the third round of the FA Cup, which took place less than a month after the trial finally reached its conclusion. Prior to the game O'Leary suggested that the tie be moved from Ninian Park to the Millennium Stadium, boasting that his team were strong enough to begin and end their cup run at the same ground. It was an unusual display of bombast from the Irishman and he was made to pay dearly for it. The Welsh side were only playing in the third tier of the league at the time but they soon cancelled out Leeds's opening goal, were a man up after Alan Smith was sent off and then, with just three minutes left to play, scored a surprise winner.

That defeat in Wales was followed by a host of others, with Leeds failing to win a league game for two months as well as being knocked out of the UEFA Cup in the fourth round by PSV Eindhoven. Their poor run of form dropped them to sixth place in the table and, despite winning four of their last five league games, they could only manage a fifth-place finish.

That season saw the introduction of four places in the Champions League for English clubs but, once again, Leeds just missed out. The financial consequences of failure were severe with the club making large losses as the cost of paying players' wages and servicing debt started to outstrip their falling revenues. In an attempt to put the club's finances back on to an even footing some of the crown jewels were auctioned off to the highest bidders, with Rio Ferdinand being sold to Manchester United for £30m. That netted Leeds a huge profit on the sum they had paid for him but still wasn't enough to stem the tide of debt that threatened to overwhelm the club. A host of other players were also sold, but at values far less than Leeds had paid for them, with the club becoming locked into a devastating spiral of falling attendances, decreasing revenues and lacklustre performances on the pitch.

In the weeks following Leeds's fifth-place finish in the Premier League David O'Leary was sacked, his failure to get the club back into the Champions League ultimately counting against him. He had come close to winning a number of trophies but his inability to get his team across the line had resulted in the press cruelly dubbing him 'David O'Nearly'.

Leeds's subsequent fall from grace was one of the most spectacular seen in the history of football, with the club being relegated from the Premier League just three seasons after appearing in the semi-finals of the Champions League. Then, three years after that, they suffered the humiliation of going down to League 1. The club's finances, which had been in a precarious state for a number of years, finally collapsed and Leeds were declared insolvent. The club went into administration with the 15-point deduction imposed on them by the Football League making a swift return to the Championship almost impossible. The proud club that had beaten AC Milan in the San Siro were forced to rub shoulders instead with the likes of Hartlepool, Walsall and Yeovil, enduring three seasons in the third tier of English football before rising again.

In retrospect, 2001 was clearly the high watermark for David O'Leary's young Leeds side. Not only did they have an incredible run in the Champions League but they also racked up more points in the Premier League than any other club. If only the season had run from January to December, rather than from August to May, then Leeds would have been champions. If only the referee had disallowed Valencia's first goal for handball, or Bowyer had been available for the game, then perhaps they would have reached the Champions League

Final. If only Leeds had managed to qualify for the Champions League a second time, either in 2001 or 2002, then maybe the club would have avoided financial meltdown. If only. If only. If only.

. . . .

Bayern Munich had spent the last few minutes of the 1999 Champions League Final desperately defending their goal and now the situation was reversed, with the Germans frantically laying siege to the Leeds goal. The calm, considered football normally played by Hitzfeld's side was jettisoned in favour of a much more urgent, more instinctive style of play, which would not have been unfamiliar to those that regularly watched football in the lower leagues. The ball was repeatedly pumped into the Leeds penalty area, with Jancker being the principal intended target, but that just played to Ferdinand's and Matteo's strengths; the two centre-backs revelling in their aerial duels with the Bayern striker.

In front of the penalty area Lee Bowyer was tireless in his efforts to thwart the Germans, barely catching breath as he chased every loose ball, cementing his status as a Leeds idol. His club had successfully appealed against his three-match ban for violent conduct in the first leg of the semi-final; his punishment being commuted to a one-match ban which he served in the second leg. Alan Smith's late equaliser in that game, taking Leeds through on the away goals rule, had also been contentious, just as the disallowing of Valencia's first goal for handball had been, but it was nowhere near as controversial as what happened next at the San Siro.

With normal time morphing into injury time, Effenberg lofted another high ball into the Leeds penalty area. Ferdinand dealt with it easily enough, climbing above Élber to head the ball away, but his clearance only got as far as Owen Hargreaves who was standing a few yards outside the penalty area. He quickly side-stepped a challenge from Dacourt and found himself in enough space to smash the ball at goal, his shot threading its way through the massed ranks of Leeds players and past Martyn's dive. As the Cornishman's body hit the turf he heard the ball cannon off the post behind him but, before he had the chance to get to his feet, he glimpsed Jancker's boot connecting with the loose ball, pushing it into the empty net.

As the Bayern players mobbed the bald-headed striker, piling their bodies on top of his prone frame, Martyn instinctively raced to the referee, knowing in his heart that the big German had been standing in an offside position when Hargreaves had struck his shot. The Dutch referee was immediately surrounded by frenzied Leeds players, all of them excitedly joining in Martyn's protest. He calmly walked away from them and made a beeline for the assistant referee, who had not raised his flag at any point during this incident.

The length of their discussion was commensurate with the gravity of the matter that they were adjudicating on, with the Bayern players nervously halting their jubilant celebrations to see what its outcome would be. Up in the stands, Franz Beckenbauer, the president of Bayern Munich, looked on imperiously, with images of a similar incident a quarter of a century earlier flooding his worried mind. With a dramatic flourish the referee eventually blew his whistle, raised his arm in the air and then brought it down decisively with his finger pointing towards Martyn's goal, indicating a free kick awarded in Leeds's favour.

Cyril's memories of what happened in the next couple of minutes would later become a bit of a jumble, with the last few moments of football fusing with the sight of furious Bayern players chasing the referee around the pitch. The chaos on the pitch was mirrored by the mayhem in the stands, with white-shirted Leeds fans celebrating wildly, many of them in tears at what they were witnessing. It wasn't just that their side had won the Champions League, or that they could now legitimately call their side the best in Europe, but that something buried deep inside them had finally been released.

The injustice of Paris had been rectified; the triumph that should have been theirs a quarter of a century earlier rightfully awarded to a new generation of stars. When the over-sized trophy was later given to Rio Ferdinand the Leeds fans instinctively chorused, 'We are the champions, champions of Europe!' And, finally, they were.

Bibliography

I have consulted numerous sources during my research for this book and those which have been of greatest use are listed below. If you want to find out more about the great teams and players covered in this book then I strongly recommend them to you.

1. Triumph in Montevideo
Uruguay v Scotland, World Cup Final 1930

Perhaps unsurprisingly, there aren't many histories of Uruguayan football written in the English language. The most useful books I found were Chris Taylor's *The Beautiful Game: A Journey Through Latin American Football* (Victor Gollancz, 1998, revised edition Phoenix, 1999) and Tony Mason's *Passion of the People? Football in South America* (Verso, 1995). Cris Freddi's delightfully thorough *Complete Book of the World Cup 2002* (CollinsWillow, 2002), Brian Glanville's well-respected *The Story of the World Cup* (Faber and Faber, 2001) and Hyder Jawad's *Four Weeks in Montevideo: The Story of World Cup 1930* (Seventeen Media, 2009) were also of great help, as was Eduardo Galeano's poetic *Football in Sun and Shadow* (translated Mark Fried, Fourth Estate, 1997) and Jon Spurling's, *Death or Glory! –*

The Dark History of the World Cup (Vision Sports Publishing, 2010).

Paul Joannou's authoritative *Wembley Wizards: The Story of a Legend* (Mainstream Publishing, 1990) was a valuable source of information on that great Scotland side. Also of use was the same author's *The Hughie Gallacher Story* (Breedon Books, 1989), Peter J. Beck's *Scoring for Britain: International Football and International Politics, 1900–1939* (Routledge, 1999). John Harding's *Alex James: Life of a Football Legend* (Robson Books, 1998), Brian James's *England v Scotland* (Sportsmans Book Club, 1970), John Keith's *Dixie Dean: The Inside Story of a Football Icon* (Robson, 2001), John Rafferty's *One Hundred Years of Scottish Football* (Pan, 1973), Ivan Sharpe's *40 Years in Football* (Hutchinson, 1958) and Paul Smith's *Rangers' Cult Heroes* (Know the Score Books, 2007).

2. The Italian Job
Italy v England, European Championships Final 1968

The most thorough chronicle of Italian football is John Foot's *Calcio: A History of Italian Football* (Fourth Estate, 2006). Also of assistance was Brian Glanville's *For Club and Country: The Best of the Guardian's Footballing Obituaries* (Guardian Newspapers Ltd, 2008) and Richard Williams's s*The Perfect 10: Football's Dreamers, Schemers, Playmakers and Playboys* (Faber and Faber, 2006). Cris Freddi's *Complete Book of the World Cup 2002* (CollinsWillow, 2002) and Brian Glanville's *The Story of the World Cup* (Faber and Faber, 2001) were of help once again.

One legacy of England's 1966 World Cup triumph is a copious array of autobiographies from that era, including Alan Ball's *Playing Extra Time* (Pan, 2005), Gordon Banks's

Banksy: My Autobiography (Michael Joseph, 2002), Bobby Charlton's *The Autobiography: My England Years* (Headline, 2009), Jimmy Greaves's *Greavsie: The Autobiography* (Time Warner Books, 2003), Norman Hunter's *Biting Talk* (Hodder and Stoughton, 2004), Geoff Hurst's *1966 and All That: My Autobiography* (Headline, 2006), Brian Labone's *Defence At The Top* (Pelham Books, 1968), Martin Peters's *The Ghost Of '66: The Autobiography* (Orion, 2006) and Alan Mullery's *Alan Mullery: The Autobiography* (Headline, 2006). Useful biographies include Leo McKinstry's *Sir Alf* (HarperSport, 2006), Ivan Ponting's *Sir Roger: Roger Hunt of Liverpool and England* (The Bluecoat Press, 1995) and Jeff Powell's *Bobby Moore: The Life and Times of a Sporting Hero* (Robson, 1993). Also of assistance were Graham Betts's *England Player by Player* (Green Umbrella, 2006), Niall Edworthy's *England: The Official FA History* (Virgin Books, 1997), Arthur Hopcraft's *The Football Man: People and Passions in Soccer* (Aurum Press, 2006) and Ivan Ponting's *The Book of Football Obituaries* (Pitch Publishing, 2008).

3. Clough vs. Cruyff
Ajax v Derby County, European Cup Final 1973

The most authoritative source for the history of the great Ajax side of the early 1970s is David Winner's superb *Brilliant Orange: The Neurotic Genius of Dutch Football* (Bloomsbury, 2000). Ben Lyttleton's *Match of My Life European Cup Finals: Sixteen Stars Relive Their Glory Nights* (Know the Score Books, 2006) was also a useful mine of information, as was Frits Barend and Henk van Dorp's *Ajax, Barcelona, Cruyff: The ABC of an Obstinate Maestro*, translated by David Winner and Lex den Dam (Bloomsbury, 1997), Brian Glanville's *For Club and*

Country: The Best of the Guardian's Footballing Obituaries (Guardian Newspapers Ltd, 2008) and *The European Cup 1955–1980* by John Motson and John Rowlinson (Queen Anne, 1980).

Brian Clough's eventful time at Derby County has been the subject of numerous books, of which I found Jonathan Wilson's *Brian Clough: Nobody Ever Says Thank You. The Biography* (Orion, 2011) to be the most comprehensive. Also of great use were Brian Clough's *Clough: The Autobiography* (Corgi, 1994) and *Cloughie: Walking on Water: My Life* (Headline, 2002), Michael Cockayne's *Derby County: The Clough Years* (Parrs Wood Press, 2003), Tim Crane's *The Life of Brian* (Football World, 2004), Wendy Dickinson and Stafford Hildred's *For Pete's Sake: The Peter Taylor Story. Volume 1: The Backstreets to the Baseball Ground* (Matador, 2010), George Edwards's *Right Place, Right Time: The Inside Story of Clough's Derby Days* (Stadia, 2007), Maurice Edwards's *Brian and Peter: A Right Pair: 20 Years with Clough and Taylor* (Derby Books, 2010), Tony Francis's *Clough: A Biography* (Stanley Paul, 1987), Archie Gemmill's *Both Sides of the Border* (Hodder and Stoughton, 2005), Duncan Hamilton's *Provided You Don't Kiss Me: 20 Years with Brian Clough* (HarperPerennial, 2008), Roger Hermiston's *Clough & Revie: The Rivals who Changed the Face of English Football* (Mainstream, 2011), Dave Mackay and Martin Knight's *The Real Mackay; the Dave Mackay Story* (Mainstream, 2004), Patrick Murphy's *His Way: The Brian Clough Story* (Robson Books, 2004), Peter Taylor's *With Clough by Taylor* (Sidgwick and Jackson, 1980) and Colin Todd's *Toddy: The Colin Todd Story* (Breedon, 2008).

4. The Battle of Britain
Liverpool v Dundee United, European Cup Final 1984

There is no shortage of literature on Liverpool's greatest era. Illuminating autobiographies include Kenny Dalglish's *My Liverpool Home* (Hodder & Stoughton, 2011), Bruce Grobbelaar's *More Than Somewhat* (Collins Willow, 1986), Alan Hansen's *A Matter of Opinion* (Partridge Press, 1999), Alan Kennedy and John Williams's *Kennedy's Way: Inside Bob Paisley's Liverpool* (Mainstream, 2005), Mark Lawrenson's *Mark Lawrenson: The Autobiography* (Queen Anne Press, 1988), Phil Neal's *Life at the Kop: The Phil Neal Story* (Macdonald, 1986), Ian Rush's *Rush: The Autobiography* (Ebury Press, 2009), Graeme Souness's (with Bob Harris), *No Half Measures* (Collins Willow, 1985) and Ronnie Whelan's *Walk On: My Life in Red* (Simon & Schuster, 2012). Other informative sources were Dave Bowler's *Shanks: The Authorised Biography of Bill Shankly* (Orion, 1996), Andrew Fagan and Mark Platt's *Joe Fagan: Reluctant Champion – The Authorised Biography* (Aurum Press, 2012), Stan Hey's *Liverpool's Dream Team* (Mainstream, 2002) and John Keith's *Bob Paisley: Manager of the Millennium* (Robson, 1999).

There are more books available on the subject of Dundee United than one might expect. A personal favourite is *Jousting with Giants: The Jim McLean Story* (Mainstream, 1987) by Jim McLean and Ken Gallagher, while Peter Rundo's *Dundee United: Champions of Scotland 1982–83* (Desert Island Books, 2005) and Peter Rundo and Mike Watson's *Dundee United: The Official Centenary History* (Birlinn, 2009) were invaluable sources of reference. Other useful texts were Brian Glanville's *Champions of Europe: The History, Romance and Intrigue of the European Cup*

(Guinness, 1991), Paul Hegarty's *Heading for Glory* (John Donald Publishers Ltd, 1987), Ralph Milne with Gary Robertson's *What's it All About Ralphie?* (Black and White Publishing, 2010), Paul Smith's *Tannadice Idols: The Story of Dundee United's Cult Heroes* (Black and White Publishing, 2010), Paul Sturrock with Charlie Duddy and Peter Rundo's *Forward Thinking: The Paul Sturrock Story* (Mainstream, 1989) and Jim Wilkie's *Across the Great Divide: A History of Professional Football in Dundee* (Mainstream, 1984).

5. None Shall Sleep
Argentina v England, World Cup Final 1990

The unique relationship between England and Argentina has been the subject of two informative books: Neil Clack's *Animals!: The Story of England v Argentina* (Pitch Publishing, 2011) and David Downing's *England v Argentina: World Cups and Other Small Wars* (Portrait, 2003). The history of the 1990 World Cup has been well chronicled in Pete Davies's *All Played Out: The Full Story of Italia 90* (Random House, 1991), Cris Freddi's *Complete Book of the World Cup 2002* (CollinsWillow, 2002) and Brian Glanville's *The Story of the World Cup* (Faber and Faber, 2001).

There is a welcome abundance of books on, or by, many of the key protagonists, including John Barnes's *John Barnes: The Autobiography* (Headline, 1999), Peter Beardsley with Bob Cass's *Peter Beardsley: My Life Story* (HarperCollinsWillow, 1996), Jimmy Burns's *Hand of God: the Life of Diego Maradona* (Bloomsbury, 1996), Terry Butcher, with Bob Harris's *Butcher: My Autobiography* (Highdown, 2005), Paul Gascoigne with Hunter Davies's *Gazza: My Story* (Headline, 2004), Colin Malam's *Gary Lineker: Strikingly Different* (Arrow Books, 1993), Diego

Maradona with Daniel Arcucci and Ernesto Cherquis Bialo's *El Diego* (translated Marcela Mora y Araujo, Yellow Jersey, 2005), Paul Parker with Pat Symes's *Paul Parker: Tackles Like a Ferret* (Know the Score Books, 2006), Stuart Pearce's *Psycho: The Autobiography* (Headline, 2001), David Platt's *Achieving the Goal: An Autobiography* (Richard Cohen Books Ltd, 1995), Peter Shilton's *Peter Shilton: The Autobiography* (Orion, 2004) and Mel Stein's *Chris Waddle: The Authorised Biography* (Pocket Books, 1998).

Other useful books were Niall Edworthy's *England: The Official FA History* (Virgin Books, 1997) and *The Second Most Important Job in the Country* (Virgin Books, 1999), John Foot's *Calcio: A History of Italian Football* (Fourth Estate, 2006), Graham McColl's *How to Win the World Cup* (Bantam Press, 2010), Richard Williams's *The Perfect 10: Football's Dreamers, Schemers, Playmakers and Playboys* (Faber and Faber, 2006) and Jonathan Wilson's *The Anatomy of England: A History in Ten Matches* (Orion, 2010).

6. The History Boys

Bayern Munich v Leeds United, European Champions League Final 2001

Ulrich Hesse-Lichtenberger's *Tor! The Story of German Football* (WSC, 2002) was invaluable in understanding the history of German football and Bayern Munich's place in it. Other helpful accounts of the club's fortunes around the turn of the millennium were Alex Ferguson's *Managing My Life: My Autobiography* (Hodder & Stoughton, 1999), Ian Macleay's *Owen Hargreaves – The Biography of Manchester United's Midfield Maestro* (John Blake Publishing, 2008) and Keir Radnedge's *50 Years of the European Cup and Champions League* (Carlton, 2005).

There are a number of useful volumes on one of the most eventful periods in the history of Leeds United. Particularly instructive were David O'Leary's *Leeds United On Trial: The Inside Story of an Astonishing Year* (Little, Brown, 2002), Peter Ridsdale's *United We Fall: Boardroom Truths About the Beautiful Game* (Pan, 2008) and Don Warters's *2001 A European Odyssey: Leeds United's Champions League Season* (Leeds United Publishing Ltd, 2001). Also of help were Rob Bagchi and Paul Rogerson's *The Unforgiven: The Story of Don Revie's Leeds United* (Aurum Press, 2009), David Batty's *David Batty: The Autobiography* (Headline, 2002), Graham Betts's *England Player by Player* (Green Umbrella, 2006), Anthony Clavane's *Promised Land: The Reinvention of Leeds United* (Yellow Jersey, 2010), Richard Coomber's *Lucas Radebe: From Soweto to Soccer Superstar* (Great Northern Books, 2010), Rio Ferdinand's *Rio: My Story* (Headline, 2007) and Dominic Matteo's *In My Defence: The Autobiography* (Great Northern Books, 2011).

General

Butler, Bryon, *The Official History Of The Football Association* (Queen Anne Press, 1993)

Goldblatt, David, *The Ball is Round: A Global History of Football* (Viking, 2006)

Soar, Phil, *The Hamlyn A-Z of British Football Records* (Hamlyn, 1981)

Wilson, Jonathan, *Inverting the Pyramid: The History of Football Tactics* (Orion 2008)

Rothman's Football Year Books

Websites

I have also consulted the following websites to check facts and figures:

www.bbcsport.co.uk
www.fai.com
www.fcbayern.de
www.fifa.com
www.scottishfa.co.uk
www.uefa.com
www.youtube.com

About the Author

As a long-suffering supporter of Walsall Football Club, Simon Turner has witnessed countless 'if only' moments over the years. He lives in Lichfield with his wife Val, daughter Ellie, who has the good sense to follow athletics rather than football, and son Edward, who deliberately annoys him by supporting Aston Villa.